THE SHEPHERDS OF FÁTIMA

Manuel Fernando Sousa e Silva

BOOKS & MEDIA
Boston

Library of Congress Cataloging-in-Publication Data

Silva, Manuel Fernando Sousa e.

[Pastorinhos de Fátima. English]

The shepherds of Fátima / Manuel Fernando Sousa e Silva ; [translated by Mary Emmanuel Alves]. — 1st English ed.

p. cm.

Includes bibliographical references.

ISBN 0-8198-7121-4 (pbk.)

1. Blessed—Portugal—Biography. 2. Marto, Jacinta, 1910-1920. 3. Marto, Francis, 1908-1919. 4. Maria Lúcia, Irmã, 1907-2005. 5. Fatima, Our Lady of. 6. Mary, Blessed Virgin, Saint—Apparitions and miracles—Portugal—Fátima. 7. Fátima (Portugal)—Religious life and customs. I. Title.

BX4669.S5413 2008

282'.4690922—dc22

2008039598

Cover design by Rosana Usselmann

Cover photos and interior photos courtesy of Paulinas Editora, Lisboa, Portugal

Translated by M. Colm McCool, OP, and Mary Emmanuel Alves, FSP

Originally published in Portuguese by Paulinas Editora, Lisboa, Portugal

First English edition, 2008

Published by Pauline Books & Media, 50 Saint Paul's Avenue, Boston, MA 02130-3491

Printed in the U.S.A.

www.pauline.org

Pauline Books & Media is the publishing house of the Daughters of St. Paul, an international congregation of women religious serving the Church with the communications media.

1 2 3 4 5 6 7 8 9   13 12 11 10 09 08

Contents

Foreword

THE BEATIFICATION OF the visionaries Francisco and Jacinta has stirred a worldwide interest in the message of Fátima. Historians, spiritual writers, and theologians have pondered it without exhausting its meaning. It is always possible to draw from its riches *new things and old* (cf. Mt 13:52). There is no truth of the Catholic faith that the message does not contain, implicitly or explicitly. It is truly a synthesis of the Gospel.

Manuel Fernando Sousa e Silva's book is indeed a proof of this. This work demonstrates that the author is not only a skillful writer, but also a careful historian. He begins by describing the deeply Christian homes into which the shepherds were born: the parents were the primary educators, by word and by example, forming in reality a "domestic church."

When I was a young priest I had a meeting with Ti Marto, father of Francisco and Jacinta. I asked him whether he had easily believed what the children were saying about the Apparitions of Our Lady in the Cova. He answered calmly and severely, as if weighing his words:

> My wife kept insisting with the children, "You have to tell me what Our Lady said to you." One day Jacinta said to her: "If you had seen what we saw, Mother, you would spend your whole life weeping." I heard that, kept silent, and thought: people want to sweep God into a corner [anticlericalism was then at its height] and after having heard them, I said: "That's it, [he put his hand to his forehead], that's God's answer!"

And that was it. In its essence, Fátima is God coming to meet humanity in order to save it. It is a new intervention of God in human history. The history of the twentieth century cannot be written without referring to Fátima, as Pope John Paul II once said. In the message of Fátima, peace is entrusted to Our Lady. Thus it was in the past, and so it will be in the future. Her Immaculate Heart will continue to triumph.

There are thousands of books about Fátima, but this one will rightly be counted among the best. I congratulate the author with joy and gratitude.

Fátima, February 20, 2002
Feast of Blesseds Francisco and Jacinta Marto

ALBERTO COSME DO AMARAL
Bishop emeritus of Leiria-Fátima

Preface

FÁTIMA HAS QUICKLY come to be known throughout the world. But until May 13, 1917, the Cova da Iria was unknown even to many people in the neighborhood. Father Manuel Marques Ferreira, who served as pastor in Fátima, declared that he had never heard of a place called the Cova da Iria.[1] Today, the mere mention of the name brings joy to people everywhere.

I recall an incident that occurred during the Fifty-first International Eucharistic Congress held in Lourdes, France, from July16–23, 1981. Portugal was represented by about 700 pilgrims who traveled in a special train. They were joined by seventy Angolans, some pilgrims from other Portuguese-speaking African countries, and about 200 pilgrims from Brazil.

On Sunday, July 19, more than 80,000 people participated in the concelebrated Mass. Because our group needed to meet afterward but was dispersed through the crowd, someone had the idea of using an easy signal: a small group of Portuguese pilgrims would begin singing the Fátima *Ave*. All who spoke our language, alerted by the sound of that hymn, could then easily come together. However, something completely unforeseen happened: as soon as the first notes of the Fátima *Ave* were heard, the crown rushed to join us, mingling their voices with ours.

Known and venerated by people all over the world, Fátima has become a meeting place of all races, colors, and nations. Mary chose Fátima and made it known everywhere. From there she sent a message to the human race through the three children to whom she appeared. The choice could not have been more suitable:

> The name Cova da Iria is a term derived from the Greek word *eirene*, which means *peace*. So it can be said that Our Lady appeared during World War I in the Cova (hollow) of Peace. This becomes even more significant when we consider that the first apparition took place exactly eight days before Pope Benedict XV ordered that the invocation "Queen of Peace, pray for us" be added to the Litany of Loreto.[2]

The Queen of Peace came to the Cova of Peace, to proclaim to the whole world a message of peace. This encounter was prepared for by the angel of Portugal, who identified himself as the angel of peace.

The following story, among so many others, shows the fascination of Fátima. A group of Portuguese people traveled to Budapest in September 1989. Near the Cathedral of Saint Stephen, we met a Hungarian priest. Various priests in our group tried to speak to him in different languages—Portuguese, French, Spanish, and Italian—but without success. Then someone had the idea of speaking in Latin. *"Sumus lusitani!"* [We're Portuguese!] When he heard this, the face of this man of God, until then clouded by an expression of mistrust, lit up with a smile. He looked up to heaven and exclaimed joyfully, "Oh! Fátima!"

During the Communist oppression, the Catholics of Hungary had built in Fátima, near Valinhos, the Hungarian Calvary. Cardinal József Mindszenty, symbol of a people's resistance to a totalitarian regime, came to the Cova da Iria when he was able to leave his refuge in the U.S. embassy in Budapest. He thanked Our Lady for his liberation and begged her intercession for his country, which was still oppressed.

I also recall the contagious joy of a middle-aged woman from Colombia who visited the Chapel of the Apparitions on July 4, 1992. She felt immensely happy to be there. A humble dressmaker, she had dreamed all her life of visiting the Cova da Iria. But the money she scrimped together was always needed for some unforeseen expense and the trip always had to be put off, until someone offered to help her with the cost. She said, full of emotion: "How fortunate you Portuguese are to live so near to Fátima!" Examples like these could go on for ever.

This book will tell the story of the three shepherds to whom Our Lady appeared. They were not simply heralds of the Mother of God, they were also the first to live her message faithfully and to be its official interpreters. For this they were carefully prepared by an angel and, finally, by Our Lady herself.

It is as though Mary were telling us that, in order to live the message of prayer and penance, of conversion and solidarity with the whole Church, we need a child's heart, or, more concretely, we must become like the three little shepherds.

They were children like so many others, without anything to distinguish them outwardly. They enjoyed the same fun and games typical of all children, and they looked at the world with the same innocence and simplicity. Before strangers, they quite naturally hid their unique experiences, so much so that the mother of Francisco and Jacinta commented: "The life of these children is an enigma to me. I can't understand it!"[3]

Lúcia's mother added: "When they are alone, they talk so fast that no one can catch a word, no matter how hard you listen. As soon as someone arrives, they lower their heads and say nothing. It's all a mystery to me!" Francisco and Jacinta's father once said that his children were no different from any others.

Once in an interview, Lúcia was asked whether they were different. She answered with her usual vivacity, "What difference do you expect? We continued to play as before. Some pious people would tell us: 'You saw Our Lady: you shouldn't continue to play!' But what else could we do except play? Were we supposed to stay still on the altar, like our Foundress?"[4]

Lúcia would later become a highly qualified witness to the events in the Cova da Iria. She was the eldest of the children, and cousin of Jacinta and Francisco. In God's plan, prophesied by Mary during the apparitions, Lúcia lived much longer than her cousins in order to spread devotion to Mary's Immaculate Heart. She lived in the Carmel of Coimbra and died on February 13, 2005, at the age of ninety-seven.

Fortunately, the then Bishop of Leiria, José Alves Correia da Silva, asked Lúcia to write her memoirs. She wrote the last two parts (V and VI) at the request of the rector of the Sanctuary of Fátima, Father Lúciano Guerra. These *Memoirs* give many details about the life of Jacinta and Francisco.[5] In fact, the six *Memoirs* are indispensable for an accurate chronicle of the events of Fátima. But other testimonies and documents, besides various writings of the visionary, are available to draw from, and these sources are noted in this book.

Chapter 1

The Little Shepherds' Families

During a visit to Fátima in September 1955, I had the good fortune to meet Francisco and Jacinta's parents personally. One evening I took a walk with a friend toward the nearby village of Aljustrel. Unexpectedly, we came upon a stone house where we found Senhora Olímpia Marto, Francisco and Jacinta's mother, sitting in a wheelchair. She rested quietly, with her lips moving slightly as she slipped her rosary beads through her fingers. She was gazing into the distance and seemed not to be aware of our arrival.

Without realizing we could tire her and so worsen her frail health, we began to speak with the venerable woman. She answered us with nods of her head and whispered words difficult to hear. Then we heard from inside the house the steps of someone who gave us warning of his vigilant presence by clearing his throat. I firmly believe that Ti Marto—as we affectionately called him—did so out of courtesy, so that we would be aware of his presence and could discreetly leave.

Instead, Manuel Pedro Marto received us very well, answered our greeting, and frankly told us, "I don't want people talking to my wife. She is very ill, they tire her, and she is dying.... And when she dies, I will die too, because she is the greatest treasure I have in this world!"

The relationship between these two people deeply impressed me. They had reared children and faced great difficulties together, which only deepened their friendship. Now, bent with the weight of years, full of limitations due to illness and age, they were closer to each other than ever.

Sister Lúcia describes the families of the three shepherds:

> They were two Christian families closely related by blood ties. Aunt
> Olímpia was my father's sister, and her first husband was my mother's
> brother. They had two children, António and Manuel. After her first
> husband's death, Aunt Olímpia married Uncle Marto, who was also
> related to my mother, a cousin, in fact, though I'm not sure to what
> degree. Seven children were born of this marriage. My parents,
> António Santos and Maria Rosa, had seven children....
>
> The two families had such a close bond that the children felt as
> much at home in the house of their aunt and uncle as in their own
> home. Together they would eat bread still warm from the oven for their
> afternoon snack, and make a sandwich with fresh sardines from Nazaré
> or with slices of salted cod.... At other times, the filling consisted of
> pieces of game that provided a family feast at certain times in the year:
> rabbits caught in ingenious traps, partridges caught in the hay and the
> corn fields, thrushes caught in the snares under the olive trees that were
> baited with ripe olives.[1]

FRANCISCO AND JACINTA'S PARENTS

A happy marriage

Francisco and Jacinta's parents were Manuel Pedro Marto and
Olímpia de Jesus. When they married, Olímpia was a widowed mother
of two children.[2] She had first married José Fernandes da Rocha, a
brother of Lúcia's mother, on February 6, 1888.[3]

> José Fernandes da Rocha returned from Mozambique and brought
> back enough money to renovate his parents' house, giving it the form it
> has today, and to build a house for his own family when he married
> Aunt Olímpia. The servants of God, Francisco and Jacinta Marto,
> were later born in that house. José died eight years after the marriage,
> leaving as heirs to his home and possessions his young wife, who
> received half, and his two orphaned children, António and Manuel do
> Santos Ferreira Rosa, who received the other half.[4]

Olímpia had seven children in her second marriage: José, Teresa
(who died at two years of age), Florinda, Teresa (who died from pneumonia in 1921), João, Francisco, and Jacinta. These last two were the
younger visionaries of Fátima.

Manuel Pedro Marto and Olímpia de Jesus lived generously the mutual self-giving of marriage. They joyfully accepted their seven children, along with Olímpia's two others. They understood, intuitively, that children are a sign of God's trust in the parents. With patience, wisdom, and consummate skill, they formed their children's hearts in the human virtues: love of truth, joy, a spirit of service, generosity in work, fortitude, and compassion for the most needy.

Even when the children were young, their parents taught them to pray the Rosary while guarding the sheep on the hill. Accustomed to obeying, they finally discovered a childish strategy to make this obedience a little easier. Lúcia describes it in all simplicity.

> We had been told to say the Rosary after lunch, but as the whole day seemed too short for our play, we worked out a good way of getting through it quickly. We simply passed the beads through our fingers, saying only "Hail Mary, Hail Mary, Hail Mary...." At the end of each mystery, we paused awhile, then simply said "Our Father" and so, in the twinkling of an eye, as they say, we finished our Rosary.[5]

The parents taught their children to do the work they could, without interfering with a normal, happy childhood, and entrusted them with the care of the flocks.

Olímpia de Jesus Marto

Senhora Olímpia gave her children a rich example of faith. Various references in the writings about Fátima give us a glimpse of this. For example, Olímpia was extremely careful about safeguarding her children's innocence, as a dialogue between Jacinta and Lúcia shows:

> [Jacinta:] "Will your mother let you go today?"
> [Lúcia:] "No."
> [Jacinta:] "Then I'm going with Francisco over to our yard."
> [Lúcia:] "And why won't you stay here?"
> [Jacinta:] "My mother doesn't want us to stay when those other children are here. She told us to go and play in our own yard. She doesn't want me to learn these bad things, which are sins and which the Child Jesus doesn't like."[6]

The children's mother was naturally timid in the middle of all the agitation about the apparitions, as her husband explains: "My Olímpia was always fearful, yes, always distraught. She would always turn to Our

Lady. She foresaw everything in another way, because the priests and other people predicted that it would work out badly."[7]

At first Senhora Olímpia had great difficulty in believing her daughter's account of the apparitions. "She allowed them to go, but she was afraid that the people might harm them, thinking that they were deceiving them. One day she spoke of wanting to punish her son and daughter, so that they would not keep on deceiving the people."[8] But she was ready to defend them at the cost of her own life, when, in the days before October 13, 1917, veiled threats to the children surfaced.

Other sufferings followed. In just fifteen months, she saw four of her children die in the influenza epidemic: Francisco (April 4, 1919), Jacinta (February 20, 1920), Florinda (May 7, 1920), and Teresa (July 3, 1921).[9] Olímpia sorrowfully accompanied the two visionaries' ascent to Calvary, especially Jacinta's. Whoever has observed a mother's persistence in seeking a cure for her child, furtively wiping away her own tears at her child's bedside, even when everyone else has lost hope, can imagine how Olímpia suffered. She went with Jacinta to the hospital in Vila Nova de Ourém, and later to Lisbon. Though her daughter remained in Lisbon, awaiting her final journey, Senhora Olímpia returned to Aljustrel while her mother's heart remained in the capital.

Olímpia spent the last days of her life with the rosary in her hand, helpless, in a wheelchair, until the Lord came to receive her into his arms and bring her to heaven. Olímpia de Jesus departed to meet the Lord and her children on April 3, 1956,[10] after a life of generous self-giving to God in the persons of her husband and her children.

Manuel Pedro Marto

The writings about Fátima often refer to Ti Marto, as he was popularly known, since he often gave testimony about the apparitions. Manuel Pedro Marto was a courageous man who could not be intimidated. He had served in the Portuguese military and had seen action in Mozambique.[11]

When the administrator of Vila Nova de Ourém served him a notice to bring his children before a tribunal, Marto took a courageous stand: "He said that he would not bring his children there and present them before a tribunal because they were too young to be responsible for their actions. It was too far for them to walk to Vila Nova de Ourém, he declared, and added, 'I will go see what they want.'"[12]

When the children were imprisoned around August 13, Marto saw not only human malice but, above all, the hand of God drawing good from evil. When some men wanted to attack the parish priest of Fátima because they thought he was involved in the children's abduction by the administrator of Ourém, Ti Marto shouted: "Hey, boys! Behave yourselves! Neither the parish priest nor the administrator caused this, rather it was the power of the Most High."[13] With these words and with his mind firmly made up, he pacified those who wanted to attack the rectory. This supernatural intuition, fruit of a docile submission to the Holy Spirit's action, led him to believe in the apparitions from the very first moment.[14]

Ti Marto loved his children deeply and had no inhibitions about showing it. When he heard that the children had been released from prison and were on the parish priest's veranda, he himself confessed how he reacted. "I hugged Jacinta and kissed her, as my tears ran down her little face. I took her up in my arms."[15]

As June 13 approached, the day for the second visit of the Mother of God to the Cova da Iria, Ti Marto found himself in a quandary. He recounted the dilemma with his usual sincerity:

> "What a problem!" I thought, totally perplexed. "Should I go to the Cova da Iria with the youngsters ... but what if nothing appeared? ... Let them go there on their own with all those people there for the feast? ... Hmmm! That's not right either." Then an idea came to me: "There is a fair tomorrow in Pedreira, I'll go there and buy oxen...." I said to my wife, Olímpia, "Tomorrow we'll go to the fair and buy oxen. By the time we get back, the problem of the youngsters will be sorted out." It was all such a muddle![16]

He also showed his courage when he decided to accompany his children and wife to the Cova da Iria on October 13. Rumors had surfaced about what the crowd might do if the promised miracle did not occur, and the parents wanted to be there to defend them in case of danger.

As a father, Ti Marto was very concerned with bringing his children up properly. "In this house there is always peace and quiet," he would say. "And it was a family of eight. I want everything to be as it should." But he always acted prudently, never rushing to rebukes and punishments. First, he found out what had happened and only then did he make the necessary correction.

> Once someone came to our house to talk about something, but the children were making a racket. I put up with it without scolding them,

but when the visitor left, I turned to them and said, very seriously, "If you do this again, you'll see what will happen!" That was enough to quiet them down. From then on, when a stranger came into the house, they all cleared out at once.[17]

Manuel Pedro Marto closed his eyes on this world on February 3, 1957,[18] certainly filled with longing to meet once more his wife and his children who had gone before him to heaven.

LÚCIA'S PARENTS

Maria Rosa Ferreira married António Santos in the parish church of Fátima on November 19, 1891. This couple received seven children from God: Maria dos Anjos, Teresa de Jesus, Manuel Rosa, Glória de Jesus, Carolina de Jesus, Maria Rosa, who died at birth, and the youngest, Lúcia de Jesus.

While seated around the supper table one winter's evening with their children, the parents spoke to them in a way that reflected their profound convictions about family life. Lúcia's sister Glória had asked a question reflecting her doubts about continuing a friendship with a certain boy. Her mother responded: "You should choose a good Christian who fulfils his obligations, works hard, and is honest and respectable. If someone tries to lead you to sin, don't even speak with him, turn your back to him, because his actions are a sign that he is neither honest nor chaste. Such a person will never give you a good life. It is better to stay single than to marry the wrong person."[19]

Lest anyone think she said this only to encourage her children to practice virtue, it is worth adding a statement the father made: "I will tell you something that I never told you before. When I was engaged to your mother, the first thing we agreed upon together was to preserve the flower of our chastity pure until the day of our wedding, in order to offer this to God in exchange for his blessing and for the children he desired to give us. Thus he blessed us, giving us this little family."[20]

Compared with the false image of her father arising from an incorrect interpretation of the four previous *Memoirs*, Lúcia explains: "It is true that the picture I give in the *Memoirs* is very inadequate because I wrote amidst several difficulties—lack of time and of the necessary conditions to improve the text by rereading and correcting it. Then they were published before I knew about it."[21]

Besides the four previous *Memoirs* already published, Lúcia agreed to write two more: part V, dedicated to her father, and part VI, dedicated to her mother. But because their lives were so linked together, making it impossible to speak of one without reference to the other, this book will present a portrait of them based on the six memoirs, with special reference to the last two.

A happy couple

António Santos and Maria Rosa lived in wonderful harmony, even with the normal difficulties of family life. António would always consult his wife about any decision, even if it were only about giving alms—a rare attitude for a man at that time. Maria Rosa did likewise. Both of them had a very high idea of matrimony and lived it out.

Sister Lúcia began by declaring emphatically: "I remember my parents as admirable examples of a Christian family, united in faith, hope, and love."[22]

As if by a supernatural intuition, her father understood that he and his wife formed *one flesh*, and both of them communicated this exemplary charity to their neighbors:

> One day my father was sitting at home shelling beans on the steps of a staircase leading to the attic. My mother was sitting in front of him, leaning against the firewood, peeling potatoes. I was small and was playing in the courtyard—our courtyard was closed by a large gate with wooden shingles. I saw a poor person next to the gate asking for alms. I ran into the house and told my father: "There is a poor man outside asking for alms."
>
> My father got up and went over to the fireplace. With his pocket knife he cut a string of black pudding [a type of sausage] ... and holding it in his hand he asked my mother, "Look here, can I give this to the beggar? Will we miss it?"
>
> My mother answered, "You can, we will never lack what we give to the poor."
>
> My father happily went to the gate to bring the black pudding to the beggar who, seeing it, raised his hands and prayed the Our Father and Hail Mary.... When the beggar finished his prayer he said: "May God give you and your little girl good fortune." My father responded: "Good-bye, brother, until you return." And he went back into the house. I ran behind my father and said to my mother, "The poor beggar prayed for father and me that God would give us his blessing."
>
> My mother answered: "And for me, nothing?"

I didn't know what to say, so my father replied: "For you, too, because you and I are one; everything that is mine is yours and our children's." My mother responded smiling: "So then it is fine."[23]

Lúcia's parents had a very good relationship and they had no inhibitions about showing their affection in an appropriate way in the presence of their children. An incident that Lúcia recounted shows how ready António Santos was to spend time with his children and help them.

> When my father arrived home one evening I said to him: "Father, don't bring me to the dance because I can't go."
>
> "Why not? What happened?" he asked. I answered that I had asked my mother to make a shawl of blue wool with red stripes to wear when I kissed Baby Jesus for the first time on Christmas. Mother said yes, but that she had to make two, one for me and another one for the poor girls who had none and would ask for them. She said she would not have enough time.
>
> My father answered, "There's enough time; I'll help you."
>
> "But Father, you don't know how to crochet."
>
> "That's true, but I can wind the wool for you." And he pulled up a chair next to me. He went to the drawer of the machine to get an empty spool and took out a skein of wool yarn. Then he threaded the spool and sat down next to me to wind the wool.
>
> My mother, who had been working in the kitchen, saw the wool and realized what was happening. Very sweetly she embraced my father from behind the chair and said: "What a good man you are! But look, you can't wind wool like you wind cotton. Wool is wound on your fingers to make a fluffy ball so the wool won't lose its softness." And she taught my father how to wind the wool on the fingers of his left hand. Father looked at his hand, smiled, and said, "I just learned how to do something else: to wind wool on my fingers."[24]

This couple never lost an opportunity to show each other their mutual love. Here is another example: "My mother would come with a refreshing drink of honey prepared with cool water fresh from the well, so that my father could drink it.... And she would then sit beside my father, happily conversing and laughing, feeling so content."[25] And do not suppose that these were scenes from their honeymoon. The one who describes these delightful scenes was their youngest daughter.

A close-knit family

In later years, Lúcia would affectionately recall her childhood. For example, she relates how her family spent their evenings together:

During winter while my mother cleaned the kitchen, my sisters worked the loom and sewed, and my brother took care of the animals, giving them their last food for the day. My father would cut the chestnuts and sweet acorns and then put them in the embers to roast. They could be eaten in the evening to the sound of guitars, folk songs, and the ballads that poor blind people sang.

If it was summer we would go to the threshing floor, where there was always something to do. If it wasn't a day for husking, we would peel beans in the moonlight or the light from lanterns hung on posts nearby: broad beans, peas, beans, chickpeas. Their seeds were set apart to plant, and we would strain the seeds of cabbage, lettuce, and turnips while we breathed the pleasant fresh air. [26]

Good neighbors

António and Maria Rosa did not live wrapped up in their own concerns. They made their home a domestic church, open to anyone who needed help, even at the cost of great sacrifices on their part. Thus, their relationship with their neighbors—another important part of family life—reflected a deep Christian faith.

Our house was like all the other homes: it had a door where people knocked and where everyone was welcomed. Sometimes they came to ask if we had bread, if we could loan them one or two loaves because they had finished theirs before the day to bake a new batch. My mother always had some: "Take it, it's there!"

In the summer they would come to ask for jugs of water because their wells had run dry and it was too far to go and get it from a new well.... My mother—and my father if he was home—would always agree ... saying, "go there and fill your jugs." God would bless that generosity because the well never ran dry.

Other times people would come to ask if we could spare any onions, because theirs had run out.... "Go over there" my mother or father would say, "and take from the baking room whatever you need."

My parents had them hanging from woven grass cords tacked up on the wooden beams in the baking room. And it was always like that. [27]

The trust and generosity between the thirty-three or so families in Aljustrel extended even further, as Sister Lúcia tells us:

The entire village was so united that it seemed like one single family! Everyone knew the place in the wall where the lady of the house would leave the key when she went out. If a neighbor needed anything, she knew that she could go in and help herself to whatever she wanted, and

would always give it back later. Usually, the bread would run out sooner than expected; and then one would ask one's neighbor for some.
Later, when a new batch had been baked, the borrower would pay it
back with some fresh bread straight from the oven. [28]

António and Maria Rosa were always attentive and available to their
neighbors, especially in times of sickness. Their daughter has many
examples of this:

> The neighbors would often come to ask my mother to go to their
> homes because someone was sick. My mother would leave everything
> that had to be done to some of my older sisters who were home.
>
> I remember one day my godmother Teresa was in our house talking
> with my mother. A little boy, the son of Aunt Prazeres (Maria dos
> Prazeres, wife of Manuel Gonçalves da Silva) ... came to ask my
> mother to go to his house because his mother was sick. My mother got
> up quickly to go. My godmother Teresa said to her: "You'll wear your-
> self out, daughter, wanting to take care of everyone!"
>
> My mother answered: "Never mind, I help others and God helps
> me."
>
> If they called her at night, my father would get up and go help.
> Afterward he would bring the message to my mother, and while she
> was getting dressed he lit a lantern so she wouldn't stumble on the way.
>
> During the influenza epidemic in 1918, only my parents, my broth-
> er Manuel, my sister Glória, and myself were at home. I think that my
> sister Carolina was in Leiria. The epidemic struck everyone. My moth-
> er and my sister Glória went from house to house caring for the sick.
> One day Ti Marto went to warn my father not to let my mother or
> daughters go to the homes to care for the sick because the influenza
> was contagious and they could get sick, too.
>
> When my father arrived home that night he forbade my mother
> and his daughters to go out and visit the sick. My mother listened
> silently to everything my father said and then answered: "Look, you are
> right. It is exactly as you say. But how can we leave these people alone
> to die without anyone to give them a cup of water? It would be better
> if you come with me to see their condition and then decide if we can
> leave them abandoned like that."
>
> Then, pointing to a big pot hanging from a chain in the chimney
> over a fire in the fireplace, she said, "Do you see this pot? It's full of
> chickens. Some are not ours; I brought them from the houses of the
> sick because we didn't have enough for everyone. They're boiling to
> make broth, and I already have some small pots over there to bring to
> them. If you want to come with me you could help carry baskets of
> warm bread, then see for yourself and decide what needs to be done."

My father accepted. They filled the pots with broth and they went together, each carrying two baskets, one in each hand. A little later my father returned with a baby in a little basket and said to my sister Glória and me: "Take care of this baby. His parents are both in bed with fever and they can't look after him." He went outside again and after a little while returned with two more children old enough to walk, but unable to care for themselves. So he said: "Take care of these two also. They only know how to cry next to their parents' bed, but the parents are sick with fever and can't help them." So he brought more like them. I don't remember how many.

The next day he came to say that everyone in Aunt Olímpia's house was also in bed with the fever. My parents went there to take care of them too. Everyone recovered, but four of them had some traces of the illness that hindered their recovery and left them weak. One after the other, all four of them died within a few years: Francisco, Jacinta, Florinda, and Teresa. In those days my parents did nothing else but go from house to house treating the sick....

The need was so great that my parents didn't hesitate to let me stay some nights with a widow who lived alone with her son, who was in the final stages of tuberculosis. So she could rest, knowing that there was an eleven-year-old girl who could bring a cup of water or a bowl of broth to her son, or to call her if he needed anything else.... The sick youth passed the nights sitting up in bed propped with pillows, struggling to breathe.

Sometimes I would go to the kitchen to get the fan to cool him and give him a little air. When he saw me there he was so happy and said that he spent those nights better.

Some people warned my father that he should not leave me there because I might get sick too. My father responded: "God will not repay with evil the good I do for him." And so it was! The confidence my father had was not in vain. I am almost eighty-two years old and I never had even the slightest trace of that disease. [29]

Besides all this, the family generously took in a little orphan who had lost her mother at birth.[30] What a magnificent school of charity for the children of this family!

António Santos

Some writings and films have given a rather unfavorable impression of Lúcia's father. But when we read carefully the *Memoirs* that his daughter wrote, together with other documents, we get a very different picture. António Santos appears as a very honorable man. From what his daughter wrote about him, we can see the beauty of a simple soul.

A tireless and diligent worker

Although farming was difficult work, António diligently dedicated himself to it. He also knew how to use his free time for other occupations:

> On rainy days when he couldn't work in the fields, my father stayed in the house cutting wood to the exact size to use in the oven and fire-place, piling them on the patio to dry. Afterward he would put them in the shed and in the baking room to stay dry so they would burn without smoke. If he happened to be home on the days my mother made bread, he would help by putting the wood in the oven. When it was hot he would take out the embers and clean the oven while my mother knead-ed the bread. Then he would put it in the oven to cook.
>
> If my sister Maria dos Anjos had a lot of work, he would sit by the spindle holder to fill the spindles [bobbins] for the loom. If he saw my mother get the water jugs, he would take them from her hands and go fetch water at the well. My mother said that when the infants cried at night, he would get up to take care of them. He would bring them to my mother in bed to give them milk so she wouldn't have to get up. [31]

An honest and generous man

From a practical point of view, the apparitions in the Cova da Iria put the family in financial difficulty because they couldn't grow anything on their farmland. The continual parade of people on their land made it impossible to cultivate. The people who came to the Cova da Iria com-pletely destroyed the crops and the fruit trees. They took away tree branches and plants for souvenirs, forgetting that the land belonged to others and that they should respect private property.

Besides this, the peace of the home was invaded without respect for the family's privacy. Curiosity and the desire to talk to the visionaries, especially the eldest, brought people to enter António Santos' house from morning to night as if it belonged to them. All of this interfered with work and made any private family time impossible.

Despite all this, the head of the family refused categorically to make money from this situation. People began to leave money in the house, as almost always happens when visiting a holy place. But António Santos refused to touch this money, making it quite clear that he would not accept any financial profit from the situation. Once more, Lúcia affirms:

> After the apparitions, my father began to see that more and more peo-ple were going there, instead of the numbers dropping off as he had hoped. They were transforming that site into a sacred place of faith, prayer, and penance, where pilgrims were flocking with faith and

confidence in the maternal protection of the Mother of God. So he then said: "We've lost Cova da Iria forever. We can't count on the produce from that land anymore, but if this is the work of God he will help us get along without it."

When someone told him that people were leaving money near the little holm oak where Our Lady had appeared, and that the money was collected and left for him to compensate for the loss of the land, he said: "God forbid that I should keep this money! It doesn't belong to me. It belongs to Our Lady! Nor do I want anyone in my family to keep as much as five cents of that money! As for the loss of the land, Our Lady will repay me and she will help us."

This was how Senhora Maria Carreira—who got the name of "Ti Maria da Capelinha"—began to keep the money so that it would not be stolen. Later on, they went to ask my father's permission to build the small Chapel of the Apparitions (Capelinha). He not only permitted it but he wanted to contribute, giving for' that purpose twenty square meters of land, including a strip of land for access from the road to the Capelinha. At first he had thought of putting up an iron fence as a barrier to prevent people from crossing over, so he could continue to cultivate the remaining land. But then he realized the crowds could not be held back, so it was useless.

The number of people coming continually to our home, wishing to see me and to speak with me, was greater than ever. My mother did not know what to do! She discussed the situation with my father, to see how to resolve it. She could not constantly go to the field to fetch me, nor did she have anyone to take my place. But the people would not leave unless I met them and went to the Cova da Iria to pray the Rosary with them. People came from everywhere, from far and near, rich and poor, priests, learned and simple people from the villages, and many with their sick who were so pitiful! My father suggested selling the sheep. My mother replied: "I too already thought of that. But how can we get along without the produce of the sheep? The wool we use here in the house and that which we sell, the lambs we slaughter each year for the family's sustenance, the hogs and sheep we sell to help with the house expenses, the milk and cheese! We already have no produce from the Cova da Iria. How can we make it without all this?"

My father responded: "Maybe we could make it with what we grow on the land we have here [around the house]. We could try it. Then if we see later that we can't make it without the sheep, we will go back and buy some."[32]

A peaceful, good-humored man

We find a further description of António Santos in his daughter's notes:

My father was by nature peaceful, joyful, and agreeable; he liked music, feasts, and dances. So even though the Santos family had its own style, he adapted himself well to the ways of the Ferreira Rosa family. He did not have quarrels with anyone, neither with the family nor with strangers. He loved to please everyone and see everyone happy. For example, there were some fig trees on our property near the well … and my father gave that land to a certain family because they had complained that they didn't have even one fig tree next to their house.[33]

The way he spoke to his children, especially his youngest daughter, shows a joyful spirit, simple and full of good humor. He had a melodious voice and loved to sing, especially in the family circle, as Lúcia tells us: "And to the sound of the squeaking shuttle, the reeds clacking on the weaver's loom … and the spinning wheel that my sister Teresa turned gently, he would start to sing."[34]

A good Christian

António Santos lived out his faith with great trust in divine providence, accepting his children as a gift from God. His wife recalled: "When I told him that God was going to grant us a seventh child, he responded: 'Don't be troubled! It is one more blessing from God. Therefore, we will not lack bread on the table or oil in the jar.'"[35]

Lúcia remembers: "My father loved to see the children in our house, and, when it happened that he was at home, he amused them by telling them stories and playing with them."[36]

Nothing in the testimonies about Fátima indicates that António was in any way negligent in his religious duties. On this point his wife's testimony, quoted by his daughter, is important: "One day I heard a conversation between my mother and the vicar of Olival (Father Faustino José Jacinto Ferreira, 1853–1924) who was asking about my father. My mother said: 'He was always a good Christian, a practicing Catholic, and a good worker, even as a youth. I liked this about him and we got married. He always remained very committed to his religious and civil obligations. He was a great friend to me and the children.'"[37]

He never forgot his Christian duties:

On Sundays and holy days of obligation, my father went with the whole family to assist at Mass—almost always at noon. We would get up a little later than usual in the morning, take care of the animals, tidy the house, prepare the dinner, and then we would all go to Mass without being anxious about anything.

When I was still small my father would carry me on his back or let me sit on his shoulder. When we arrived at church, he would give me to my mother because in those days the men were separate from the women in the choir and the sanctuary. After Mass he would return home with the family. [38]

In her memoirs Lúcia noted other examples of his religious practices, such as his care to have his children baptized. He understood the importance of Baptism and never delayed in having his children baptized as soon as they were born. He also followed religious customs such as praying the Angelus: "When the church bells rang for the Angelus, my father would stop work. With his head uncovered he would pray the three Hail Marys and come home." [39]

Everyone in the family of António Santos and Maria Rosa Ferreira joined in prayer, which was usually led by the father.

"Often in the evening, the poor came asking for a place to rest. We always made room for them somewhere to lie down and shared our supper with them. They prayed grace after meals with us, which my father led, and then the Rosary, if it was a day on which it was prayed." [40]

Besides praying with his family, António taught his children about their religion with great skill, in a way suited to their age. At that time it was not typical for a father to teach the catechism to his children; this task was generally left to the mother. But this was not the case in Lúcia's home. Lúcia relates how her father would explain the truths of the faith to her in a way she could understand:

> He would take my tiny hand to teach me how to trace the sign of the cross on my forehead, lips, and heart. Afterward he would teach me to pray the Our Father, Hail Mary, Creed, Confiteor, and Act of Contrition, and he would also teach me the Ten Commandments. Then often when we were eating supper together he would have me repeat all that I had already learned. Pleased, he would turn to my mother and say: "See! It was I who taught her." My mother answered with a smile: "And you are a very good man! May you always be like that...."
>
> Sometimes he would bring me to the threshing floor in the barn and we sat down to enjoy the fresh breeze. He would point at the sky and say: "Look up above, there are Our Lady and the angels: the moon is Our Lady's lamp and the stars are the lamps of the angels. Our Lady and the angels light them and place them in the windows of heaven so that we can see our way at night. The sun that you see rise every day, over there behind the Serra, is our Lord's lamp. He lights it every day to warm us and to enable us to work." This is why I would tell the

other children that the stars are the lamps of the angels and the sun is the lamp of Our Lord.

There in the barn he would teach me catechism, and to sing and to dance. Sometimes my mother and my older sisters who were in the house would come to watch us from behind the fig tree branches and say laughing: "She looks like a little spinning top with her arms in the air, trying to imitate her father's dance steps."[41]

Belief in the apparitions

The apparitions in the Cova da Iria, in which their daughter played a key role and which took place on their own land, could have benefited the Santos family. Instead, in God's mysterious plan, it brought them trials such as the destruction of their crops. Besides that, Lúcia's mother thought that her daughter was lying, despite many proofs to the contrary. Her father tried to restore peace in the family and to smooth things out. Lúcia tells us: "When the apparitions occurred, my mother was very distressed, but my father kept an attitude of faith and trust. When my mother became even more upset, thinking that we were making it all up, my father would say: 'Don't get upset! We don't know if it's true, but we also don't know if it's a lie. Let's wait.'"[42]

António Santos believed very early on that something supernatural was happening and that his youngest daughter was telling the truth. This contrasted with the attitude of others in the family, including his wife, who always doubted the truth of the apparitions.

In an affectionate way, and so as to inspire her confidence, António tried to bring his daughter to confess that she had invented the whole story. But later he fully accepted the truth about the events in the Cova da Iria. Here is how Lúcia describes one of his careful attempts to discover the truth about the apparitions:

> One day while the apparitions were still occurring—it must have been toward the end of July—my father came home, called me, and said: "Let's go for a walk to the well." We went. He sat on the edge of the well, and I sat beside him. Then he said to me: "Look, tell me the truth about whether or not you saw this Lady in the Cova da Iria. Don't be afraid to tell me that you didn't see her, that you said this as a joke and people believed it right away—or simply that you lied. There are many people in the world who tell lies; don't be afraid to tell me if you did. Then people will stop going to the Cova da Iria and everything will be over."
>
> I answered: "I know. But if I saw her how can I say that I didn't? The Lady said to continue coming every month until October." My father got up, and we went to the house.[43]

One of Lúcia's nieces, who later became a religious, asked her mother, Carolina, one day:

"And my grandfather, your father, did he also scold Lúcia because of the apparitions?"

"As far as I know, no. He kept quiet, but if he had spoken, it would have been to say: 'We'll see later. Right now we don't know whether it is the truth or a lie. But it does not seem like lies to me, because all three of them are too young to invent so much that they claim to have heard from that Lady.' "[44]

In fact, the day after he had questioned Lúcia in the farmyard and urged her to tell the whole truth, António Santos talked to Lúcia again. After supper, he said to her:

"While your mother and sisters clean up the kitchen, come with me to the barn." We went there, my father sat on one of the chairs we had there and motioned for me to sit beside him. Then he said to me: "Tomorrow morning, very early, take the sheep to the Cova da Iria. I'll go with you."

I answered: "I feel bad that Jacinta can't come then, for her mother certainly won't let her go that early."

My father answered: "That doesn't matter. Just go and tell Aunt Olímpia that you'll go to the Cova da Iria with our sheep very early in the morning. Jacinta and Francisco can come later if they want to. Tell her that you're going early because it's far away, and after midmorning you'll come home because of the heat...."

I went to give the message to my aunt, who responded: "All right, but for now I'm not going to say anything to Jacinta so she won't start crying. I'll tell her tomorrow morning."

Very early the next morning my father called me and I got up. We ate breakfast while my mother milked the sheep, and we went by way of the heath field so we wouldn't meet people on the way. It was still hard to see. We arrived at the Cova da Iria when the first rays of sun were beginning to appear behind the mountains, in the direction of Aljustrel.

We crossed the road and went down the slope between the olive trees, leading the sheep down the path in a zigzag because they could not go straight down to the Cova....

We went down the hill by the side of the big holm oak. In front of it, a bit lower, was the little holm oak where the Lady appeared. My father went over and looked at it and asked: "Is this where the Lady appears?"

"Yes, it is," I answered.

"How many more times will the Lady come?"

"Until October," I answered.

"If the Lady doesn't come back, the people will also stop coming, and by next year we can go back to cultivating the Cova da Iria like before."

Then he asked: "What do the people do here?"

"They come to pray the Rosary, and they all want me to pray with them."

"So then," my father said, "pray the Rosary with me, too."

"Yes, I will pray."

My father knelt with me in front of the little holm oak and we prayed the Rosary. When we finished, my father got up and said: "Now you stay here with the sheep. I'm going to go with your brother who is working in the heath (barren land). When it gets hot, go home with the sheep."

And so I stayed alone.... By midmorning groups of people appeared. The first one came from the direction of Moita and Santa Caterina. We had barely finished the Rosary with this group when another appeared ... and I prayed another Rosary with them, too. Then I went home with my sheep because it was already getting hot. My father came for lunch, too, and told my mother all he had seen.[45]

Despite so many difficulties, Lúcia's father never relinquished his responsibilities as head of the family, nor did he simply let things take their course. He looked at the problems in their proper perspective and then took whatever measures he deemed most appropriate.

The false portrayal of this good man

Unfortunately, some negative aspects crept into the popular image of António Santos. He was portrayed as a heavy drinker, given to wasting the family's income on gambling. He was also said to have had conflicts with the parish priest. Lúcia deals firmly with this slander:

Neither I nor my sisters (whom I asked about this) ever heard anyone say that my father drank so much that he would get drunk, or that he would come home speaking nonsense, or mistreat anyone, either in word or action. He never disturbed the peace and tranquility of the family atmosphere. But people were thinking such things when they exaggerated my father's conduct.[46]

This falsehood stemmed from an incident that occurred in the Cova da Iria on July 13, which some people falsely attributed to an excess of alcohol. When his wife asked him about this, António Santos explained simply what had happened, just as his daughter reports:

They came to get me, saying that I should go to the Cova da Iria to send the people away, since they had already greatly damaged that year's crop. I went, but when I arrived there and told them to leave the area, one of them darted toward me with such force, which I wasn't expecting, that it threw me to the ground. I got up, but seeing that I couldn't do anything in the face of so many people, I went away.[47]

Another falsehood that circulated was that he left his family to wrestle with their problems while he went off and wasted the family's money on gambling. But the truth is that toward the end of the apparitions, people would crowd into António's house. They robbed him of peace and quiet and nagged his daughter with endless questions, and sometimes they were aggressive. To avoid these crowds António Santos would leave the house and return home only at the end of the day.

Lúcia's mother would send her to call her father home for supper. When he saw her, he would ask if all the strangers had gone:

> When I said they had, my father would get up, say good-bye to his friends, and take me by the hand. In good spirits he would eat supper with the family, listening carefully to what I said and to the problems my mother talked about. When we finished eating, he would give thanks to God as he always did. If there was "peeling" [husking corn] or other work to be done in the threshing floor … he took part in it all. He would direct the work while he enjoyed the fresh breeze that blew pleasantly around us in the moonlight, with the lanterns hanging from the railings around the threshing floor. When it was time, he brought the day's work to an end and, with his family, retired to rest....
>
> [Concerning card playing, Lúcia explains:] Card playing was the only entertainment available for men at that time, and the stakes they played for were not high enough to ruin a family. Each player would place a coin on the table. The players would agree on the amount: perhaps 10 réis or 1 vintém or at most 1 tostão. The winner took all the coins, but he had to treat all the players to a glass of wine. Thus, each one lost a little and gained a little.[48]

António Santos enjoyed this pastime. After a week of hard work in the fields, he joined his friends for a game on Sunday afternoons while the children were playing nearby and his wife was talking to her friends.

But what of the accusation that he had conflicts with his parish priest? In those days, Easter duty could be made only in one's own parish. The parish would note in a register whether the parishioner had gone to confession, received Holy Communion, and contributed to the support of the parish.

Lúcia explains what happened:

> There had been an uproar in the village against the pastor. My father didn't want to get involved in this, but it made a bad impression on

him. Because of that, he stopped making his Easter duty as he had been doing, and stopped going to confession to the parish priest. But he didn't stay away from the church. He continued to go to Holy Mass every Sunday and on all the holy days of obligation. But he would go to Vila Nova de Ourém for confession, and every year he went to the feast of Our Lady of Ortiga, where he would confess and receive Communion in order to gain the jubilee indulgences. He went there until the end of his life, and he brought me with him a few days before his death. Afterward we went to eat supper at the house of my sister Teresa, who lived nearby in a place called Lomba.[49]

In fact, something had happened in the parish of Fátima, as has happened in many parishes, "a sad episode that turned all the people of the parish against the parish priest."[50] Lúcia was silent about the reason for the disagreement. Always discreet and charitable, she said only what was necessary to defend her father.[51]

António Santos changed parishes because of the bad impression left on him by these disagreements, but he never abandoned his Christian duties. However, his wife felt it would be better for him to participate fully in his own parish instead of attending another one, if only to avoid attracting attention. So she tried to help her husband overcome this difficulty.

António Santos had a magnanimous heart and a deep faith, and he never allowed himself to harbor the slightest resentment. This became very clear when he approached the end of his earthly life.

António Santos' sudden death

António had always enjoyed robust health despite the heavy labor on the farm. Along with his good health, he had a pleasant disposition that helped him face the most difficult situations. He greatly supported his wife through the problems that arose from the events of May 13, 1917.

His sudden death in the summer of 1919 added to the family's sufferings. Lúcia tells us:

> My father was a healthy, robust man who said he didn't know what it was to have a headache. But suddenly, in less than twenty-four hours, an attack of double pneumonia carried him to eternity. My sorrow was so great that I thought I would die too. He was the only one who always showed himself to be my friend. When discussions arose against me in the family, he was the only one who defended me.
>
> "My God, my God," I exclaimed, secluded in my room. "I never thought you had so much suffering marked out for me! But I suffer for

your love, in reparation for sins committed against the Immaculate Heart of Mary, for the Holy Father, and for the conversion of sinners."[52]

Before his death, António Santos gave an example of humility and a spirit of faith by his readiness to receive the pastor into his house, regardless of all that had happened previously. His daughter's statement leaves no doubt whatever:

> Happily my father finished well his "mission" on earth.... He fell sick on July 30, 1919. My mother called the doctor, who said it was a case of double pneumonia. He prescribed a remedy, but the medicine was to no avail. On the following morning, feeling very sick, my father asked my mother to go and call the priest for confession and the last sacraments. My mother warned him that she might find only the pastor. "It doesn't matter!" my father responded, "as long as it is a priest."
>
> My mother sent to call him, but the pastor, thinking it wasn't an urgent case, delayed in coming. My father died in the arms of my mother and her sister Olímpia, repeating the prayers that they suggested to him, which were used at the time in such cases.[53]

António Santos went to the Father's house on July 31, 1919, at 10:00 A.M., a victim of pneumonia.[54]

Maria Rosa Ferreira Santos

Maria Rosa Ferreira personified the valiant woman of Sacred Scripture.[55] She was born on July 6, 1869, in Perulheira, in the parish of Nossa Senhora dos Remédios do Reguengo do Fetal, in the municipality of Batalha and the Diocese of Leiria. Born into a devout Catholic family, she was baptized in the parish church on July 18. Her parents put her under the protection of Our Lady, as Lúcia tells us:

> In this way God wanted to put this child, from the cradle, under the special protection of Our Lady, to take care of her and prepare her for such a close association with the message that would be sent to us forty-eight years later.[56]

In 1883 or 1884 she went with her parents—Joaquim Ferreira and Rosa da Incarnação—to live in the village of Aljustrel, her father's hometown. He was accompanied by his wife and six children. His daughter Justina was already married. Lúcia's grandfather welcomed them with great joy.

Maria Rosa already had a taste for good literature, which she later sought to pass on to her youngest daughter. Maria Rosa had inherited several books from an aunt: *Exercises of Perfection and Christian Virtues* by Father Afonso Rodrigues, S.J.; *A Short Mission* by Father Manuel José Gonçalves Couto; and *The Imitation of Christ* by Thomas à Kempis.

After a happy childhood, Maria Rosa began her courtship with António Santos, the man she would marry at the age of twenty-one. She and her husband stayed in her family home to take care of her aging parents. Her mother died on November 26, 1891, a year after Maria Rosa's marriage; her father died on August 1, 1907, at the age of 84.[57]

Maria Rosa Ferreira looked on matrimony as a road to holiness. She understood from the beginning of her marriage that the love of God had to encompass the love of one's spouse and children. She lived in harmony with the man who had brought her to the altar, accepting generously their difference in temperament. They later told their children how seriously they had both prepared for marriage, especially by being chaste throughout their courtship. It is no wonder that, on a certain occasion, Maria Rosa's husband exclaimed enthusiastically: "God has given me the best wife in the world!"

Attentive to her neighbors' needs

As we have already seen, many people knocked at the door of this couple's home. In all simplicity, neighbors would ask Senhora Maria Rosa for help. The good woman would leave everything to help them. Her husband collaborated generously in these acts of charity, as has been noted. This charity never grew less, even when economic losses burdened the family. "Despite everything, my mother never stopped helping the poor. She would say: 'We have little, but the little we have has been given that we might help those who have even less than us.'"[58]

Maria Rosa Ferreira had a special gift for looking after the sick. She understood, as few do, the value of the works of mercy, especially almsgiving, good advice, and care of the sick. She was unsurpassed in this, and she drew her husband and her children to the same generosity.

A loving mother

Maria Rosa was gentle and loving with her children, but she did not allow them to indulge in whims. She was exacting in this, never passing over anything she thought was wrong. For example, Lúcia recounts an incident in which she learned a good lesson:

One day [my mother] had prepared for our supper some broad beans and potatoes cut into small pieces with slices of sausage.... When my mother gave me my plate I didn't take it from her, saying I didn't eat beans because I didn't like them.

My mother responded: "Well, my little girl, here we don't eat only what we like, we eat what we have, like everyone does. Until you eat the beans, you won't get anything else." She put the plate on top of the table, expecting that I would take it and eat. Everyone told me to eat because it was very good, but my stubbornness wouldn't let me. Every so often my father would reach over with a bean or a slice of sausage on his fork, wanting to put it in my mouth so I could taste how good it was. But no! I wouldn't eat it.

At the end of the meal, my mother took out all the food that was in the drawer of the kitchen table: the bread, cheese, olives, etc. She put everything up high on a board that was hanging from the ceiling, which I couldn't reach. She closed the pantry door, put the plate with the beans in the table drawer and said: "Your dish is here until you decide to eat. Unless you eat the beans, you won't eat anything else."

I spent the afternoon feeling very hungry. Once in a while I went into the kitchen and checked the table drawer, but only the plate with the beans was there. I looked up and saw the board that had the bread, cheese, olives, etc., but I couldn't reach it.

I went out to the courtyard as far as the well, but the trees didn't have any fruit yet.... At last suppertime arrived, and I was hoping my mother would give me some stewed peas with rice and rabbit meat, which we were having for supper. But my mother took the plate of beans out of the table drawer and said to me: "Take this, here is your plate. If you refuse to eat the beans, you won't get anything else."

I was so hungry by then and I realized that I had no way out, so I took the plate of beans and forced myself to eat them.... When I had eaten about half, my mother took away the plate of beans and gave me another plate with a serving of peas, rice, and rabbit meat, saying: "Now that you have conquered your stubbornness, eat what the others are eating, and then you can have a bowl of curdled milk and bread, like the rest of us."

I learned a lesson for life. I never again had the temptation to say: "I won't eat this because I don't like it."[59]

Maria Rosa also sought to develop generosity and a family spirit in her children. Lúcia recounts an incident concerning how her mother strove to teach her children to be generous in sharing:

My mother knew that her youngest daughter was very fond of fruit. One day she noticed how the child was looking to see when the first figs would ripen; as soon as she discovered a ripe one, she picked it secretly and ran back to the house to give it to her mother to eat. My mother, moved, took the gift into her hands, kissed her daughter and told her to keep the fig until that evening so that her father and the rest of the family could share it! One fig among so many is nothing, but the love that accompanied the little piece that everyone received from the first fig that had ripened on their own fig trees that year meant a great deal to them. It made everyone happy, stirring up in them a feeling of joy and satisfaction.[60]

A good catechist

In educating her children, Maria Rosa was guided not only by her heart, but also by her intelligence and her faith. She trained them in the human virtues: a spirit of sacrifice, solidarity with others, generosity, temperance, love of work, and above all truthfulness. She detested lies, as will be seen when she became immersed in a sea of doubts about the veracity of the apparitions. She took advantage of the warm summer afternoons and evenings, when no farm work could be done, to instruct her children. She would also teach other neighborhood children, as they would gather around her house to play with her children.

Doubts about the apparitions

It seems that Lúcia's mother doubted the truth of the apparitions of Fátima for her whole life. It was a difficult trial for both mother and daughter. Lúcia never had the joy of seeing her mother share her happiness over the apparitions, and that must have been a great source of sorrow for her.

When news of the events began to circulate, Maria Rosa Ferreira's first reaction was to think that it all sprang from the fertile imagination of a lively child. Besides, Lúcia was the oldest of the visionaries. So if the story was made up, it had probably come from her. Years later, in the silence of the Carmel in Coimbra, Sister Lúcia recalls how these facts about Mary's appearances became known:

> The news of the event was spreading. My mother began to worry, and she wanted at any cost to make me deny what I said. One day before I went out with the flock, she wanted me to confess I had lied. To this end she didn't spare caresses, threats, or even the broomstick. Failing to obtain any response other than silence or the confirmation of what I had already said, she told me to take out the sheep. She said that during the day I should think about how she would never allow her children to tell a lie, much less one of this type. She warned me that by the

evening she would make me go to those people I had deceived, confess I had lied, and ask their forgiveness.[61]

Maria Rosa tried a second time to get her daughter to admit that she had lied. She even brought Lúcia to the parish priest in the hope that she would tell the complete truth. This was a great trial for Lúcia, especially because the priest suggested it all might be the work of the devil. That idea troubled Lúcia. But she kept to her original story, further exasperating her mother.

As the events unfolded, Maria Rosa was deeply concerned that the whole affair was getting out of hand. She thought it was the work of the devil because of its negative effects: the disturbances caused by the apparitions, the crowds of people at the Cova da Iria who not only destroyed the crops—an important source of income for the family— but also made any future cultivation impossible, and other difficulties.

The endless stream of visitors continued to increase. This took up her daughter's time and obliged Maria Rosa to have somebody always at hand to fetch Lúcia from the pasture where she was minding the flock. At times Maria Rosa would exclaim with exasperation:

> "Every day more and more people come from everywhere.... Never have I seen anything like it in my life. We have the church right there with the Eucharistic Lord, and instead of going there they go to the Cova da Iria to pray in front of a holm oak. Where have you ever seen such madness? Spare us, Lord! If this little one would just decide to say she lied, everything would stop once and for all."[62]

She remained firmly convinced it was all a lie. After the apparition of July 13, all the doubts that had been assailing Lúcia vanished. But her mother's doubts remained. Not even the miracle of the sun that occurred on October 13 changed her convictions, as Lúcia relates:

> After that day people asked my mother: "So, Maria Rosa, now do you believe Our Lady appeared there in the Cova da Iria?" My mother answered: "I'm still not sure if all this is true!"
>
> "But didn't you see the miracle of the sun?" they asked.
>
> "I saw it, I saw it, but it seems to me to be something so great that we are not worthy of it! I'm still wondering if this could be true! I don't know!"[63]

A miraculous cure

Not even the grace of a sudden cure that Maria Rosa received could make her change her mind. A serious illness had brought her to the point of death. Lúcia stayed at her bedside, in anguish, and heard her exclaim, in great distress:

> "My poor daughter! What will become of you without a mother? I am dying like one nailed to a cross, and the thought of you pierces my heart." She burst into bitter sobs and pressed and hugged me tighter and tighter without letting me go. My sister forcibly tore me away from her arms and brought me into the kitchen, forbidding me to go back to my mother's room. She said: "Mother is dying of grief because of you and all the trouble you have caused."
>
> I knelt down, leaning on a bench with the most profound bitterness and sorrow I have ever felt in my life and offered this sacrifice to God that my mothers' health would improve. A little while later my sisters Maria and Teresa came to me and said: "Lúcia, if you really saw Our Lady, go now to the Cova da Iria and ask her to cure our mother. Make any promise to her that you want, and we will fulfill it. Then we will believe."
>
> I got up and went, taking the short cut through the barren field so I wouldn't meet anyone on the way, praying the Rosary as I went. I finished it on my knees at the holm oak where Our Lady had appeared. Shedding many tears, I asked Our Lady to cure my mother. At the same time I promised to go there for nine consecutive days with my sisters to pray the Rosary on our knees, while going from the end of the road to the place where the holm oak was.... On the last day I promised to bring nine poor children home and then give them supper.[64]

Today, pilgrims to Fátima still pray the Rosary on their knees, sometimes painfully and with great effort. Lúcia was the first to carry out this act of penance. She continued to relate this moving story:

> Encouraged with the hope that Our Lady would grant me this grace, I got up and went home. When I arrived, my sister Glória was in the kitchen and she said to me: "Lúcia, come here. Mother is already better."
>
> My father was sitting with my mother in the bedroom. When he heard us talking, he came to meet me, took me by the hand and said: "Come and give your mother a hug. She is much better."
>
> My mother was sitting up in bed sipping a bowl of chicken broth. My father held it so that she could hug me.[65]

Maria Rosa asked whether Lúcia had gone to pray for her at the place of the apparitions, and told Lúcia that she was already feeling much better. As can be imagined, the whole atmosphere of the house changed to joy, although the mother prudently remained in bed until she had completely recovered. They prayed the Rosary, while Maria Rosa intoned hymns and said she wished to go on her knees from the road to the apparition site. António, however, did not want her to do that just then, for fear that his wife's health would again deteriorate.

After she recovered, the whole family went to fulfill the promise. They said the Rosary, and Maria Rosa began the hymn "Hail, Noble Patroness." Yet the cloud of doubt in Maria Rosa's mind did not dissipate. From time to time, she would say, as if thinking aloud, "I don't know how it is! Our Lady cures me and still it seems that I cannot believe!" Even when saying good-bye to Lúcia as she left for the College of Vilar, in Porto, her mother said to her, "Off you go, daughter, and if you really did see Our Lady, she will take care of you. I entrust you to her. But if you were telling lies, I don't know what will happen to you."[66]

Many years later, Maria Rosa gave the same explanation for her attitude. It is the last testimony we have of her opinion about the apparitions. She had a conversation with José Alves Correia da Silva, Bishop of Leiria. He had invited Lúcia's mother to spend a few days in an estate in the suburbs of Braga called the Quinta da Formigueira.

> One day when we were eating supper, the bishop asked my mother: "Senhora Maria Rosa, what can you tell me about the apparitions of Our Lady at the Cova da Iria?"
>
> She replied: "Your Excellency, I don't know what to say. It is something so great that we are not worthy of, so it seems impossible to me that it could be true."
>
> The bishop answered: "That's true, but don't you know that God gives graces to those who don't deserve them, as he did with Saint Paul who was thrown down off a horse, in order to transform a sinner into an apostle?"
>
> My mother replied: "Only in that way."[67]

Then she went back into the silence of the doubt that had always tormented her, the doubt about the truth of the apparitions, and she carried it with her into eternity. She had, however, a certain logic to her reasoning: "Why do so many people go to prostrate themselves in prayer in a deserted field, while the living God, the God of our altars in the Eucharist, remains alone, abandoned in the tabernacle? Why do they leave money under the holm oak for no purpose, while renovations to the church cannot be completed for lack of funds?"[68]

Maria Rosa gives Lúcia permission to enter religious life

During their stay in Braga, Lúcia, now eighteen years old, asked her mother for permission to enter religious life. Her mother answered bluntly, with her usual prudence:

"Look daughter, I don't know anything about that kind of life. I will ask the bishop."

She went downstairs to look for the bishop, who was sitting on a bench in front of the porch, reading in the shade of the trellised vines. As soon as the bishop saw her, he called her and had her sit next to him on the bench. I watched from above the porch. I didn't hear what they were saying, but my mother came back after a long conversation. She was happy to tell me yes, on the condition that I would let her know if I wasn't happy and it didn't work out well.[69]

The Portuguese used to have a tradition that the youngest daughter—whether married or single—would stay at home with the parents until they died. Lúcia knew she was the youngest in the family, so she asked her sister Maria dos Anjos to carry out this duty for her. Maria willingly agreed.

Lúcia's mother went to visit her at Túy for her final profession in the Congregation of Saint Dorothy, on October 3, 1934. Perhaps it never occurred to Maria Rosa that she would never again see her daughter in this world. At the end of the ceremony, Lúcia was alone with her mother for a few moments, and they talked about the apparitions of Fátima. Hoping to remove the doubt from her mother's heart, Lúcia asked her:

"Mother, you told me you would let me go away to see if everything would stop once I had gone. It's been thirteen years since I left and I have never returned. Has everything stopped?"

My mother answered promptly, with a certain disillusionment: "Nothing stopped! It keeps getting worse!"

"So you see it wasn't I who was there to deceive people, it is God and Our Lady who are there."

My mother replied: "If I knew for sure it was Our Lady who appeared to you, then I would be pleased to give her the Cova da Iria and all that I have. But I am not sure!"[70]

Maria Rosa's departure for heaven

As death approached and she was unable to travel, Maria Rosa wrote to Lúcia asking her to come to see her and to give her a farewell embrace. She did not want to die without seeing her daughter once more. The rules of Lúcia's congregation did not permit such a visit, and Maria Rosa had to be satisfied with a letter from her daughter, encouraging her to offer this sacrifice to the Lord and promising her prayers.

Upon hearing this refusal her mother sobbed, "So they won't let her return to Fátima even to assist at my death! If I had known this would happen, I wouldn't have let her go there! But I offer God this great sacrifice so that he will watch over her and always help her to be good."[71] Crying, she bowed her head, holding it in her hands while leaning on her knees.

A few days later, feeling that death was near, and wanting to at least hear Lúcia's voice on the telephone, she asked her daughter Teresa to call. She did, but to her great sorrow, Teresa was told no, with an explanation that this was not allowed, either. When she heard this, the holy woman said with resignation: "This is the last drop that God reserved for me in the depths of the chalice that I still had to drink on this earth. I will drink it for his love."[72]

Lúcia, busy with her duties, knew nothing then about her mother's request; she found out about it later.

Maria Rosa asked to draw her last breath in her daughter Lúcia's room. A priest, sent expressly from the Sanctuary of Fátima, gave her the last sacraments and the apostolic blessing. She went to meet the Heavenly Father at the age of seventy-three, on July 16, 1942, the feast of Our Lady of Mount Carmel, to whom she had a great devotion and whose scapular she wore.

Chapter 2

The Shepherds: Lúcia, Francisco, and Jacinta

TWO FAMILIES FROM the Serra d'Aire, located in the center of Portugal, unknowingly prepared the heralds of Our Lady, who would bring her message to the whole world. Our Lady appeared to three children in the Cova da Iria: Lúcia, the eldest, age ten, and her cousins, Jacinta, age seven, and Francisco, age eight, who were the two youngest children of the Marto family. They were all born in the same area in the parish of Fátima. Lúcia's memoirs provide the details of the story.

A village in the solitude of the Serra d'Aire

Aljustrel is about a kilometer from Fátima... and about two kilometers from the Cova da Iria, which belonged to my parents when the apparitions occurred. The village of Aljustrel has one street with a few little curves.... Coming from Fátima, we first arrive at Jacinta's parents' house, the eighth on the right. Continuing down the road, perhaps after a two or three minute walk ... my parents' house is the eighth one on the left. It is a standard height, whitewashed inside and out. The side facing the road has a door with a porch and two windows: the first was my parents' bedroom; the other is a room that had two looms: my eldest sister used one of them, and various young girls learned to weave on the other.

Between these two rooms was a square room that we called the outdoor house. It was entered by a door that opened onto the street, and then one had to climb four stone steps. Five doors opened off this room

... first, my parents' room; next, the room where my three eldest sisters slept; then the room where I slept with my sister Carolina; then another door that led to the kitchen; and the door to the room with the looms.[1]

LÚCIA DE JESUS

Birth and Baptism

The eldest of the three shepherds, Lúcia de Jesus Santos was born on March 28, 1907. She tells us:

> Asked when I was born—I heard my mother recount in an interview with Father Manúel Formigão, who had asked her my date of birth— my mother answered: "We say it is on March 22 because she is registered as having been born on that day, but this is actually not true. She was born March 28, 1907." Only then did I learn the real date of my birth. This wasn't surprising, because in Fátima at the time we didn't attach any importance to one's birthday, nor did we celebrate it; we did not speak about the subject.[2]

Lúcia's mother tells us what happened the day Lúcia was born: "It was Holy Thursday morning, I went to Holy Mass and Communion, expecting to return later to visit the Blessed Sacrament. But that was not to be, because that afternoon she was born."[3]

Lúcia was baptized two days after her birth, on Holy Saturday, then known as Alleluia Saturday. An unusual circumstance regarding her baptism explains why her birth date had been given as March 22, as her mother relates:

> Her father took care of getting her baptized right away. He couldn't arrange for it to take place the following week because of his work. But because it was required for fathers to bring their children for baptism eight days after birth, her father decided to give Lúcia's birth date as March 22. Thus, the pastor baptized her on Holy Saturday, which was March 30.[4]

At the baptism, the godfather was Anastácio Vieira, a friend of Lúcia's father. The godmother was Maria Rosa Marto, the daughter of José Pedro Marto, who was Jacinta and Francisco's uncle. The godmother's father insisted that the child should be called Lúcia. The visionary herself recounts the story:

[My father] invited a young neighbor to be my godmother. She was the goddaughter of my mother.... She gladly accepted and asked her father's permission.... Her father asked what they would name the little girl. She told him it would be Maria Rosa, because her mother already had four daughters and none of them had that name.... Her father said: "No! You have to name her Lúcia! If not, I won't give you permission to be her godmother." She went to tell my parents, who were surprised and asked: "But where did your father get that name?"[5]

Lúcia's family was amazed because in Fátima, as in other parts of Portugal, it was customary to give the youngest daughter her mother's name, or a boy, his father's. However, it is worth emphasizing the coincidence: "Lúcia" means "she who shines." This child, entrusted by Our Lady with the task of spreading the message of Fátima throughout the world, was baptized with a name appropriate for her future mission.

Maria Rosa still tried to prevent the godmother from giving her child such a name, begging her not to listen to the strange suggestion. But "she couldn't do anything, because she resting in bed for the thirty days of recuperation that was the custom after the birth of baby girls (forty days for boys)."[6]

When the rest of the family returned home after the Baptism, Maria Rosa asked anxiously whether the child had received her name. They answered, "No, it is Lúcia." Gazing at the child in the cradle beside her bed, Maria Rosa murmured, sadly, "Ah, Lúcia, where did they get such a name?"

Her parents used to tell Lúcia that she had come from heaven surrounded by roses and flowers in "a little wicker basket we had in the house."[7]

Lúcia's childhood

Lúcia grew up an ordinary child in a healthy family under her parents' watchful, demanding, and loving care. She was healthy and robust. As can be seen in her photographs, Lúcia had a round face, dark eyes, and full eyebrows. She gave the impression of being resolute, serious, and thoughtful. She liked to dress well, especially at feasts. She would wear a gold chain, large earrings that reached her shoulders, and an attractive hat decorated with gilded beads and feathers of different colors.[8]

Her sister Maria dos Anjos tells us: "We loved her very much because she was very intelligent and loving. When as a little girl she would return home with the cattle, she would throw herself into her mother's arms. Holding her closely, she would play with her, hugging and kissing her."[9]

Lúcia was a great friend of all the children and they took to her readily. There might easily be ten of them in the yard of her home. At one time, her mother put her in charge of some local children while their mothers worked in the fields.

"She would dress up the little children with flowers or ivy, hold processions with holy pictures, and organize games.... If they were in the church, she would sing hymns to Our Lady ... and end everything with a blessing."[10]

She loved to play "hide-and-seek," and she had a gift for story-telling—some were stories she had heard, others she made up herself—and the children listened with great interest. She was popular with the little ones.

> They would run up next to me, excited and happy, and when they knew I would be taking my flock around the village, groups of them would come along to spend the day with me. My mother used to say: "I don't know what attraction you could have; the children run to be with you as if there were some feast!" But as for me, I often felt ill at ease in the midst of so much screaming, and so for that reason I would try to hide.[11]

The visionary of Fátima cherished many memories of her happy childhood at home, from the pastimes she enjoyed to the games she played with other children. She was blessed by God "with the use of reason from my earliest childhood,"[12] and she learned to pray very early on in her mother's arms. Lúcia testifies: "The first thing I learned was the Hail Mary, because my mother used to hold me in her arms while she taught it to my sister Carolina."[13]

Lúcia recalled how her sisters would dress her when she accompanied them to festive celebrations: "I had the most elegant clothes used by the peasants of my region at that time. I wore a pleated skirt, a shiny belt, a cashmere kerchief ... and a hat with golden beads and bright-colored feathers."[14]

She talked like a parrot, to use her own expression, and she went with her sisters to dances suitable for families, where the people of the village enjoyed themselves.

With such a happy childhood, Lúcia continued to grow and develop in every way. Meanwhile, unknown to Lúcia, the Lord was preparing her for the mission he would soon entrust to her. While still a small child, she learned from her mother the practice of charity, helping the sick and needy:

> Sometimes my mother would prepare a small basket ... with gifts that she sent me to bring to various persons whom she knew didn't have much.... Sometimes it was a basket of chestnuts, and when she sent me to bring them to Ti Coxa's house or to the old lady ... she would send me there with a bundle of dry firewood—because theirs was wet since they couldn't guard it from the rain—so they could light the fire and roast the chestnuts. So I would leave, carrying the chestnuts on my arm and the bundle of firewood on my head.[15]

Learning to live a virtuous life

In her daily family life, by means of the small tasks that her mother gave her, and by her keen spirit of observation, Lúcia learned how to live a virtuous life. As a child, she had her occasional tantrums. In all simplicity, the visionary of Fátima tells us about them. Fortunately, her mother did not let Lúcia indulge her whims but corrected her faults, as she did when Lúcia refused to eat her plate of beans. Another incident occurred when Lúcia was trying to find the nests with the eggs the chickens had laid:

> The next day I was spying on [the chickens] and I saw them fly over the courtyard gate and go down the path toward the well. I ran after them and saw that they went under some thistle on a low wall that supported the soil next to the well. My father had some beehives there. Burrowing under the thistle, the chickens disappeared behind the beehive.... I took a stick and tried to move the thistle, wanting to see where the chickens were and what they were doing there. Instead, I saw bees buzzing all around me, stinging me on every side. I threw away the stick, and shaking them off I ran to the house, calling for my mother: "Mother, help! The bees want to eat me!"[16]

Besides going to her daughter's aid, Lúcia's mother gave her some advice so that, next time, she would be less curious and more prudent.

Lúcia had her difficulties, too, resulting from childish ways that she slowly grew out of with the help of grace. She herself concluded that it is part of human weakness to slip and fall. She recounts one incident that had particular significance for her:

> It must have been around Christmastime, which was when my mother would make offerings. She took three good clusters of grapes that she

had in the loft, arranging them well in a small basket ... and she sent me to Fátima to bring them to the pastor. I went there, but on the way I began to nibble on the top bunch of grapes ... so that by the time I arrived at the square in front of the church, I realized that the cluster of grapes was in no condition to offer to the pastor. I ate the rest of them and threw the stem over the wall around the cemetery ... and went to give the two remaining bunches of grapes. I walked up the steps of the rectory, knocked on the door, and the pastor's sister answered the door, smiling and grateful.

I went down the steps and across the square, heading to the church to visit the Blessed Sacrament.... I then realized that if the pastor went to tell my mother that there were two bunches of grapes and not three, she would scold me and ask what had happened to the rest. So with this fear, I went into church, knelt down next to the altar rail and prayed: "Please don't let the pastor tell my mother that there were two bunches, not three." So I prayed I don't know how many Our Fathers and Hail Marys. I prayed like that all the way home ... and God granted my prayer. I believe my mother never found out, because she never said anything to me.[17]

A childhood marked by a life of prayer

In her family, Lúcia learned the various popular devotions the Portuguese people practiced. She tells how her family celebrated the May devotions at home. People from various districts in the parish gathered to participate:

In the month of May we would pray the Rosary as a family every day. My mother would start this prayer at night after supper.... At the end of every mystery we would sing to Our Lady a verse of the hymn, "Hail, Noble Patroness." Many other people came from the surrounding villages.... Sometimes there were so many people that they could not fit inside our small house. They stayed outside on the road and in the courtyard, joining their voices with ours, praying and singing the praises of God and of Our Lady, asking their blessings and protection.[18]

Learning the catechism

From an early age, Lúcia was attentive to what she saw and heard. But she interpreted things with the mind of a child, as the following delightful episode indicates. One day she heard her mother asking her father what fruits from the farm were ready to be picked:

[My father said:] "The fruits that are now ready for the Holy Spirit [it was near Pentecost] are fava beans, peas, and cherries." I had this in my mind, and when on Sunday after Mass the pastor taught catechism to the children, he asked: "Now then, children, which one of you can tell me what the fruits of the Holy Spirit are?"

I stood up very quickly and said: "I can!"

"Yes?" he answered, adding, "tell us what they are."

"They are beans, peas, and cherries." I was very surprised when I saw the pastor laugh, along with my mother and all the other people who were in church.... Then the pastor asked me: "Tell me, my little one, who taught you that?"

I answered: "I heard my father say it to my mother." [19]

Lúcia's mother, of course, hastened to explain why Lúcia had given that answer.

A joyful family atmosphere

Lúcia grew up in a healthy family that enjoyed dialogue and shared experiences. The following is one example among so many presented in the *Memoirs:*

Supper was a happy and serene meal, shared in peace and contentment. Each one freely recounted the events of the day, while the others laughed or made comments.... Life in our house was like that, peaceful, serene, and happy. We had no worries other than those arising from our daily work, which each one did according to what our parents decided without refusals or discussions. My father took charge of the work in the fields, while my mother looked after running the house.... [20]

In her six *Memoirs*, Lúcia recreates for us [21] not only her childhood, but also family customs and events with such detail that we seem to be witnessing them.

First Holy Communion

Lúcia made her first Communion at the age of six. [22] She owed that grace to the intervention of the Servant of God, Father Francisco Cruz, who happened to be preaching in her parish at the time. With her prodigious memory, Lúcia tells us about that unforgettable day:

The day approached that the pastor had designated for the children of the village to make their solemn first Holy Communion. My mother thought that her little daughter knew her catechism and because she was six years old, she could receive her first Communion. For this purpose she sent me with my sister Carolina to the catechism classes that the pastor was giving the children to prepare for that day. I went there bursting with joy, hoping that I would soon receive my God for the first time. The priest was teaching while seated on a chair up on a platform. He called me next to him, and when some child didn't know an answer, he would have me answer....

The evening before the great day, the pastor sent all the children to church to tell them definitely who would make their Communion in the morning. I was so disappointed when the priest called me ... and said I had to wait to until I was seven years old! I immediately started to cry, and since I was next to my mother, I put my head on her knees, sobbing. Just then another priest came into the church, one whom the pastor had asked to help with confessions.[23] He asked the reason for my tears, and after finding out he took me to the sacristy and questioned me regarding doctrine and the mystery of the Eucharist. Then he led me by the hand to the pastor and said: "Father Pena, you can allow this little one to make her Communion. She understands better than many of the others."

"But she's only six years old," objected the good priest.

"It doesn't matter! I'll take the responsibility for that myself."

"All right then." The good pastor said to me. "Go and tell your mother that tomorrow you can make your first Communion."

Off I went, clapping my hands with joy, and running all the way to give my mother the good news. She immediately began to prepare me to go to confession that afternoon.[24]

A "public" confession and a smile from the Mother of God

Lúcia prepared for the Sacrament of Reconciliation with all the seriousness possible at such a tender age. The confessor was Father Francisco Cruz, and Lúcia would always remember this moment with nostalgia and gratitude:

Upon arriving at church I told my mother that I wanted to confess to the visiting priest [Father Cruz]. He was hearing confessions in the sacristy, sitting on a chair. My mother knelt down in front of the altar near the door, next to the other women who were waiting for their children. There in front of the Blessed Sacrament my mother gave me her last advice. When my turn came, I knelt down at the feet of our good God, represented by his minister, to implore pardon for my sins. When I finished I saw everyone was laughing. My mother called me and said: "My daughter, don't you know that when you go to confession you should speak softly, that it's a secret? Everybody heard you! Only at the end you said something no one heard."

On the way home my mother tried several times to find out what she called the secret of my confession; but the only answer she got was complete silence. Now, however, I am going to reveal the secret of my first confession. After he heard me, the good priest said these brief words: "My daughter, your soul is the temple of the Holy Spirit. Keep it always pure so that he may continue his divine action in it."

On hearing this, I felt at awe of my interior and asked the good confessor what I should do. He replied: "Kneel down over there at the feet of Our Lady and ask her, with great trust, to take care of your heart, to prepare it to worthily receive her dear Son tomorrow, and to keep it for him alone."

The church had several statues of Our Lady. But since my sisters took care of the altar of Our Lady of the Rosary,[25] I always used to pray near that statue, so I went there then. I asked her very fervently to keep my poor heart for God alone. Upon repeating this humble request several times with my eyes fixed on the statue, it seemed to me that she smiled with a look and a gesture of goodness, and told me yes. I was so overwhelmed with joy that I could barely say a word.[26]

Lúcia's experience before the image of Our Lady of the Rosary has a prophetic quality. At the end of the apparitions in the Cova da Iria, on October 13, 1917, the Mother of God—who had promised in May, "In October I will tell you who I am and what I want"—identified herself as "the Lady of the Rosary."

Lúcia would never forget the advice the kindly priest gave her. Years later, they would meet again, before and after the apparitions, and Lúcia would again benefit from his advice in order to live a more intense union with God. Lucia never revealed what she whispered into the ear of Father Cruz.

The great day arrives

Lúcia's first Communion was to take place on the feast of the Sacred Heart of Jesus. The joy her family felt at the first Communion of the youngest involved all of them in a night of work. Lúcia tells us:

My sisters spent the night making me a white dress and a wreath of flowers. I couldn't sleep because I was so happy, and the hours dragged on slowly. I constantly got up ... to see if they wanted me to try on the dress and wreath, etc. Finally daylight dawned, but it seemed forever until 9:00 A.M. I put on my white dress, and my sister Maria brought me to kitchen to ask pardon of my parents, to kiss their hands and ask for their blessing. After this ceremony my mother gave me some last advice. She told me what she wanted me to ask Our Lord when I had received him in my heart, and sent me off with these words: "Above all, ask Our Lord to make you a saint." Her words made such an indelible impression on my heart that they were the first words I said to Our Lord when I received him.[27]

Her first Communion was certainly an important day for Lúcia, because many years later she still remembered details that could easily have been forgotten:

> I set out on the way to church with my sisters, and my brother carried me the whole way so the dust from the road wouldn't get me dirty. As soon as I arrived at the church, I ran to the foot of Our Lady's altar to renew my request. I stayed there contemplating her smile from the previous day, until my sisters came to get me and took me to my place.
>
> There were many children. They formed four lines, two of boys, two of girls, from the back of the church to the altar rail. As I was the smallest, I wound up next to the angels on the altar rail step. The sung Mass began, and as the moment approached, my heart beat faster in expectation of the visit of the great God who would descend from heaven to unite himself to my poor soul.... I had the good fortune to be the first. I prayed: "Lord, make me a saint, keep my heart pure, only for you." Then it seemed to me that our good God spoke these distinct words to me in the depths of my heart: "The grace you received today will remain in your soul, producing fruits of eternal life."[28]

Although the ceremony did not end until about 1:00 P.M. Lúcia's mother came looking for her, distressed because she thought Lúcia would be hungry.[29] Lúcia confesses: "Filled to overflowing with the bread of angels, I found it impossible to take any food whatsoever."[30] This event marks another decisive step, as she relates: "From then on, I lost the taste and attraction that I was beginning to feel for the things of the world, and I only felt well in some solitary place where, all alone, I could recall the delights of my first Communion."[31]

Lúcia did not record the date of this memorable event. According to her statement that she made her first Communion at the age of six, and because she was born March 28, 1907, it must have taken place in 1913.[32]

Work and play

Lúcia continued to enjoy a carefree childhood and the warmth of her loving family. When her sisters grew and took up other work—at the loom or in the fields—Lúcia began to take their place as a shepherdess.[33] She was then almost eight years old. She did this work until she was ten, when it became impossible for her to remain with the flock because people were continually looking for her. The tasks her parents entrusted her with helped to develop her sense of responsibility.

But she also had time to play. Everywhere children have favorite games that change according to the time of year. Lúcia recalled what life was like in the early twentieth century in that corner of the Serra d'Aire: "The games we knew and liked best were pebbles, catch, pass the ring, buttons, hit the mark, quoits [a lawn game similar to horseshoes], and cards.... We had two packs of cards; I had one and the other was theirs. Francisco preferred to play cards."[34] Between games and the duties their parents had given them, the children grew up in a wholesome atmosphere.

Festivities were organized, especially at carnival time, with dances among friendly families. Most participants were young people, enjoying themselves under the affectionate but attentive eyes of their parents. A meal prepared especially by the youngest members was always part of the festivities.

Lúcia was the life and soul of these gatherings until her mother put a definite end to them when the new pastor of Fátima began to discourage these amusements in his Sunday sermons. When someone remarked that until the new pastor arrived it wasn't a sin to dance, Maria Rosa answered: "I don't know.... All I know is that the pastor doesn't want dancing, and as far as I'm concerned my daughters will no longer go to those gatherings. At most I would let them dance in the family because the pastor said there is no harm in that."[35]

Spiritual help

In his providence, God makes use of other people to help us in our spiritual life. Lúcia was no exception. She testifies to the help she received after the apparitions began:

> I think it was during this month [August 1917] that Father Formigão came here for the first time to question me. His interview was serious and very detailed. I liked him very much because he spoke to me about the practice of virtue, teaching me some ways to put it into practice. He showed me a holy card of Saint Agnes, told me the story of her martyrdom, and encouraged me to imitate her. His Reverence continued to come every month to question me, at the end of which he

always gave me some good advice that helped me spiritually. One day he said to me: "You have an obligation to love Our Lord very much for the many graces and favors he is granting you."

These words were so deeply engraved in my soul that to this day I acquired the habit of constantly saying to our Lord: "My God, I love you in thanksgiving for the graces you have granted me." I shared with Jacinta and her little brother this prayer that I liked so much. Jacinta took it so much to heart that in the midst of our most entertaining games, she would ask: "Did you forget to tell our Lord that you love him for the graces he has given us?"[36]

The death of Lúcia's father

Her father's unexpected death, referred to in the preceding chapter, must have been very painful for the little shepherdess of the Serra d'Aire. It was an experience of suffering quite unlike any other. Her testimony in this respect is striking: "My pain was so great that I thought that I too would die."

Apart from her filial affection for her father, she missed him because in the midst of all the confusion and hostility aroused by the apparitions, he alone in the family understood her and believed firmly in her sincerity. "He was the only one who continued to be my friend, and the only one who defended me when discussions arose in the family against me."[37]

Lúcia learns to read

The Lady of the Cova da Iria had told Lúcia to learn to read, thus preparing her for the mission in the world with which she would entrust her. At that time girls in her village were not usually taught to read. Lúcia relates: "At home they told me that it was only because of vanity that I wanted to learn to read. Until then, little girls almost never learned to read; school was only for the boys. It was only later that a school for girls was opened in Fátima."[38]

One reason Lúcia did not attend school was because she had to bring the flock out to pasture every day. When the family later had to sell the sheep, the door opened for her to enroll in the primary school. Jacinta also attended. Their teacher, Maria de Jesus Carreira, found the two little girls to be good students.

Lúcia would complete her education some years later, in the College of Vilar, run by the Dorothean Sisters.

FRANCISCO MARTO

Francisco and Jacinta were the two youngest children of Manuel Pedro Marto and Olímpia de Jesus Santos. Both children were born in the village of Aljustrel, in the parish of Fátima. Francisco Marto was born on June 11, 1908, and was baptized on June 20. Francisco and Jacinta resembled each other, but Lúcia writes: "Francisco didn't seem to be Jacinta's brother, except for his facial features and the practice of virtue. Unlike her, he wasn't capricious and lively. On the contrary, he was naturally peaceful and agreeable."[39] His mother described him: "Francisco had a rounder face. His eyes were lighter and more expressive than mine were when I was young."[40]

Francisco had "a round, chubby face, somewhat dark, with a small mouth, thin lips, and a prominent chin. The color of his eyes resembled his mother's."[41] His father added that he was "very gentle."[42]

Dr. Carlos de Azevedo Mendes described Francisco as having a "closely fitting hood, very short jacket, vest with a shirt underneath, suitable trousers, in summary, a little man. Handsome boy's face! Lively expression and boyish countenance. Responded to my questions in an honest way."[43]

Francisco's qualities

The *Memoirs*, as well as other testimonies, describe Francisco as a typical boy, with certain notable qualities. From the accounts of the apparitions, it seems that Francisco remained a bit in the shadow. For example, he only saw the angel and Our Lady, and did not hear what they said, nor did he speak with the heavenly visitors. This may seem to make Francisco stand out less than the other children. Nevertheless, Francisco was a delightful character. Lúcia compares him with his sister Jacinta:

> Francisco was ... always smiling, always kind and friendly, playing with all the children without distinction. He didn't get angry or yell at anyone. He would just go away when something wasn't good....
>
> I remember that one day he came to my house with a handkerchief in his pocket that had an image of Our Lady of Nazaré imprinted on it, which someone had brought for him from the seaside. He showed it with such joy, and all the children were admiring it. It was passed around and then suddenly it was gone. He looked for it but didn't find

it. A little later I found it in the pocket of another little boy. I wanted to take it but he insisted it was his own, that someone had also brought him one from the seaside. So in order to stop the quarrel, Francisco came over, saying: "Let him have it! What does a handkerchief matter to me?"[44]

Lúcia's temperament was completely different from Francisco's. At first they had no special bond except for the ordinary one that exists between cousins who live near one another. But that changed as they became involved with the apparitions. Francisco developed a great affection for Lúcia, especially after the three apparitions of the angel and the six of our Lady had put them all on the same adventure. Lúcia herself explains the reason for this preference:

> My aunt sold her flock before my mother sold hers. From then on before I left in the morning I would tell Jacinta and Francisco where I was going to pasture the sheep, and as soon as they could get away they would go there. One day when I arrived, they were already there waiting for me.
> "How did you get here so early?"
> "I came," Francisco answered, "because—I don't know how to put this—before you didn't matter to me, and I came because of Jacinta. But now in the morning I can't sleep because I want so much to be with you."[45]

The soul of a poet

When we think of Francisco working as a shepherd, we could imagine him perched on a rock overlooking the grazing flock, playing the pipe he always carried, gazing at the horizon or enjoying the beauty of the flowers that grew on the hills. He absorbed all this and gave it his own childish and poetic interpretation, especially at night when, with his cousin and his sister, from the threshing floor of Lúcia's parents, he watched the first stars and the moon appear in the sky.

The three children amused themselves while they waited for Our Lady and the angels to light their lamps, as they said, in their childish ideas about nightfall and the appearance of the stars. Francisco loved to count the stars—the angels' lamps—but the spectacle of the setting sun delighted him most of all.

"No lamp is as beautiful as Our Lord's," [i.e., the sun] he would say to Jacinta. But she preferred Our Lady's lamp [the moon], because, she explained, "it doesn't hurt your eyes."[46]

Courageous and playful

Senhor Marto spoke of Francisco as being a boy of unusual courage for his age. "He wasn't afraid of things at all. He would go without any fear or protest to any dark place at night. He played with lizards, and when he found snakes he liked to roll them around his stick and put sheep's milk in the hollows of stones for them to drink. He would go looking for hares, foxes, and moles."[47]

His games didn't always please everyone. His mother complained that "he would go after wall lizards ... and bring them home.... But he was like that. He was very daring."[48]

Francisco was a playful boy with a good sense of humor. His father recalls a trick he tried to play on his brother João while he was sleeping one afternoon: "This mischievous boy got up stealthily, took an old stick and was on the verge of putting it into his brother's mouth when I caught hold of his arm."[49]

Sometimes the children would quarrel, as is the case in any family. "Sometimes they quarreled among themselves, but I always made them stop right away."[50]

Sincere and humble

Francisco was sincere and transparent in his words. He didn't know how to deceive others. Manuel Pedro Marto testifies to this.

> I was never concerned that these two [Francisco and Jacinta] would ever take part in anything deceitful. Jacinta would reprimand anyone who did not tell the truth, even if it was her mother.... When her mother misled her, saying that she was going down to the cabbage patch when she was really going farther, Jacinta told her: "So, Mother, you lied to me? You said you were going here and you went there?... Lying is an evil thing!"[51]

Lúcia gives us more details about her cousin, saying that Francisco "was naturally peaceful and agreeable. When someone would try to deny him his rights as a winner, he would give in without fighting, saying simply: 'You think you won? That's fine! It doesn't matter to me.'"[52]

In her *Memoirs*, Lúcia declares:

> He showed no love for dancing, as Jacinta did; he much preferred playing the flute while the others danced. In our games he was quite lively; but few liked to play with him because he almost always lost.
>
> I admit that I myself did not always feel kindly disposed toward him, as his naturally calm temperament exasperated my own excessive

vivacity. Sometimes I caught him by the arm, made him sit down on the ground or on a stone and keep still; he obeyed me as if I had real authority over him. Afterward I felt sorry and went and took him by the hand, and he would come along with me as good-humoredly as though nothing had happened.[53]

Ti Marto believed in the apparitions in the Cova da Iria from the very beginning because of Francisco's attitude. When his mother asked him if Jacinta was telling the truth, Francisco found himself in a difficult position. He could not deny it, because that would be telling a lie; neither could he affirm it because that would be failing to keep his promise.

He later explained to his cousin what he said and why: "As for me, when my mother asked me if it were true, I had to say that it was, so as not to tell a lie."[54]

Possibly it was humility and not shyness that led him to avoid meeting people who came looking for him because of the apparitions. He was also afraid of being inaccurate in the statements he would have to make. Once, when he felt a group of people were on their way, he quickly disappeared. When Lúcia and Jacinta returned at the end of the afternoon and asked where he was, Senhora Olímpia answered crossly:

"How do I know! I am tired from looking for him all afternoon. Some ladies came to see you. You were not here. He vanished and can't be found. So now you look for him yourselves."

We sat a little while on a bench in the kitchen, thinking to go afterward to the cave of Cabeço, certain that he would be there. But scarcely had my aunt left the house, when he spoke to us through a hole in the attic ceiling. He had gone up there when he heard people coming. From there he saw everything that happened, and he said to us later: "There were so many people! God spare me, if they had caught me here alone! What could I have told them?"[55]

Delicate conscience

Francisco's sincerity was lived out in all its dimensions. He was also sincere with himself, showing a great delicacy of conscience. He tried to express frankly what seemed to him to be the will of God.

For example, he advised Lúcia not to go dancing at the carnival and suggested an excuse for not doing so. "Do you know how you could do it? Everyone knows that Our Lady appeared to you; so then you can say you promised her not to go to the dances anymore and for that reason you are not going."[56]

On Sunday, August 19, when Lúcia and Francisco, accompanied by his brother João, saw the first signs that Our Lady was about to appear, João went home to call Jacinta, because the house was nearby. After the apparition, she was preparing to stay there, but Francisco intervened and said: "No! You have to leave because today mother didn't let you come with the sheep." And to encourage her, he accompanied her home.[57]

The delicacy of Francisco's conscience had its roots in his deep humility. One particularly moving incident occurred shortly before his death when he asked his cousin and his sister to help him to remember his sins, so that he could make his last confession.

This same delicacy and humility also led him to react when he was treated unjustly. When he was being examined before his first Communion, possibly because of an understandable nervousness, he "faltered" when reciting the Act of Contrition. The parish priest, his patience exhausted by the noise and restlessness of so many children, said sharply: "You aren't going to make your first Communion this time because you made a mistake!" Francisco, his voice broken by sobs, protested: "Grown-up people also make mistakes and they still go!"

Taste for prayer

It is not easy to say exactly when Francisco began to develop a taste for prayer. Could it have been in his family, when they prayed together? He showed this attraction for prayerful silence after the three encounters with the guardian angel of Portugal, and especially after the apparitions in the Cova da Iria. He would leave the company of his sister and his cousin and go off by himself to pray, so that sometimes they called him and he did not hear. As Lúcia describes him:

> Francisco was a boy of few words. When he prayed and offered his sacrifices, he liked to hide from Jacinta and me. Often we would go to surprise him behind a wall or a clump of blackberry bushes, where he camouflaged himself so he could kneel and pray, or, as he would say, to think "of Our Lord who is sad because of so many sins." I asked him: "Francisco, why don't you ask me to pray with you, and Jacinta, too?"
>
> "I prefer to pray alone," he answered, "to think and to console Our Lord who is so sad."
>
> One day I asked him: "Francisco, what do you prefer: to console Our Lord or to convert sinners so more souls don't go to hell?"
>
> "I would rather console Our Lord. Didn't you notice how sad Our Lady was in that last month when she said that people must no longer

offend God Our Lord, who is already so much offended? I would want
to console Our Lord and then after convert sinners so they won't
offend him anymore."[58]

Love of nature

Francisco had the soul of an artist. As we have seen, he loved to contemplate the night sky when it was full of stars. "Enraptured, he
watched the sun's rays glinting on the windowpanes of the homes in the
neighboring villages, or glistening in the drops of water on the trees and
woods on the hills, making them shine like so many stars; in his eyes
these were a thousand times more beautiful than the angels' lamps."[59]

He also loved to play his reed flute, which he brought with him when
he went up the hills with his sister and his cousin to tend the sheep.
Lúcia testifies: "He especially loved to go to the mountains and sit on top
of the highest rock to play his flute or sing. If his little sister came down
to run races or play tag, he would stay there enjoying his music and
songs."[60] Lúcia remembers:

> He liked little birds a lot, and he couldn't bear to see anyone rob the
> nests. He always crumbled a piece of the bread that he had taken for a
> snack, and left it on the rocks for them to eat. Going away a short dis-
> tance, he would call them, as if they understood him, and he did not
> want anyone to go near them and frighten them away. "Poor little things!
> You are so hungry," he would say to them. "Come, come and eat!"
>
> One day we met a little boy who had in his hand a little bird he had
> caught. Full of compassion, Francisco promised to give him two coins if
> he let it fly away. The boy accepted the deal, but he wanted the money
> first. So then Francisco ran all the way home from Lagoa do Carriera
> ... to get two coins in order to free the prisoner. After he saw it fly
> away, he clapped his hands for joy and said: "Be careful! Don't get
> caught again."[61]

He would stop to enjoy the beauty of the flowers along the road. He
was, in short, a contemplative who gazed in wonder at the beautiful
things that the Lord has scattered so lavishly over our earth.

Spirit of service

Francisco loved to help people and never expected thanks. The satisfaction of helping others was enough for him, as Lúcia describes.

> There was an elderly woman whom we called Ti Maria Carreira, and
> her children would sometimes send her out to care for the flock of
> goats and sheep. These animals were somewhat wild and at times wan-

dered off in every direction. When we met her in such distress,
Francisco was the first one to run to her aid. He would help her lead
the flock to pasture, gathering for her the ones that had wandered off.
The poor old woman overwhelmed Francisco in a thousand thanks and
called him her guardian angel.

When we met any sick people he was full of compassion and said,
"I can't bear to see these people like that. It makes me very sad. Tell
them I will pray for them."[62]

Seriousness and honesty

Part of Francisco's character was the seriousness with which he regarded everything, despite his cheerful disposition. The following event,
which occurred after the apparitions, illustrates this:

> One day when Francisco was already sick but was still able to walk, I
> went with him to the cave of Cabeço and to Valinhos. When we
> returned home, we found the house full of people. A poor woman
> stood next to a table pretending to bless several religious objects:
> rosaries, medals, crucifixes, etc. Jacinta and I were soon surrounded by
> many people who wanted to question us. Francisco was caught by that
> lady trying to bless things, and she invited him to help her.
>
> "I can't bless," he answered seriously, "and neither can you! Only
> priests can bless."
>
> The words of the little boy immediately spread through the crowd
> … and the poor woman had to go away immediately amidst the insults
> of those who demanded back from her the objects they had just hand-
> ed over to her.[63]

Francisco often spoke with a wisdom more advanced than his years.
He had a way of looking at things far superior to what is typical for his
age. Lúcia relates one such example, from among many:

> One day when I arrived at his house, I said good-bye to a group of
> children from school who had come with me. I went in to visit him and
> his sister. Since he had heard the noise of the children he asked me:
>
> "Did you come with all those children?"
>
> "Yes, I did."
>
> "Don't go with them, you could learn to commit sins. When you
> leave school, stay for a little while at the feet of the hidden Jesus, and
> afterward go home alone."[64]

Areas of growth

In what areas did Francisco Marto need to grow to greater maturity?
His cousin points out only one:

"It seems to me that, if he had lived to manhood, his principal defect would have been his attitude of 'never mind.'"[65]

Perhaps it would be more accurate, however, to look at that attitude in a different way. Francisco was not apathetic, but his temperament did not incline him to react with overenthusiasm to things and events. Without doubt, he had a strong emotional side—such as his love of music, his delight in contemplating flowers, birds, and stars—but still he reacted to things in a quiet way. Along with these qualities, he had a great desire to serve, to be agreeable, even engaging in activities that did not naturally attract him:

> When he insistently asked his mother to let him go with the flock so he could come with me, it was more to please Jacinta, because she preferred his company to that of her brother João. One day when Francisco's mother, already quite annoyed, denied him permission, he answered with his natural calm: "For me, Mother, it doesn't matter; it's Jacinta who wants me to go."
>
> Another time he confirmed this very same attitude. One of my friends came over to my house and invited me to go with her because she had a good area for pasture that day. Because the sky was overcast, I went to my aunt's house to ask if Francisco was coming with Jacinta, or if her brother João was coming. My aunt had already decided that since it was raining, João would go. But Francisco still wanted to go and went to his mother to ask insistently. Upon receiving a very strong no, he answered, "For me it's all the same. It's Jacinta who feels worse about it."[66]

Francisco's attitude was not apathetic but shows he had a certain readiness to accept events as they occurred.

Francisco had his limitations and the whims proper to his age. His father recalls an occasion when his son was about to be punished because he had run off instead of praying with the family:

> I got up and went to the attached house where he was hiding. When he saw me coming toward him ... he shouted at once: "Here's my good father!" And right away he decided to pray with the family. That happened before Our Lady appeared; afterward, he would never miss prayers; instead, those two [Francisco and Jacinta] urged everyone to go to the Rosary.[67]

According to his father, "He had more courage but was more restless than his little sister. At times he didn't have much patience and would fidget a lot, almost like a calf."[68] However, his humility and sincerity in confronting his defects and shortcomings are truly moving.

JACINTA MARTO

Jacinta, the seventh and youngest child of her parents, was born on March 11, 1910. On March 19, the feast of Saint Joseph, she became a child of God through Baptism.

Her father used to refer to the birth of his youngest child with humor: "Seven months after the birth of the little one, the Republic came to Portugal, and after another seven—seven years this time—Our Lady appeared."[69]

Lúcia described Jacinta:

> She was of average height for a six-year-old, well developed, robust, more thin than plump; with a healthy complexion from the sun and the fresh air of the hills; she had big, brown eyes that were very bright and protected by long lashes and black eyebrows; and she had a sweet, gentle, and lively expression. (In the photograph we have of her she looks serious because it was taken in the sun. That was not her natural expression).[70]

In a letter to his fiancée, Dr. Carlos de Azevedo Mendes describes Jacinta:

> [She wore] a headscarf with a floral pattern, the ends tied behind her head. It was old and slightly worn. A little jacket, a bit dirty. A reddish skirt, very full, as was typical in that place.... I would love to describe her small face, but I don't think that anything I could say would do it justice.... Dark eyes that sparkled vivaciously, an angelic expression, showing a goodness that attracted people, her whole appearance so extraordinary.... Very shy, for it was difficult to hear the few words she spoke in response to our questions.[71]

Childhood games

Jacinta's favorite games were the typical ones enjoyed by children of her age. Lúcia, her biographer and childhood companion, gives some details about the games they played in the Santos' yard:

> Once there, Jacinta would choose the games we would play. Her favorites were pebbles and buttons. We played them while sitting on top of the well that was covered with concrete slabs, shaded by an olive tree and two plum trees.[72]
>
> [Another] of her favorite games was forfeits, in which the winner could order the loser to do whatever the winner wanted. She loved to

send us running after butterflies until we caught one and brought it to her. Other times she sent us to pick whatever flower she chose. [73]

The little shepherdess enjoyed other pastimes, typical in a child's life. Her cousin tells us:

> Jacinta loved to hear her voice echo in the depths of the valleys. That's why one of our favorite things was to climb to the top of the hills, sit on the biggest rock, and yell out names. The name that echoed best was Maria. Sometimes Jacinta would say the whole Hail Mary like that, repeating the next word when the preceding one had stopped echoing. [74]
>
> Jacinta also greatly loved to hold the little white lambs, placing them on her lap, embracing and kissing them. At night she would carry them home on her shoulders so they wouldn't get tired. One day on our way home she walked along right in the middle of the flock.
>
> "Jacinta," I asked her, "what are you doing there in the middle of the sheep?"
>
> "To do the same thing that Our Lord is doing in that little holy card you gave me. He was just like this, in the middle of them all, with one on his shoulders." [75]
>
> We also liked to sing hymns, along with the various popular songs that unfortunately we knew quite well. Jacinta preferred "Hail, Noble Patroness," "Pure Virgin," and "Angels, Sing with Me." [76]

A love of dancing

Along with playing games and singing, Jacinta liked to dance, as Lúcia relates: "Jacinta really loved dancing, and had a special aptitude for it. I remember that one day she was crying about one of her brothers who had gone to the war and was thought to have been killed in action. To distract her, I arranged a little dance with two of her other brothers. The poor child went to dance, all the while wiping away the tears that ran down her cheeks." [77]

One incident must have taken place after the apparitions: "She had such a great love for dancing that at times if she merely heard some instrument that the shepherds were playing, she would begin dancing all by herself. When the feast of Saint John and the carnival approached, she told me:

"I'm not going to dance any more."

"And why not?"

"Because I want to offer this sacrifice to Our Lord." [78]

Some shadows

The mission of parents and educators is to form children's consciences so they may learn to distinguish good from evil, and to help them to overcome their faults before these become so deeply rooted they are difficult to eradicate. Jacinta, like all children, had her faults and inclinations to sin that she needed to overcome.

She was "capricious and vivacious."[79] Lúcia even admits that before the events of 1917, except for their being related, she would not have felt drawn to her cousin.

Her company sometimes annoyed me because she was overly sensitive. The slightest dispute or quarrel that arose among the children while playing was enough to make her sulk in a corner.... To coax her back to the game, not even the sweetest expressions of affection that children know how to use on such occasions were enough. We would have to let her choose the game and the partner with whom she wanted to play.[80]

Jacinta could also be very attached to things. In this she was completely opposite Francisco. Lúcia tells us in her *Memoirs*:

Playing the game of buttons I often found myself in trouble, because when they would call us to eat, they would find me without buttons on my clothes. Usually Jacinta would win them, and that was enough for my mother to scold me. I had to sew them back in a hurry. But how could I get her to give them back, since besides being inclined to pout, she was possessive! She wanted to keep them for the next game so she wouldn't have to take off her own. Only when I threatened her that I wouldn't ever come back to play with her was I able to get them back![81]

Jacinta's virtues

But Jacinta was richly endowed with notable human qualities, apart from her shadow areas, as Lúcia says: "However, she had a very good heart. God gave her a sweet and gentle character that made her both amiable and endearing."[82]

With careful and wise guidance, her parents knew how to form a delicate conscience in their child. One incident illustrates these qualities:

One day we were playing the game of forefeits in my house and I won, so I could tell Jacinta to do something. My brother was sitting next to the table writing. So I sent her to give him a hug and a kiss, but she answered: "No, not that! Give me something else to do. Why don't you send me to kiss Our Lord over there?" A crucifix was hanging on the wall.

"Yes," I answered, "certainly. Climb up on a chair to get it, bring it here, kneel down and give him three hugs and three kisses, one for Francisco, one for me, and another for you."

"To Our Lord I'll give as many hugs and kisses as you like." Then she ran to get the crucifix. She kissed it with so much devotion that I have never forgotten it.[83]

Sincerity

Jacinta was spontaneous in showing her feelings, and this led her to blurt out what had happened on May 13. The little girl confessed honestly to Lúcia that she had told her family about the apparitions in the Cova da Iria, saying exactly what she had revealed. Jacinta begged pardon for breaking her promise of secrecy and promised that from then on she would never mention it again. Lúcia tells us:

> On that afternoon we were caught up in wonder and pondered what had happened, and Jacinta kept on exclaiming with enthusiasm: "Oh, the Lady is so beautiful!"
>
> "I can see what will happen," I told her, "you are going to tell others about it."
>
> "No, I say no!" she answered. "I'll be quiet."
>
> The next day, when Francisco ran to tell me that Jacinta had told her family about it, she listened to the accusation without a word.
>
> "You see? I knew that would happen," I told her.
>
> "I had something inside that wouldn't let me keep quiet," she answered tearfully.
>
> "Well, don't cry now, and don't say anything else to anybody about what the Lady told us."
>
> "But I already said it!"
>
> "What did you say?"
>
> "I said that the Lady promised to bring us to heaven!"
>
> "And right away you went and said that!"
>
> "Forgive me, I won't say anything else to anyone."[84]

She showed the same sincerity after the apparitions:

> One day they told us that a very old priest was coming to interview us, and that he could perceive what was happening inside a person's heart. So he was going to find out if we were telling the truth. So then Jacinta said, full of joy: "When will this priest come who can see inside us? If he can see inside, he will know very well that we are telling the truth."[85]

Compassion for others

When she heard about Our Lord's sufferings, Jacinta was moved to tears. Many times afterward she would ask to hear again the story of the Passion. She cried with sorrow and would say: "Our poor dear Lord! I can never commit another sin. I don't want Our Lord to suffer more!"[86]

She was deeply impressed by the vision of hell the children saw on July 13. She often lamented that with a little effort those souls could have avoided such great suffering. This thought gave her a strong desire to do penance for the conversion of sinners, which became more and more noticeable in her.

She was very grateful that the Virgin had given them a promise of their salvation, saying, "How good that Lady is! She has already promised to take us to heaven."[87]

Jacinta's kindness

Describing her cousin, Lúcia begins by stating that, despite having the ordinary faults found in any child, Jacinta's heart was kindly, compassionate, and inclined toward good. Lúcia said the Lord had endowed Jacinta with a sweet and gentle character, making her lovable and attractive. Dr. Carlos de Azevedo Mendes said something similar in a letter to his fiancée after having met the three little shepherds.

In relation to Lúcia, along with many signs of affection, Jacinta had one that was especially expressive. Many flowers grew on the hillside where the three children so often prayed together after the angel appeared. Among these were many irises—the flower Jacinta loved best of all.

After her parents sold their flock, she would wait for Lúcia in the evening. Jacinta would pick an iris, or, if there were no irises, some other flower to give to Lúcia. Or sometimes she would run to her cousin, pluck the petals from the flower and strew them over her.[88] Lúcia remembers:

Jacinta also loved to go at night to the threshing floor in front of the house to see the beautiful sunset and the sky full of stars. The beautiful moonlit nights enraptured her. We competed to see who could count the most stars, which we called the lamps of the angels. The moon was Our Lady's lamp and the sun, Our Lord's. Sometimes Jacinta would say: "I still like Our Lady's lamp best because it doesn't burn or blind us as Our Lord's does."[89]

Devotion to the Blessed Sacrament

Lúcia's sister Carolina belonged to the Sodality of the Sacred Heart of Jesus. That entitled her to bring her younger sister to renew her first Communion in a special ceremony. Olímpia brought Jacinta to see the ceremony. The little girl was thrilled with the sight of children dressed as angels, strewing flowers near the Blessed Sacrament during Benediction.

Fascinated by this gesture, the little shepherdess frequently left her brother and her cousin, gathered an apron full of flowers, and came back to strew them over Lúcia. Jacinta said that she was doing it in order to imitate the angels.

Carolina used to select and dress some children as angels in the Corpus Christi procession. They would walk beside the canopy under which the priest carried the Blessed Sacrament in the monstrance. Their duty was to strew flowers before the Lord in the Eucharist.

Naturally, Lúcia's sister always chose her as an angel. Once when Lúcia was trying on the dress for the feast, she told Jacinta that she was going to strew flowers before Jesus in the coming feast. Jacinta also wanted to do this, and the two of them went to Lúcia's sister to ask permission. It wasn't difficult to get what she wanted, and Lúcia's sister began at once to make a dress for Jacinta.

She rehearsed with the two little girls, explaining everything to them and showing them how to throw the flowers. Jacinta was delighted and could not resist asking at one of the practices:

"Will we see him?"

"Yes," my sister replied. "The pastor will carry him."

Jacinta jumped for joy and constantly asked if the time for the feast had come. The longed-for day finally arrived, and Jacinta was beside herself for joy. They put the two of us by the side of the altar, and then in the procession by the side of the canopy, each one with her basket of flowers. At the places marked by my sister, I threw my flowers to Jesus. But despite all the signals I gave to Jacinta, she didn't scatter even one. She constantly looked at the pastor and nothing else. When the ceremony was over, my sister brought us outside the church and asked:

"Jacinta, why didn't you scatter your flowers for Jesus?"

"Because I didn't see him."

Afterward she asked me; "Did you see the Child Jesus?"

"No! But don't you know that you don't see the Child Jesus in the host, he is hidden! He's the one we receive in Communion."

"And when you go to Communion do you speak to him?"

"I do."

"So why don't you see him?"
"Because he is hidden."[90]

This conversation stirred in Jacinta a great desire to receive Holy Communion. She decided at once to ask her mother to allow her to attend catechism class, but Lúcia tried to dissuade her, saying that it was too soon, because the pastor would not give her first Communion before she was ten. But Jacinta protested, asking why Lúcia had been allowed to go to Communion even though she wasn't ten yet. Lúcia told her it was because she knew the entire catechism but Jacinta didn't.

From then on, at the request of Jacinta and Francisco, Lúcia became their catechist. However, at a certain point she had exhausted all her knowledge. The two cousins then went to their mother to ask if they might attend the catechism classes in the parish, but she refused for the same reason as before: the pastor would not allow them to make their first Communion until they were ten.

So they had to wait. But it wouldn't be long before these three children, Lúcia, Francisco, and Jacinta, with their lights and shadows, virtues and defects, were caught up in a great heavenly drama. The workings of grace would transform them and lead them into unforgettable events.

CHAPTER 3

At the School of the Angel of Peace

AT THE END of the first decade of the twentieth century, a name completely unknown until then began to be heard all over the world. People were talking about an apparition of Our Lady to three shepherd children at a place called the Cova da Iria, in the parish of Fátima, in the center of Portugal, in the mountain region called Serra d'Aire.

The place was so little known to the people of the area that many of them admitted that, at the time of the apparitions, they had never even heard of it. But nothing happens by chance when the initiative comes from heaven. In all the events of Fátima we can see a providential coincidence in which various elements converge toward a single purpose.

As already noted, the word *iria* derives from the Greek word for "peace" *(eirene)*. Thus, during the First World War, Our Lady appeared in the Cove of Peace. To prepare for the apparitions of the Blessed Virgin Mary in the Cova da Iria, God sent a messenger from heaven, and the messenger called himself the angel of peace.[1]

In a way, the angel introduced the shepherds to the message that the Lady of Peace would soon give them. Because they had to be the first to live the message, the angel taught them how to put it into practice.

Devotion to the guardian angel of Portugal

The mysterious personage who appeared to the little shepherds at the Loca do Cabeço in the spring of 1916 identified himself as the guardian angel of Portugal. The three little shepherds, who had taken shelter from the rain amid the rocks of that place, had perhaps never heard about such an angel. In the history of the Church, it is the first time we know of that an angel presented himself as the guardian angel of a specific nation.

The Catholic faith teaches that angels can assist human beings throughout their lives by protecting and praying for them. They are called guardian angels to indicate their role. Besides our own personal guardian angel, it is a pious belief that each nation has its own angel to protect it. Portugal has honored its own guardian angel with special devotion, including a proper Mass and Office.[2]

In response to the request of King Manuel I, Pope Leo X (1513–1521) gave permission for this special liturgical feast, which dates from the beginnings of Portugal's existence as a nation. For more than three centuries, Portugal remained the only nation in the world to have an official devotion to its guardian angel.[3]

> In the nineteenth century, Spain also established a liturgical feast to honor its guardian angel. It was granted by Pope Leo XII, who was the Pope from 1823 to 1829. This feast in Spain unfortunately disappeared with the liturgical reforms that followed Vatican II, so Portugal is again the only nation that has an official devotion in honor of the angel given to it by God to guide its destiny.[4]

Splendid statues of the guardian angel of Portugal may be found in some of the great national monuments, such as Jerónimos Monastery, the Church of Conceição Velha in Lisbon, the Convent of Christ in Tomar, the Church of the Holy Cross in Coimbra and in Mafra, and in a public park in Ponta Delgada, on the island of Saint Miguel in the Azores.

The story of the apparitions at Fátima begins with the appearance of an angel who called himself the guardian angel of Portugal. The precise dates of the three apparitions of the angel in 1916 are not known.

THE APPARITIONS OF THE ANGEL IN FÁTIMA

Two vague apparitions in 1915

The first apparition of the angel in Fátima seems to have taken place some time in the summer of 1915. Lúcia, only eight years old at the time, was a devout child with a spirit of initiative. She had invited three little girls to say the Rosary with her at Cabeço, a little hill near Valinhos a short distance from Aljustrel. They climbed almost to the top of the hillock, by the slope facing north. It was here that the first and rather indistinct apparition took place.[5]

Lúcia describes it thus:

> Around noon we ate our lunch. Afterward I invited my companions to pray the Rosary with me, and they happily agreed. We had hardly begun when right before our eyes we saw a figure that seemed to be suspended in air over the trees. It looked like a statue of snow that seemed transparent through the rays of the sun.[6]

The children were frightened, so they stopped praying for a few moments. They kept looking at the unusual figure. Still feeling apprehensive, they asked one another what it was, but none of them knew.

They could not explain what was happening but continued to pray, trying not to lose sight of the strange figure. It disappeared when their prayer ended. Lúcia proposed that they keep silence about the whole thing. Her companions, however, talked about the event, and Lúcia's mother came to hear of it.

Maria Rosa questioned her daughter, but was convinced that it was all a figment of a child's imagination.

> "Look here! People are saying that you saw something up there. What did you see?"
>
> Because I didn't know how to explain it, I said, "It seemed like a person wrapped up in a sheet." Wanting to explain that I couldn't make out any features, I added: "I couldn't see any eyes or hands."[7]

Lúcia's mother was not concerned about it, because no one took the children seriously. She concluded that it was just childish nonsense.

The same apparition was repeated some time later, when Lúcia was minding the flock with three companions. The three companions spoke about it again. Lúcia relates what followed: "Some people began to make fun of us. And because after my first Communion I would sometimes be lost in thought, my sisters would then ask me almost with disgust: 'Are you seeing someone wrapped in a sheet?'"[8]

What did the angel intend in these two apparitions, neither uttering a word nor making the slightest gesture? We can only speculate, but perhaps he wanted to encourage them for praying the Rosary and to approve of the way Lúcia had tried to find better company. Indeed, the first day Lúcia went out with the sheep, she came home very sad, because

the other shepherds were not good company for a young girl. Aljustrel
had its fair amount of people who neglected Christian morality.

The child confided in her mother, as she always did, and her mother
chose three good companions for Lúcia: Teresa Matias, her sister Maria
Rosa, and Maria Justino. Later, Francisco and Jacinta, because of their
insistent appeals, began their life as shepherds and accompanied their
cousin in looking after the flocks.

The way in which some people who had heard the story of the angel
made fun of it, and the fear that her mother would reprimand her must
have had a decisive influence on Lúcia. That is probably why she strongly urged her cousins to say nothing to anyone when the later apparitions
occurred. After all, as will be seen, Our Lady did not command them to
keep secret all that had happened, except for the secret revealed in July,
when she said: "You must not tell anyone about this."

When Lúcia took care of the flocks with Jacinta and Francisco, they
pastured them together. When they arrived home at the end of the day
the flocks went to their respective pens. Lúcia's previous companions,
without abandoning their friendship, stopped going with her because she
no longer needed them. It was exactly at this point that the little shepherds were to receive a visit of the guardian angel of Portugal, preparing
them for the meeting with the Lady of the Cova da Iria.

First apparition of the angel of peace

One morning in the spring[9] of 1916 the three little shepherds went
to a place called Chousa Velha, which belonged to Lúcia's parents. To
avoid the persistent light rain, they climbed the hill as the sheep followed
them and took shelter among some rocks.

Lúcia gives her account:

> Then for the first time we entered into that blessed grotto. We spent the
> day there even though the rain had passed and the sun had come out,
> beautiful and clear. We ate our lunch and prayed our Rosary. I don't
> recall if we said it the way we did when we were anxious to play ...
> saying only the words "Ave Maria" and "Our Father" on each bead.
> Our prayers finished, we began to play the game pebbles.
>
> We had been playing only for a little while, and then a strong wind
> started shaking the trees. We got up to see what was happening because
> the day was calm. Then we saw above the olive trees the figure I
> already spoke about walking toward us. Jacinta and Francisco had
> never seen it, and I had never told them about it.

As he approached us, we were able to distinguish the features: it was a youth about fourteen or fifteen years old, whiter than snow; transparent as crystal in the sunlight, so very beautiful. When he came near to us he said: "Don't be afraid! I am the angel of peace. Pray with me."

Kneeling on the ground he bowed down until his head reached the ground. He made us repeat these words three times: "My God! I believe, I adore, I hope, and I love you. I ask you pardon for all those who do not believe, do not adore, do not hope, and do not love you." Afterward, he got up and said: "Pray like this. The hearts of Jesus and Mary are attentive to the voice of your supplications." [10]

He then disappeared. Lúcia describes the profound impression that this event made on the three of them.

The supernatural atmosphere that enfolded us was so intense that we almost weren't aware of our own existence, remaining for a long time in the position in which he had left us, always repeating the same prayer. God's presence made itself felt so intensely and intimately that we didn't even dare to speak to each other. The following day, we felt our spirits still enwrapped in this atmosphere, which disappeared very slowly. [11]

From then on, we spent much time prostrated like the angel, repeating the words he said, until we became tired. [12]

It didn't occur to us to speak about this apparition, nor did we think of telling each other to keep it secret. The apparition itself imposed secrecy. It was so intimate, it was difficult to speak of it at all. Perhaps it made such a great impression on us because it was the first such manifestation. [13]

In spite of this, Lúcia did not forget to enjoin silence on her cousins, having learned from the experience of the previous year. Francisco saw the angel but did not hear anything that he said, so he had to learn the prayer by hearing his sister and his cousin praying it along with the angel. Very interested in knowing everything, he continually questioned Lúcia and Jacinta about the details.

During the apparition of the angel, Francisco prostrated himself like his sister and me, carried by the supernatural force that moved us; but he learned the prayer by listening to us repeat it, since he heard nothing from the angel. When afterward we would prostrate ourselves to recite this prayer, he was the first to get tired in this position, so he would remain kneeling or sitting, praying until we finished. Later he would say: "I am not able to stay like that for a long time like you. My back hurts so much that I can't." [14]

Francisco had to make a double effort, by making the prostration and by paying attention to what his sister and his cousin were saying so that he could repeat it.

Second apparition of the angel of Portugal

Toward the end of July the angel returned to meet with the children. This time, the meeting took place in the yard of Lúcia's parents, as Lúcia tells us:

> Some time passed, and one summer day we had gone home for the siesta. We were playing on top of the well that my parents had in the yard that we called the Arneiro.... Suddenly, we saw next to us the same figure, or the angel, as it seemed to me, and he said, "What are you doing? Pray much. The most holy hearts of Jesus and Mary have designs of mercy for you. Offer prayers and sacrifice constantly to the Most High."
>
> "How are we to sacrifice ourselves?" I asked.
>
> "In everything you can, offer to God a sacrifice as an act of reparation for sins by which he is offended, and humbly beg God for the conversion of sinners. In this way you will draw down peace on your country. I am its guardian angel, the angel of Portugal. Above all, accept and bear with submission the suffering that the Lord will send you." [15]

Some time after giving this account, Lúcia felt the need to be more explicit about the date and the reason they were in her parents' yard at that hour: "The second apparition must have been at the height of summer, on those days when it was the hottest. Then, we would go home with the flock at mid-morning and let them out again only in late afternoon. We would go to spend the hours of the siesta in the shade of the trees that surrounded the well that I have already mentioned a few times." [16]

In this second apparition, Francisco could still not hear what the angel said to Lúcia and Jacinta. Besides that, he did not understand the meaning of the angel's words once they told him what had been said:

> At the second apparition by the well, Francisco waited a few minutes and then asked: "You spoke with the angel; what did he say to you?"
>
> "You didn't hear?"
>
> "No. I saw him speak to you and I heard what you said to him, but I don't know what he said to you."
>
> Since the supernatural atmosphere in which the angel had left us still lingered, I told him to ask me the following day, or to ask Jacinta.

"Jacinta, tell me what the angel said."

"I will tell you tomorrow. Today I can't speak."

The next day, as soon as he came up to me, he asked me: "Did you sleep last night? I keep thinking about the angel and what he said."

So then I told him all that the angel had said in the first and second apparitions. But he seemed not to understand what the words meant, and he asked: "Who is the Most High? What does it mean to say: 'The hearts of Jesus and Mary are attentive to your supplications'?"

And having received an answer, he remained thoughtful, only to quickly interrupt with another question. But my spirit was still not completely free, and I told him to wait until the following day because at that time I still couldn't speak. He waited happily, but didn't lose the first chance to soon ask new questions that led Jacinta to say to him: "Look, we shouldn't talk much about these things." [17]

Third apparition of the angel of Portugal

The angel of Portugal appeared a third time to the three children at the Loca do Cabeço, while they were minding their flocks just above Valinhos. It was in an olive grove belonging to Lúcia's parents, a place called Pregueira. The apparition took place around the end of September 1916. Having eaten the lunch they had brought with them, they decided to pray in the cave on the other side of the hill. On their way, they went past Pregueira as far as Lapa, turning at the slope of the hill on the side of Aljustrel and Casa Velha.

As soon as they arrived at Loca, they recited the Rosary. Then, on their knees, they pressed their foreheads to the ground and recited the prayer that the angel had taught them at the first apparition, "My God I believe, I adore, I hope, and I love you...." Lúcia relates:

> I don't know how many times we had repeated this prayer, and then we saw an unknown light shine over us. We got up to see what was happening and we saw an angel holding a chalice in his left hand. Above it a host was suspended, from which some drops of blood fell into the chalice. The angel left the chalice suspended in the air and knelt next to us, and had us repeat three times: "Most Holy Trinity, Father, Son, and Holy Spirit, I adore you profoundly. I offer you the most precious Body, Blood, Soul, and Divinity of Jesus Christ, present in all the tabernacles on earth, in reparation for the outrages, sacrileges, and indifference with which he is offended. And through the infinite merits of his most Sacred Heart and of the Immaculate Heart of Mary, I ask of you the conversion of poor sinners."

Then he got up and took in his hands the chalice and the host. He gave to me the sacred Host, and he divided the Blood of the chalice for Jacinta and for Francisco, saying at the same time: "Take and drink the Body and Blood of Jesus Christ, horribly insulted by ungrateful men. Make reparation for their crimes and console your God."

Prostrating himself again to the ground, he repeated with us another three times the same prayers: "O Most Holy Trinity…" and then disappeared. We remained in the same position, always repeating the same words. When we finally got up, we saw that it was already night and that it was time to go home.[18]

Although he was profoundly impressed and immersed in this supernatural atmosphere, Francisco realized that night was approaching and thought to bring the flock home.[19]

Francisco did not at once understand what had happened, but he did not want to remain in doubt. His lack of comprehension is very understandable because, apart from his being only a child, Communion under the species of wine was not practiced at that time. Jacinta must have received special lights so that, in spite of her young age, she could answer her brother with such conviction.

When a few days passed and things had returned to normal, Francisco asked: "The angel gave you Holy Communion, but what did he gave to me and Jacinta?"

"It was also Holy Communion," answered Jacinta with unspeakable happiness. "Didn't you see that it was the Blood that fell from the Host?"

"I felt that God was in me but I didn't know how!"

Then, prostrating himself on the ground, he remained for a long time with his sister, repeating the prayer of the angel: "Most Holy Trinity…."[20]

Later, Sister Lúcia gave more details about this third apparition of the angel. With reference to the place, she says, "When he came nearer to a small stone by the cave entrance, he left the chalice and the host suspended in the air, in the same position as he had carried them."[21]

Questioned later as to whether, in fact, she had received Communion, she answered, "I think that the Communion was real, because I felt contact with the Host just as in ordinary Communions."[22] She was also to say that she remembers having swallowed the Sacred Host.[23]

To the question of Don José Pedro da Silva as to whether the angel of peace and the angel of Portugal were one and the same, she replied, "I don't know. It seems to me that they are the same."[24]

When she was asked if there was any difference regarding the second apparition's garments, etc., Lúcia said, "I don't recall noticing any difference." In another passage she clarified, "At a distance, one saw only light; nearer, a person of transparent light.... I cannot explain in words exactly what it was like."

She added: "The outlines of the angel were perfectly defined. The voice did not sound like a human voice, but it could be understood as if it were human.... The figure didn't have wings!"[25]

Concerning the actual time of the third apparition, she is a little more explicit: "It seems to me that the third apparition took place in October or the end of September, because we were no longer returning home for siesta."[26]

Desecration of the Holy Eucharist

When the angel of Portugal spoke of the desecration of the Eucharist, he may have been referring to events in the following year when many churches were vandalized and the consecrated hosts desecrated:

[The desecrations] began on January 4, 1917, when the churches of Olival, Vila Nova de Ourém, and Pousos were broken into, and the vessels containing the sacred hosts were taken.... On January 31 ... the parishes of Vilar do Pinheiro e Mosteiró, Vila do Conde and those of Caridelo, Gaia, Alfena, and Valongo were broken into and the sacred hosts were scattered over the floor and the altars.

February began with a failed attack on February 7 against the chapels of the Sanctuary of Bom Jesus do Monte and ended on February 28 with a similar attempt on the parish church of Serzedo.

In March attacks began on the fourteenth with robberies in the churches of Saint Pedro dos Arcos at Val-de-Vez, Gesteira, Soure the Ega chapel, and in Condeixa, where the consecrated hosts were left on the ground....[27]

Attacks continued to occur throughout the year, with many churches being vandalized. In Lisbon alone, between 1910 and 1917, at least forty-two churches and chapels were vandalized and desecrated.[28]

The profound impression left by the encounters with the angel

Not knowing quite how to explain what was happening to them, the little shepherds bore witness to what took place within them after each apparition.

When we spoke about the angel, I don't know what we felt. Jacinta would say: "I don't know what I feel. I can't talk, sing, or play anymore, and I don't have strength for anything."

"Me too," answered Francisco. "But what does it matter? The angel is more beautiful than anything else. Let's think about him."

In the third apparition the presence of the supernatural was even more intense. For some days even Francisco didn't dare to speak. He said afterward: "I love to see the angel, but the worst part is that after we aren't able to do anything. I couldn't even walk. I don't know what was wrong with me."[29]

The children went on with their life as usual, without their families noticing any difference. But grace was transforming them interiorly, preparing them for the great day that was approaching. They never forgot the angel's lessons. Even when Francisco was ill, he loved to visit the Loca do Cabeço.[30] When he was near death and very weak, he would get out of bed and, prostrate on the floor, say the angel's prayer until he no longer had the strength to continue.

The Loca do Cabeço continued to hold a very important place in the lives of the little shepherds. When Jacinta was ill, Lúcia tells us:

Whenever I could, I loved to go to Cabeço, our favorite cave, to pray. Since Jacinta loved flowers so much, on the way back I would pick a bunch of flowers on the hillside—irises and peonies when they were in bloom—and bring them to her, saying: "Here! They are from Cabeço." She would take them and sometimes say with tears running down her cheeks: "I can never return there! Nor to Valinhos, nor to the Cova da Iria! I miss them so much!"[31]

Lúcia also took refuge there to pray in difficult moments, such as when Jacinta was hospitalized in Lisbon: "As soon as I could, I withdrew to the Cabeço, and stay alone in the rocky cave. There, alone with God, I could vent my sorrow and pour out abundant tears in my grief. Coming down the hill, everything reminded me of my dear companions."[32]

Today, in the Loca do Cabeço, stands beautiful white marble sculptures representing the scene of the third apparition. Every year, on the feast of the Guardian Angel of Portugal, the National Children's Pilgrimage takes place there, organized by the Sanctuary of Fátima.

A reasonable doubt

Lúcia made no reference to these apparitions until 1946. Why this silence? When Lúcia was later asked about this, she replied:

A few other little girls and myself had seen a vague apparition of the angel in 1915, when Jacinta and Francisco were not yet coming with me to mind the flock. I had never told anyone about this marvelous event [though the others did]. People began to make fun of it. When the angel appeared to us in 1916, I had still not forgotten that lesson. After the apparition of the angel at Cabeço, we decided not to say anything about it to anyone....

After Jacinta had talked about the first apparition of Our Lady, people kept on pestering us with the most detailed questions. So we made this resolution: "When people ask us again: 'Did you see Our Lady?' we will say: 'Yes,' and if they keep on asking: 'What did she say?' we will tell them, 'That we should pray the Rosary.' And we will keep silent about the rest." [33]

A slight doubt still remains. It is understandable that these apparitions should be kept secret at first. But was there any reason to hide them until 1946? Lúcia was too humble to allow herself to be guided solely by her own thinking in a matter of such importance. She herself gives the reason for this long silence:

The archpriest of Olival, the Bishop of Leiria, and the circumstances [we found ourselves in]: all these advised us to be silent. Wasn't this enough to keep the secret, until the bishop obliged me to speak? [34]

In fact, the three children found themselves completely alone in a matter of such relevance, and previous experiences had taught them to keep silence as, indeed, they did. In the meantime, the three children continued their usual life, tending the flocks, playing games, and offering up sacrifices as the angel had recommended. They did not suspect that an event that would revolutionize the world was approaching.

CHAPTER 4

May 13: An Unforgettable Day

IN THE APPARITION near the well at Poço do Arneiro, the guardian angel of Portugal had told the little shepherds: "Pray much! The most holy hearts of Jesus and Mary have designs of mercy for you." The three children could not imagine how far-reaching these words were. They began at once to put generously into practice the recommendations of the angel, without suspecting that they were being prepared for an immensely more important meeting.

DEVOTION TO OUR LADY IN PORTUGAL

Portugal was born under Our Lady's mantle and has always been able to count on her help at the decisive moments of its history. Devotion to Our Lady is inseparable from the history of Portugal. The land is dotted with oratories and beautiful churches in honor of the Mother of God, proclaiming to everyone the love of her children.[1] A few years after the restoration of national independence on December 1, 1640, the king, Dom João IV, proclaimed Our Lady of the Immaculate Conception the patroness of Portugal.

It was declared that from that day on, Our Lady of the Immaculate Conception was to be not only patroness "but Queen of the kingdoms and domains of Portugal"; a solemn promise was made to donate "an annual offering of fifty gold cruzados" as a sign of tribute and fealty to Our Lady; and also to confess and defend always, even at the cost of life that "the Virgin Mary, Mother of God, was conceived without original sin."[2] The solemn oath was made in the royal chapel on March 25, 1646, the feast of the Annunciation, which fell on Palm Sunday that year. From then on, the kings and queens of Portugal never again wore their royal crowns, because there was only one queen: Mary, the Immaculate Conception.

The Rosary crusade

After the First Republic was proclaimed in 1910, the anticlerical government made life difficult for the Church. It seized some Church lands and outlawed various expressions of popular religiosity such as certain festivals. In this time of great trial, the Portuguese Christians turned with complete confidence to Mary, their patroness and queen. In 1916, a Rosary crusade was organized throughout the country and thousands of men, women, and children from every area and social condition were enrolled in it. Priests were requested to establish the Confraternity of the Rosary in every place where it did not yet exist. All made a solemn commitment to:

— Pray the Rosary every day, preferably as a family and always in a group, for the temporal and spiritual resurgence of the country.

— Pray the Rosary once a week in common with the group to which each of the associates belonged. It could be recited in a church or in a public place, on a day and at a time fixed by the directors.

— Receive Holy Communion every Sunday, or, at least, on the first Sunday of every month, for the intentions of the crusade.

— Enthrone a statue or, at least, a picture of Our Lady of the Rosary in the home.

The recitation of the Rosary had been part of popular tradition since the fifteenth century; it was only a case of fanning into flames the hidden embers of Marian devotion. The traditional devotion of dedicating the month of May to Mary grew in an extraordinary way in 1916. "Thanks to the Rosary crusade, the month of May 1916 became, from the north to the south of our country, a daily prayer to the patroness of Portugal, beseeching her for peace and the joy of living."[3] The enthusiasm was so great that, in Lisbon, even some army officers, in uniform, took part in these devotions, though this provoked an unpleasant political reaction.

From all over Portugal a chorus of suppliant voices rose up to the Mother of God, praying the Rosary in her honor. Heaven's answer was not long delayed, and it came with undreamed of magnanimity.

THE DRAMA BEGINS

On the way to the Cova da Iria

On the morning of May 13, 1917, the three little shepherds went to the parish church of Fátima to assist at what was called the Mass of the Souls. Dressed in their Sunday clothes and with sleepy faces—the Mass usually began at 6:00 A.M.—the children walked from the hamlet of Aljustrel to the church. The morning was cold and dry and promised sunshine.

When Mass was over, while some men stayed in the churchyard discussing the latest events in the village, the children returned home quickly. They changed their clothes and ate the breakfast their mothers had prepared for them: "a bowl of hot vegetable or rice soup, with a little olive oil and some home-made bread."[4]

They put on the shoulder bags that held their lunch and then opened the sheep pen. Usually they brought with them "bread, olives, some codfish or a sardine, cheese, and fruit."[5] Their mothers sent them off, reminding them to say the Rosary on the hill and to be very careful of the flock.

The two flocks—belonging to the parents of Francisco and Jacinta and to Lúcia's parents—were brought to the little barreiro, or pool, outside the hamlet on the road to Gouveia.[6] The sheep wandered around to eat the grass on the sides of the road while the lively children ran, jumped, and sang. They enjoyed the sense of freedom this gave them. When they had to decide where to pasture the sheep that day, Lúcia, the eldest and undisputed leader of the group, said unhesitatingly: "We'll go to the Cova da Iria." Perhaps she chose this area because her parents owned a small plot on the spot where, today, the Chapel of the Apparitions stands.

Lúcia's parents had repeatedly warned the children to keep the sheep away from the vegetables growing at the Cova da Iria when they went there. In the middle of May the crops in that plot were fresh and appetizing: wheat, corn, beans, and potatoes.[7] The sheep had to be watched carefully lest they eat the plants. Later, as has been noted, this small plot was destroyed by the first pilgrims.

The place of the apparition

The journey to the Cova da Iria had been slow because the sheep were grazing along the way. Once they arrived, the children ate their lunch and recited the Rosary. Next, they planned their game, having first moved the sheep from the area around the plot to the top of the slope. They decided to build a wall around a furze bush,[8] approximately on the spot where the Basilica of Our Lady of the Rosary of Fátima stands today. Francisco acted as architect, engineer, and builder, while Lúcia and Jacinta assisted him and brought him the building materials.

Suddenly, what seemed to them a vivid flash of lightning made them stop what they were doing. The three of them looked up at the sky for storm clouds. But the sky had no clouds at all! It was completely clear, showing the incomparable azure hue characteristic of Fátima. The children decided not to risk being caught in a thunderstorm and began to bring the flock home as quickly as possible. The sheep were coming down by a shortcut toward the road, when, "A little more or less than halfway down the slope that goes from the place of the apparitions to the top of the hill, just before the big holm oak tree,"[9] a second flash of lightening caused them to hurry along.

But a little farther on, when they were nearing the spot where the Chapel of the Apparitions stands today, beside the big holm oak, another flash of lightening, as vivid as the first two, made them stop. A few steps away, before them on a bush, they saw "a lady all dressed in white. She was more brilliant than the sun, and she radiated a light more clear and intense than a crystal glass filled with sparkling water, with rays of the burning sun shining through it."[10] How is it possible to describe in human words this supernatural vision?

The children stopped for a few instants, surprised. What else could they do? Their first instinct was to withdraw in fear. As Lúcia was to explain later, the fear they felt, "was not really of Our Lady but of the thunder" and the flashes of lightning. "Our Lady does not cause fear, but only surprise, peace, and joy."[11]

Lúcia also corrected a rumor that had been going around for some time. It is not true that Francisco told Lúcia to throw a stone at the apparition to see if it was human.[12]

Our Lady visits the children

Lúcia gives us an account of this great event, insofar as it is possible to express it in human words: "We were so close that we were within the circle of light that surrounded her, or that she radiated. Then Our Lady said to us: 'Don't be afraid. I will not harm you.'" The heavenly messenger spoke to the children in a language they could understand. Overwhelmed by such an unusual event, it is natural that they felt ill at ease in the presence of such a beautiful but unknown person. Mary repeated the calming words that Jesus had spoken to the apostles on several occasions. Lúcia continues: "It seems to me that Our Lady, by telling us not to be afraid, wanted to relieve our fear of what we supposed was an approaching thunderstorm, because we were used to seeing lightning only when there was a thunderstorm."[13] Encouraged by this invitation to enter into conversation, Lúcia spoke:

"Where do you come from?" I asked her.

"I am from heaven."

"And what do you want of me?"

"I have come to ask you to come here six months in a row, on the thirteenth day, at this same hour. Afterward, I will tell you who I am and what I want. Later on I will come here for a seventh time."[14]

"Will I also go to heaven?"

"Yes, you will go."

"And Jacinta?"

"Yes, she also."

"And Francisco?"

"Yes, he too, but he must pray many Rosaries...."

"Do you wish to offer yourselves to God by bearing the sufferings he wills to send you, as an act of reparation for the sins that offend him, and to humbly beg for the conversion of sinners?"

"Yes, we want to."

"Go then, you will have much to suffer, but the grace of God will be your comfort."

Upon pronouncing these last words (the grace of God will be your comfort) she opened her hands for the first time, communicating to us a light so intense that as it streamed from her hands, its rays penetrated our hearts and the deepest recesses of our souls. It made us see ourselves in God, who was that light, more clearly than we see ourselves in the best of mirrors. Then, moved by an interior impulse communicated to us, we fell to our knees and repeated deep within our hearts: "O Most Holy Trinity, I adore you, my God, my God, I love you in the most Blessed Sacrament."[15]

Our Lady did not communicate her message only in words, but also in gestures, by the light that radiated from her hands. She would do this in four of the six apparitions, in May, June, July, and October. Each one would contain a different message.

The children saw themselves in God and understood his infinite greatness. This vision awoke in them the fear of the Lord: the greatness of the Creator and the littleness of the creature. In consequence, they felt themselves penetrated by a profound humility that led them to adore the Most High. Our Lady did not have to teach them this prayer, for it arose from their inmost hearts, through the action of the Holy Spirit.

> After a few moments, Our Lady added: "Pray the Rosary every day, in order to obtain peace for the world, and the end of the war."
>
> Then she began to rise serenely, going toward the east, until she disappeared in the immensity of space. The light that surrounded her seemed to open a path before her in the heavenly court of the stars, and so that is why we sometimes said that we saw heaven opening.[16]

Just as in the apparitions of the angel, Francisco saw the apparition but did not hear any words, so the others had to tell him all that Our Lady said. They told him about the promise of going to heaven and how the Lady had said that Francisco would need to pray many Rosaries.

The children's reaction

The children remained enraptured for some time, scarcely aware that the Lady had already disappeared. When they recovered, Lúcia was alarmed. Their parents had told them so many times not to let the sheep eat the vegetables growing in the plot at the Cova da Iria that her first act was to look anxiously in that direction. In fact, "the sheep were peacefully grazing in the shade of the holm oaks."[17]

When Don José Pedro da Silva asked whether Our Lady had said that the sheep were not eating the chicken weed, Lúcia replied:

> As far as I remember, Our Lady did not mention the chicken weed. During the first apparition, the sheep did go into a neighbor's field that had chicken weed, but we only knew that when the owner, after the apparition, came out shouting that the sheep were eating the chicken weed. He himself drove them off and then noticed that the chicken weed had not been touched.[18]

Relieved to see that the sheep had not damaged the crop, the little shepherds discussed whether they should tell their parents what had happened. Our Lady did not them to keep everything a secret. She wanted the message to be made known. However, the children agreed among themselves not to tell anyone what had happened, and Lúcia insisted on this. Why would they have decided this?

We could point out various reasons: Spiritual matters tend to foster an atmosphere of instinctive reserve. Those who have mystical experiences tend not to talk about them casually. The children had acted in this way after the three apparitions of the angel in 1916. The difficulty they met in making themselves understood when describing their actual experience, and, above all, the painful memory of what Lúcia had to bear when people ridiculed her about it, made them reticent. Even apart from this, the little girl may have already guessed how much suffering awaited her once the news reached her mother's ears.

The children did not play. They remained immersed in the supernatural atmosphere surrounding them. It was time to internalize the message more fully. Jacinta, however, could not keep such happiness to herself and periodically exclaimed, "Oh, what a beautiful Lady!"

Lúcia's joy was mixed with sadness, because she kept remembering Our Lady's question: "Do you wish to offer yourselves to God by bearing the sufferings he wills to send you, as an act of reparation for the sins that offend him, and to humbly beg for the conversion of sinners?"

The story slips out

Jacinta and Francisco's parents had gone to the fair in Batalha that day to buy a young pig. Jacinta waited impatiently for her mother's return. The child was not used to keeping secrets from her mother and she wanted to share with her the tremendous joy she felt. While her father was busy tending to the little animal when they returned, Jacinta ran to meet her mother and held tightly to her legs in a way she had never done before. Unable to keep the great news to herself, she said it at once, as if it were the most important thing in the world. "Oh, Mother," she shouted excitedly, "I saw Our Lady in the Cova da Iria today."

Laughing at this childish thought, her mother kept on with her work, answering ironically: "I believe you, daughter! You are a great little saint to have seen Our Lady." Jacinta's first reaction was disappointment and sadness. How could her mother scoff at something that was so important? Hoping to convince her mother, Jacinta followed her around the house and kept on repeating, "But I saw her!"

When she saw, at last, that her mother was paying some attention to what she was saying, Jacinta began to tell her what had happened in the Cova da Iria that morning. Senhora Olímpia, however, did not set much store by her daughter's words and paid little attention to them. In any case, it would be quite some time before she believed in the truth of the events in the Cova da Iria.[19]

Night fell, and the family gathered around the hearth, waiting for the supper their mother was preparing. At last, in the family circle, and feeling more serene, Senhora Olímpia was ready to listen in the presence of the whole family. Jacinta recounted enthusiastically all that had taken place. Worried, Francisco added his part, unable to do anything to stop Jacinta. Besides, she had already said that he had been there also, whereupon his father asked him to confirm what Jacinta had said.

Francisco was in a difficult situation: he did not want to be untruthful but neither did he want to break his promise to Lúcia to say nothing about what had happened. He found an intelligent way out. He turned to his sister and said in a tone that reminded her of her broken promise: "There you go, saying everything!"

After these words, their father no longer doubted. He knew that Francisco was incapable of lying and that if nothing had happened in the Cova da Iria, he would have contradicted his sister. Manuel Pedro Marto passed a sleepless night, thinking about the great event, as he would confess later. After the children themselves, he was, without doubt, the first to believe that something extraordinary had happened.

Francisco, for his part, told Lúcia about the quandary he was in because of what had happened when he was questioned in front of the whole family about the occurrence. Francisco let her know that Jacinta had broken their pact about not saying anything, so that Lúcia would be prepared for the consequences of this indiscretion. He added at once, with sadness: "When my mother asked me if it were true, I had to say yes so as not to lie."[20]

A time of suffering

It was practically impossible that the great news should not spread rapidly. It was such an unusual event that anyone who heard of it immediately spread the news. Jacinta's mother told her neighbors about her daughter's story. Naturally, she also went to Lúcia's mother to confirm her daughter's statement.

Lúcia came down to earth once more when her mother asked if the news was true. Lúcia became very worried indeed, foreseeing the complications that all this could bring her. Senhora Olímpia recounts: "I never saw the child so sad. Then Francisco went to tell Lúcia that Jacinta had told the story and that, in our house, everyone already knew what had happened in the Cova da Iria."[21]

Tribulations arose for the three little shepherds, especially for Lúcia, who was rightly considered the most responsible. She had to face her mother's disbelief, the neighbors' insults, and the pastor's doubts. Furthermore, the children felt it necessary to completely change their way of life. In the first place, they would have to say the whole Rosary from beginning to end, without omitting a word. They would have to make sacrifices in reparation and for the conversion of sinners.

As had happened during the apparitions of the angel, each of the three shepherds experienced their meeting with the Lady in a different way. "Lúcia saw the Lady, spoke to her, and heard her. Jacinta saw and heard the Lady, but did not speak to her. Francisco saw the Lady, but did not hear her nor speak to her."[22]

The first believers and pilgrims

On May 13, the only witnesses of the apparition were the three visionaries. If it were not for Jacinta's providential indiscretion, the great event would have been kept secret among themselves. But during the following days, the first devotees of the events of Fátima appeared. One of them was a simple and honest person to whom the Lord entrusted an important role: Maria da Capelhina, or Maria Carreira.

Maria lived in Moita and had a son—João—who was handicapped and often ill. One of Maria's daughters, a playmate of Lúcia, often went in later years to the Carmel in Coimbra to visit Lúcia and recall various childhood events. The Lord granted that one of her daughters—a granddaughter, in fact, of Maria da Carreira—Sister Maria de Fátima, would be professed in the Congregation of Saint Joseph of Cluny. Maria da Carreira tells us how she was affected by the news of the apparition.

> I had always been sickly, and seven years earlier the doctors had even told me that I could not live much longer. Two or three days after the first apparition, my husband, who had been working with Lúcia's father, said to me one night, "Would you believe it, António [Santos] Abóbora told me that Our Lady appeared in the Cova da Iria to one of

his children, the youngest, and to two children of his sister, Olímpia, who is married to Marto. Our Lady spoke to them and promised to return there every month until October."

Then I said to him, "I'll have to find out if that is true or not. And if it is, I want to go there too, unless it is impossible for me.... But where is the Cova da Iria?" I asked. In fact the Cova da Iria is quite close to our place, in Moita ... about a ten-minute walk from my house, but I had never gone there ... no one ever mentioned that name. At that time it was not important at all....

My husband gave me directions to it and added: "Do you want to go there? You're crazy! Do you think you'll see her?"

"I know very well that I won't see her, but if we heard that the king was going there, nobody would stay at home in case they might see him. They say Our Lady is coming and we wouldn't go and see her?" Then he fell silent; and whoever is silent consents. For my part, I was determined to go there on June 13. [23]

How the apparitions affected the children

The apparitions of Our Lady had a different effect on each one of the three children. Lúcia, the chronicler of Fátima, tried to explain it in words, thus facing the insuperable difficulty of describing divine realities in human terms.

Comparing the apparitions of the angel with those of Our Lady, she notes an important difference, then goes on to explain more details about the apparitions:

> The apparition of Our Lady came to absorb us again in the supernatural, but more gently: in place of being so overwhelmed in the Divine Presence, which drained us even physically, it left us in peace and filled us with incredible joy, which did not prevent us from speaking afterward about what had happened....
>
> However, regarding the rays that Our Lady had communicated to us when opening her hands, and everything related to that light, we felt something interiorly that moved us to be silent.
>
> Afterward we told Francisco everything that Our Lady had said. To express his great joy at the promise that he would go to heaven, he crossed his hands over his chest and said: "O, Our Lady, I will say as many Rosaries as you want!" From then on he got into the habit of moving away from us as if going for a walk, and if I called him to ask him what he was doing, he would raise his arm and show me the rosary. If I told him to come play and that afterward he could pray

with us, he answered: "I will pray afterward, too. Don't you remember that Our Lady said I had to pray many Rosaries?"

Our Lady had said that Francisco would have to pray many Rosaries before he could go to heaven. Because he was the first to go to meet her in heaven, we wondered how many Rosaries he had recited.

Francisco said to me once: "I loved seeing the angel but I loved seeing Our Lady even more. Most of all, I loved to see Our Lord in that light from Our Lady that penetrated our hearts. I love God so much! But he is very sad because of so many sins! We must never sin again...."

Sometimes he would say: "Our Lady said we would have much to suffer! It doesn't matter to me; I'll suffer as much as she wants! All I want is to go to heaven."

One day I showed how unhappy I was over the persecution that was beginning to occur both within my family and from outsiders. He tried to encourage me, saying: "Let it go. Didn't Our Lady say we would have much to suffer to make reparation to Our Lord and to her Immaculate Heart for the many sins by which they are offended? They are so sad! If we can console them, we will be so happy!"

When we arrived at the pasture a few days after the first apparition of Our Lady, Francisco went up on a high rock and said to us: "Don't come here; leave me by myself."

"All right." I went off with Jacinta to catch butterflies, and as soon as we caught them, we made the sacrifice of letting them go. We forgot all about Francisco. At lunchtime we realized he was missing, and we went to call him: "Francisco, don't you want to come for lunch?"

"No, you eat."

"And to pray the Rosary?"

"Yes, later on. Come back to call me."

When I went back to call him he said to me: "Come up here to pray next to me."

We climbed to the top of the rock, where the three of us could hardly fit kneeling, and I asked him: "But what have you been doing here for so long?"

"I am thinking of God, who is so sad because of so many sins! If only I could make him happy!"

One day we began singing in chorus about the joys of the Serra. We finished the first round and were going to repeat it, but Francisco interrupted: "Don't sing anymore. Since we saw the angel and Our Lady, I no longer care to sing."[24]

From then on, the news spread everywhere and no one could stop it, drawing ever greater crowds to the Serra d'Aire.

CHAPTER 5

The Apparition of June 13

THE LITURGICAL FEAST of Saint Anthony, June 13, fell on a Wednesday in 1917. For the feast day, farmwork was reduced to a minimum. Devotion to Saint Anthony is deeply rooted in Portuguese tradition and is especially celebrated on the annual feast. In Fátima, the feast was very important also because Saint Anthony is patron of the parish.

The sung Mass was followed by a solemn procession. After that, the day brought music, fireworks, distribution of food and clothing, and an open-air festival. Boys and girls went in groups to distribute goods and clothing, while the bells pealed joyfully and packets of white bread were given out.

The men would drive ox-carts decorated with branches, flowers, flags, and quilts, in which they would bring their wives and children, along with the offering of 500 packets of food to distribute among the people. They circled the church a few times, then stopped in front of the pastor's veranda so he could bless everything. An area was marked off around the carts with a few openings for people to pass through to receive their packet.[1]

It was an important day in the humdrum life of a country village, and the children enjoyed it most of all. So the parents of the little shepherds were convinced the story of the apparitions would die a natural death once the children had to choose between the feast with all its attractions and the Cova da Iria, lost in the solitude of the hills. Contrary to what their families thought, Lúcia, Jacinta, and Francisco remained firmly resolved to give up the feast so as not to miss the meeting with the Lady clothed in light.

The reaction of the families

Lúcia describes the atmosphere in her family around June 13: "My mother and sisters had a scornful attitude, and I was very sensitive to this, which cost me as much as insults."[2]

The atmosphere was more pleasant in the home of Jacinta and Francisco, although their family tried to dissuade them from going to the Cova da Iria. "Jacinta had hardly opened her eyes when she jumped out of bed and ran to her mother's room to ask her again to go to the Cova da Iria to meet the Blessed Virgin, but she was surprised to find the bed empty. Her eldest brother came in immediately and told her that their parents had left for the day and would return home at night."[3] Her deep love for her mother made her feel great sorrow. The person she loved best in the world would not see Our Lady! What had happened?

Her father and mother feared that nothing whatever would appear in the Cova da Iria, and that their family would be made a laughingstock. They thus decided not to go to the Cova. But at the same time, they did not want to stay home with nothing to do on the feast day while their children were left to themselves. So Manuel Marto decided to go with his wife to the fair at Pedreira and buy cattle. In this way, when they returned home, the question would certainly be solved one way or another.[4]

Olímpia de Jesus narrates in all simplicity the conversation she had with Jacinta about her insistence that her mother go with her to the Cova da Iria:

> "Mother, don't go to the fair tomorrow; go to the Cova da Iria, Our Lady is coming there."
>
> The mother didn't wish to believe that and told her daughter: "You want to go to the feast for Saint Anthony, you don't want to go to the Cova da Iria," as if to help her see that it was just a pretext for going to the festival.
>
> Jacinta responded: "Saint Anthony isn't beautiful."
>
> "Why?"
>
> "Because Our Lady is more beautiful! I'm going to the Cova da Iria with Lúcia and Francisco, and if Our Lady says we should go to Saint Anthony's festival, we'll go."[5]

She ran at once to waken Francisco and to let the flock out to graze, after which the three young shepherds could arrive punctually to meet Our Lady. They were so worried about being late that they ate their breakfast on the way. Lúcia was already waiting near Barreiro, where they usually joined their flocks. They decided to go to Valinhos, where the flock could find good pasture. An hour and a half later they returned home, the sheep having eaten their fill. After the animals were put back in their pens, the children put on their Sunday clothes and prepared themselves for that day's great encounter.

Lúcia's mother, worried about the urgency of discovering the truth about the apparitions, decided to allow her daughter to go. She decided herself "to go to the Cova da Iria to see if Lúcia would return there, to observe her secretly, without being seen. She did not think that anyone else would be going there. But people appeared at once to accompany her, and so she did not go."[6]

On the way to the Cova da Iria

Lúcia recounts what happened:

Around 11:00 A.M. I left home and passed by the house of my uncle and aunt, where Jacinta and Francisco where waiting for me. From there we went to the Cova da Iria to await the desired moment. All those people followed us, asking us a thousand questions. That day I felt overwhelmed with bitterness. I saw that my mother was distressed, and she wanted to compel me at all costs, as she said, to say that I had lied. I would have satisfied her wish if I could have done so without lying. From the cradle, she had instilled in her children a great horror of lying and severely punished anyone who told a lie.

She often said: "I always managed to have my children tell the truth, and now I have to let my youngest get away with this? If it were only a small thing.... But a lie like this, that deceives so many people and brings them out here!"[7]

According to different estimates, between fifty to seventy people gathered at the Cova da Iria that day,[8] among them fourteen girls who had been Lúcia's companions at their solemn Communion that year.[9]

For the first time, Maria Carreira was present at the apparitions, with her disabled son João. Maria was hoping to obtain his cure.[10] She arrived at the spot of the apparitions before noon and did not see any-one there. To pass the time, she went toward Aljustrel to wait for the three children. She did not know them, as they were still young, but she knew their families.

She met the three children on the way, along with some people from around Torres Novas, and they all went toward the holm oak. When they arrived there, they met some women from Boleiros who had braved the criticism and ridicule of some other people.

The three shepherds awaited the time of the apparition, sheltered from the heat by the leafy branches of the big holm oak, along with the rest of those present. They behaved like normal children of their age: they ate lupine seeds that people gave them.[11] Lúcia was becoming more serious as the time passed, and then she announced that it was nearly time for the apparition, so they went to the little holm oak. People offered the children oranges, but they accepted only one each, and did not eat them.

The heavenly visitor

After everyone present had recited the Rosary, a girl asked them to recite also the Litany of Our Lady, but Lúcia said there wasn't enough time. As soon as they saw once more the flash reflecting the light that was approaching, which they called lightning, the children ran to the holm oak and knelt down. The people who were present accompanied them. Moments later, Our Lady was on the holm oak, as in the previous month. The dialogue between Lúcia and Our Lady began:

"What do you want of me?" I asked.

"I want you to come here on the thirteenth day of the next month, to pray the Rosary every day, and to learn to read. Afterward I will tell you what I want."

I asked for the cure of a sick person.

"If he is converted, he will be cured within the year."

"I would like to ask you to take us to heaven."

"Yes, I will take Jacinta and Francisco soon. But you will stay here some time longer. Jesus wants to use you to make me known and loved. He wants to establish devotion to my Immaculate Heart in the world."

"Will I stay here alone?" I asked with grief.

"No, daughter. And are you suffering much? Don't be disheartened. I will never leave you. My Immaculate Heart will be your refuge and the way that will lead you to God." At the moment she said these last words, she opened her hands and communicated to us for a second time the rays of that immense light. In that light we saw ourselves immersed in God. Jacinta and Francisco seemed to be in the part of the light that was lifted up toward heaven, and I was in the part that spread over the earth. In front of the palm of Our Lady's right hand was a heart surrounded by thorns that seemed to be piercing it. We understood that it was the Immaculate Heart of Mary, insulted by the sins of humanity, and which sought reparation.[12]

When she heard that Jacinta and Francisco would be going to heaven soon, Lúcia felt intensely alone. She was only ten years old and was living through a very difficult time. Except for her father, her family opposed her. Her mother thought the child was lying and wanted her to tell people the truth. Her sisters kept saying that, from then on, if she wanted to eat, she could take whatever was left in the plot in the Cova da Iria, which was now destroyed. Many people insulted her and even hit her.

She had only her two cousins to confide in, and they tried to comfort her as best they could. And now Our Lady was saying that she would be deprived of that support as well. Hence her question which, more than that, was a lament! "Will I stay here alone?"

In Our Lady's words we can hear the warmth of her motherly heart: "No, daughter.... Don't be disheartened. I will never leave you...."

Then Our Lady made the beautiful gesture with her hands. In the light that radiated from them, the future of the three children was shown in a symbolic manner, as if to confirm what Our Lady had already told them: she would soon take the brother and sister up to heaven. Lúcia, instead, would remain on earth to spread devotion to the Immaculate Heart of Mary.

For the first time, also, the Immaculate Heart appeared in a different form than usually shown in pictures. Previous to the Fátima apparitions, pictures of the Immaculate Heart of Mary were shown with a crown of roses. Here it was crowned with thorns, symbolizing our sins.

Discernible signs of the apparitions

The people present knew that something unusual was happening. Maria Carreira testifies: "Then we started to hear something that sounded like a very gentle voice, but we couldn't understand what was being said; it sounded like bees humming."[13] In her deposition for the official inquiry, on September 28, 1923, she expressed herself in a similar manner: "We heard a humming sound coming from the holm oak, but couldn't understand a word of the response."[14]

As soon as the dialogue was over, Lúcia exclaimed: "Look! Do you want to see her? There she goes, there she goes!"

Those present heard something like the whistle of a rocket when it is gaining upward momentum. Maria Carreira added afterward: "We saw nothing: just a small cloud, a leaf from the branch rising slowly, moving toward the east until it disappeared completely."[15] In her deposition, she is more explicit: "We looked and saw a cloud of smoke rising from the holm oak and moving upward toward the east; the little girl was pointing to it.... The cloud was a very light mist."[16]

Another curious detail: before the apparition, the shoots of the holm oak appeared fresh and straight. Afterward, in a little circle on top, possibly where the Lady clothed in light had been, they were bent toward the east. People eager for souvenirs began to pull off branches and leaves from the tree, while Lúcia asked that they take them only from the sides and the trunk, but not from the spot where Our Lady had been.[17]

At the end of the meeting with Our Lady, as was natural, questions rained on the little shepherds, but they had decided to say nothing about what had happened, answering only in monosyllables.

"Somebody said, 'Let's pray the Rosary,' seeing that people were starting to leave. But others who lived farther away said, 'Let's pray only the litany, we'll pray the Rosary on the way to Fátima' ... and they arrived there when the procession was already going down the street."[18]

The children returned home at about 4:00 P.M., followed by a crowd of people who tormented them with all kinds of questions.[19] From then on, the Cova da Iria began to be a place of prayer, with more and more people going there. Once more, Maria Carreira began this new phase. On the following Sunday she was there with her two eldest daughters, praying the Rosary at the holm oak. On the previous Sunday only the daughters were there, but other people joined them to pray. Before long many people went even during the week, their beads in their hands.

The first interrogation of the little shepherds

The next day, the three little shepherds were called to the house of the parish priest, Father Manuel Marques Ferreira. The rectory was located beside the church, on the right, in front of the side chapel (before the renovations). The priest had first heard about the apparitions on May 17. Certainly by the afternoon of June 13, the news of the latest apparition had already reached him. He quickly sought information about it without giving any great importance to the matter, simply treating it as a normal part of his duties in the parish.

Lúcia's mother was pleased that the priest had summoned her daughter to see him the following day, convinced that he would put an end to the whole matter. She was careful to prepare Lúcia for this meeting which, in her opinion, would be decisive.

> Around that time the pastor of my village knew what was happening and sent word to my mother to bring me to his house. This made her feel relieved, since she thought that the pastor would take responsibility for the events. So she said to me: "Tomorrow we are going to Mass early in the morning. Afterward you'll go to the pastor's house. He will insist that you tell the truth, in whatever way he thinks best. Perhaps he will punish you … as long as he obliges you to confess you lied, I'll be satisfied."[20]

The two cousins were also summoned, but apparently Jacinta did not say anything. When Lúcia later asked her why, Jacinta answered that she was simply keeping the promise she had made, that is, not to say anything about it to anyone. Lúcia continues narrating what happened the next day:

> I followed my mother and went up the stairs to the porch of the pastor's house. As we were going up the first steps my mother turned around and said to me: "Don't irritate me anymore! Now you will tell the pastor that you lied, so that on Sunday he can announce at church that it was a lie, and that will be the end of it. What a thing this is! All the people run to the Cova da Iria to pray in front of a holm oak!"
>
> Without saying more, she knocked on the door. The sister of the good pastor had us sit down on a bench and wait a little. Finally the pastor came. He took us into his office and indicated that my mother could sit on the bench, then he called me over to his desk.... The interrogation was very detailed and, I almost dare to say, bullying. His reverence gave me a warning, because he said: "It doesn't seem to me to be a revelation from heaven. Usually, when these things happen Our Lord commands those with whom he communicates to give an account to their confessors or pastors. This child, on the contrary, keeps it to herself as much as she can. This could also be a deceit of the devil. We will see what the future reveals to us."[21]

Lúcia withdrew thoughtfully. This was the first time that anyone had suggested to her the possibility that it might not be Our Lady who was appearing, but the devil. After that a doubt, sharp as a thorn, remained in Lúcia's mind for a long time and robbed her of peace and joy.

Meanwhile, her mother continued her attempts to get her daughter to say that she had lied. Maria Rosa insisted that the whole thing was simply the fruit of the little girl's imagination. Soon, the mother launched another attempt. "Early one morning she called me and told me she was bringing me to pastor's house: 'When we arrive there, kneel down, tell him you lied, and ask his pardon.'"[22]

This time, he questioned only Lúcia. The two smaller children stayed at the Arneiro well, praying for a happy outcome of the meeting. When she returned she met them there, on their knees.

CHAPTER 6

Events in July

THE APPARITION OF JULY 13

NEWS OF THE SECOND apparition on June 13 aroused a burning curiosity in hundreds of people. For the first time, Maria Carreira was a witness to the dialogue between Lúcia and the heavenly visitor. She brought her son João with her, hoping he would be miraculously cured.

No one can recount better than Lúcia what happened in the Cova da Iria on that typically warm Friday, July 13. First, however, some preliminary facts need to be known.

Lúcia's doubts

It was almost the end of the second week of July. The thirteenth fell on a Friday. As the day announced for the third visit of Our Lady approached, Lúcia felt herself immersed more and more in a sea of anguish. At her meeting with the priest of Fátima, she had been received with the greatest courtesy and kindness. The priest had listened to her with deep attention. The simplicity and realism with which the little shepherd girl spoke of the events in the Cova da Iria left no room for doubt about her sincerity. But the priest's suggestion that it all might have come from the devil opened a wound in Lúcia's heart.

"This could also be a deceit of the devil!" These words tore into her, and from that moment on she had no peace. "Only our Lord knows how much these words made me suffer, for he alone can penetrate our inmost heart. I began then to have doubts that these manifestations might be from the devil, who was seeking in this way to make me lose my soul."[1]

As if this inner anxiety were not enough, her mother kept repeating to her that it was all from the devil, hoping that Lúcia would retract and admit that she had lied. In Lúcia's innocent child's mind, various events were mixed together, along with ideas she had gotten from the spiritual books that her family read together in the evening. Lúcia was an intelligent child, prone to reflection. When she was away from her cousins, taken up with household tasks or in the silence of the night, she turned this question over and over in her mind. The girl twisted and turned, unable to sleep because of her inner turmoil and the summer's heat.

In light of what the priest had said, Lúcia began to analyze everything that had happened: "Since I heard it said that the devil always brings conflict and disorder, I began to think that ever since these things had happened, there was no more joy or peace in our house."[2]

Her doubt became a wound that time did not heal. In fact, it became more painful as the thirteenth approached. Her torment was made worse because she could not confide in her mother, and much less in the priest. The friendship and clear-sightedness of her cousins helped Lúcia the most at this time. Their answer, which did not come out of any great theological knowledge, brought her some peace of mind. "I made my doubts known to my cousins. Jacinta replied: 'It's not the devil! They say the devil is very ugly and that he is under the earth, in hell; but that Lady is so beautiful! And we saw her go up to heaven.'"[3]

Meanwhile, the doubt kept gnawing at Lúcia's mind, as she herself confesses with simplicity: "During that month I lost enthusiasm for making sacrifices and acts of self-denial. I debated whether I should say that I had lied just so that then everything would stop."[4] This was the exact result of the temptation that the enemy wanted: a lie that would put an end to this supernatural intervention. From the beginning, the prince of darkness must have perceived, by the fruits that the children manifested in their lives, that these events would work against him. Faced with the temptation of putting an end to all her suffering by saying that she had lied, Lucia was again helped by the youthful wisdom of her cousins, who said: "Don't do that! Don't you see that then you would really be lying, and lying is a sin?"[5]

This doubt had such a grip on Lúcia's subconscious, like a thorn that never stops hurting, that one night she awoke in terror. Her cries wakened the whole family:

> In this state of mind I had a dream that increased the darkness of my spirit: I saw the devil laughing for having deceived me, and trying to drag me to hell. Upon seeing myself in his clutches I began to scream so loudly, calling Our Lady, that I woke up my mother. She called me anxiously and asked me what was wrong. I don't remember what I told her. I only remember that on that night I couldn't sleep anymore because I was so crippled with fear. That dream left my spirit in a cloud of true fear and anguish. My only relief was to be alone in some lonely corner to cry freely.[6]

The more Lúcia thought about the matter, the more she was set against returning to the Cova da Iria. Besides, the temptation was attractive. In that way, without much trouble, she could put an end to all the complications and sufferings. Without knowing why, she began to feel annoyed at the company of Jacinta and Francisco and tried to avoid them. Her mother redoubled her efforts to dissuade her from returning to the Cova da Iria for the next apparition. Lúcia's two cousins suffered also, not because of any doubt, but because they were sorry for her, precisely because they were convinced that the visitor to the Cova da Iria really was Our Lady. They could not imagine how they could present themselves at the holm oak without their speaker.

Lúcia's dilemma

The situation became more complicated. By the evening of July 12, people were already gathering in anticipation of the next day's events. In fact, news of the apparition had spread far and wide.[7] Lúcia had to make a decision.

Tormented by doubt and an aching heart, Lúcia felt obliged to let her cousins know of her resolve not to go to the Cova da Iria the next day. This decision caused her suffering because she, too, wanted to meet the beautiful Lady—even more now that the time of the promised meeting approached—and because she was making her cousins suffer and she was very fond of them.

The month before, more and more people had come to pester the children with questions and all kinds of remarks. Francisco suffered the most from this, and sometimes he complained to Jacinta. He would tell her that if she had only kept quiet, nobody would have known about it. Now they couldn't undo what had been done.

With all his strength and all the reasons he could muster, Francisco set about convincing Lúcia she had to be present in the Cova da Iria on July 13. When he saw her perplexed, doubting, and wondering whether, in fact, it had been the devil who appeared to them, he would weep and urge her to go. He would ask her how she could possibly think it had been the devil. Hadn't she seen Our Lady in the great light? But even more, how could he and Jacinta go without Lúcia, when she did all the talking? After supper, when it was already dark, Francisco went again to Lúcia's house in a last effort to convince her. The meeting took place at the old threshing floor, the scene of so many happy moments for the three of them, looking up at the stars and talking about them in their childish fashion. Now it was a scene of sorrow. Francisco asked tearfully, hoping to get a positive answer:

> "Look, are you going tomorrow?"
>
> "I'm not going; I already told you I am not going back anymore."
>
> "That's too bad! Why are you thinking like that now? Don't you see it can't be the devil? God is already so sad on account of so many sins, and now if you don't go, you will make him even sadder! Come on, come with us!"
>
> "I already told you that I am not going; there's no use asking me." I went abruptly into the house.
>
> A few days later he said to me: "Do you believe it? That night I did not sleep at all. I spent the whole night crying and praying so that Our Lady would make you go."[8]

The imperturbable determination of Jacinta and Francisco must have impressed Lúcia deeply and increased her interior suffering. They told her resolutely: "We're going. The Lady said we were to go."[9]

Jacinta prepared to speak to the heavenly visitor—remember, in the previous apparitions of the angel and of Mary, Jacinta heard them but did not speak. Jacinta was greatly distressed at her cousin's decision not to go with them and began to cry.

In the midst of all this grief, Lúcia attempted a further dialogue that became more and more painful. She asked Jacinta why she was crying, and the girl told Lúcia it was because Lúcia didn't want to go to the Cova. Lúcia reaffirmed her intention not to go and asked Jacinta to explain to the Lady why she would not be there: "No, I'm not going. Look! If the Lady asks you about me, tell her I'm not going because I'm afraid she may be the devil."[10]

She ended the conversation as quickly as possible and went to hide behind bramble bushes on a neighbor's property near the Arneiro well. She cried her heart out and tried to get away from the questions of the people who were looking for her.

To add to her troubles, Lúcia had to bear the reprimands of her mother, who was extremely concerned to correct a daughter whom she believed to be lying. "My mother thought I was playing with the children of the neighborhood, when I was actually hiding behind some bushes on a neighbor's property.... When I arrived home at night my mother scolded me, saying: 'This is the little saint of worm-eaten wood! All the time you have left after minding the sheep you spend playing, and in such a way that no one can find you!'"[11]

The sun shines once more in Lúcia's heart

Like the sun after a storm, when July 13 dawned, Lúcia felt herself completely changed. Her clouds of doubt had scattered, her tears had dried, and she went to her cousins' house dressed in her best clothes, smiling and inviting them to go to meet the Lady. This was probably the first miracle obtained through the intercession of Francisco and Jacinta. The simplicity with which Lúcia tells us about this change has a special beauty.

> The next day, when it was nearly time to leave, I suddenly felt that I had to go [to the Cova]. I was impelled by a strange force that I could hardly resist. So I set out on the way and passed by the house of my uncle and aunt to see whether Jacinta was still there. I found her in her room with her little brother Francisco, kneeling by the foot of the bed crying.
>
> "Aren't you going?" I asked them.
>
> "We didn't dare to go without you. Come on, come."
>
> "Yes, I'm going." I answered them.
>
> Their faces lit up with joy and they left with me. So many crowds of people were waiting for us along the way that we managed to arrive there only with difficulty.[12]

At the Cova da Iria

Approximately 2,000 to 3,000 people went to the Cova da Iria that day. The reaction of the children's mothers is touching: they were still skeptical, but solicitous for the safety of their children. Shortly after the children had left for the Cova, Olímpia, who was afraid that something might happen to her children, ran to Maria Rosa's house.

"Oh, Maria Rosa," she said in great anxiety, "let's go too, or else we may never see our children again! Nobody knows what might happen. Suppose they killed them there!"

"Don't worry," Maria Rosa answered. "If it is true that Our Lady is appearing to them, she will surely look after them; if it isn't, I don't know what will happen...." But in the end, she decided to go with her sister-in-law to the Cova da Iria.

Covered up so no one would recognize them, the two good women set out, using paths through the woods. They each carried, hidden from sight, a blessed candle and a box of matches. "Because," said Olímpia, "if we see that it is something evil, we can light the candles."

When they arrived at the Cova da Iria, they hid behind some bushes where they could see the events without being noticed. They tried to observe what was happening, their hearts beating violently, "expecting something bad ... which never appeared."[13]

Senhor Marto's attitude was very different, "convinced as he was of the sincerity of the visionaries, and, consequently, of the truth of the apparitions."[14] He followed the children without wearing a disguise, because he had made up his mind not to abdicate his duties as a father and uncle. Furthermore, his solution on June 13 still weighed on his conscience. That day he had invented the need for a trip away from home so as not to be seen or to seem to give his support to what was happening.

When they arrived at the Cova da Iria, the little shepherds found thousands of people already there, praying and singing. It was the first sizable pilgrimage to this place made holy by the presence of the Mother of Jesus. When asked how many people were present, Senhor Marto preferred not to risk giving exact figures and said only that there were many people. Among them once again was Maria Carreira, the first person to take the testimonies of the visionaries seriously. She continued to cherish in her heart the hope she had shared with Lúcia a few days before the third apparition, asking her to present to Our Lady her petition for the cure of her son João.

The visit of Our Lady

Many people from varied backgrounds testified to the perceptible signs that occurred before and during the apparitions. It is true, however, that not everyone perceived these signs:

The apparition was always preceded by a flash of light, followed by an aureole of soft light that enveloped the visionaries themselves.... In the second apparition a bang was heard like the explosion of fireworks at a festival; at the same time the stalks of the holm oak showed hollows as if an invisible foot had bent them toward the ground.

From the third apparition on, many people began to see a perceptible diminution of the sun's light, reminiscent of partial eclipses, and a thin, grayish cloud was clearly visible over the holm oak during the apparitions.[15]

Kneeling beside the holm oak, the children, led by Lúcia, began to recite the Rosary. The crowd answered reverently. They had barely finished the Rosary when Lúcia rose quickly, looked toward the east, the direction from which the Lady usually came, and asked those present to close their umbrellas. Many had them up as a protection from the burning heat in the Cova, which had become like an oven.

Then the presence of Mary made itself felt by signs: a little cloud of pale grey hovered over the holm oak, something like a little boat in the blue sea of the sky. The sun's light diminished and, as Ti Marto testified, "a cool and refreshing breeze sprang up."[16] July was no exception with respect to perceptible signs during the visit of the heavenly messenger.

The people maintained a profound silence. What other attitude could they take at a moment like this? This silence enabled the father of the two little shepherds to grasp another signal: "Then I began to hear a humming sound, a buzzing like a fly in an empty pitcher."[17]

The crowd, unable to contemplate Our Lady's face, followed attentively the visionaries' reactions. First joy. Then anguish and an air of suffering. What was happening in this meeting between heaven and earth? Only the children knew. Lúcia, as before, initiated the conversation with the heavenly visitor. She relates what happened:

> Moments after having arrived at the Cova da Iria, next to the holm oak among a great crowd of people praying the Rosary, we saw the usual rays of light. Then Our Lady appeared on top of the holm oak tree.
> "What do you want of me?" I asked.
> "I want you to come here on the thirteenth day of next month, to continue to pray the Rosary every day in honor of Our Lady of the Rosary, in order to obtain peace in the world and an end to the war, because only she can help you."[18]

Our Lady had once more put off revealing her name and what she wanted, and she renewed the promise of a miracle. In this third apparition she confided a secret to the three children.[19]

THE SECRET OF FÁTIMA

The secret that Our Lady chose to reveal during the third apparition is an important part of the message of Fátima.[20] We can speak of three parts of the same secret communicated during the apparition of July 13.

Part one: The vision of hell

In the beginning of this dramatic encounter, Our Lady gave the children some motherly advice:

> "Sacrifice yourself for sinners, and say many times, especially when you make some sacrifice: 'O Jesus, it is for love of you, for the conversion of sinners, and in reparation for the sins committed against the Immaculate Heart of Mary.'"
>
> Upon saying these last words, once again she opened her hands as in the previous months. The rays of light seemed to penetrate the ground and we saw what looked like a sea of fire. Immersed in this fire were devils and souls with human forms, as if they were burning transparent coals, black or bronze, that floated in the conflagration. Carried by the flames that emerged from their very selves as clouds of smoke, [they were] falling on every side, falling into the big fire like chaff falling from wheat. [They were] falling on every side amidst shrieks and groans of pain and despair that horrified us and made us tremble with fear. (It must have been this sight that caused me to cry out, as the bystanders said they had heard.) The devils were distinguished by their horrible and loathsome likeness to unknown animals, but transparent like black live coals.
>
> Frightened and as if to ask help, we got up and looked to Our Lady, who said to us with kindness and sadness: "You have seen hell, where the souls of poor sinners go; to save them, God wants to establish devotion to my Immaculate Heart in the world. If people do what I tell you, many souls will be saved and there will be peace. The war is going to end. But if people do not cease to offend God, another worse war will break out during the reign of Pius XI. When you see a night illuminated by an unknown light, know that this is the great sign that God gives you, and he is going to punish the world for its crimes by means of war, hunger, and persecutions of the Church and of the Holy Father."

Part two: Devotion to the Immaculate Heart of Mary

> "To prevent this, I shall come to ask for the consecration of Russia to my Immaculate Heart, and the Communion of reparation on the first

Saturdays. If my requests are heeded, Russia will be converted and there will be peace; if not, Russia will spread her errors throughout the world, causing wars and persecutions of the Church. The good will be martyred, the Holy Father will have much to suffer, various nations will be annihilated. In the end, my Immaculate Heart will triumph. The Holy Father will consecrate Russia to me and there will be granted to the world a time of peace.

"The dogma of the Faith will always be preserved in Portugal.[21] Do not tell this to anyone. To Francisco, yes, you may tell him."[22]

Our Lady appeared, in fact, to Sister Lúcia at Túy, to urge devotion to the five first Saturdays, as will be related later. Also in this second part, we may include the promise made in 1925, that, by favor of the Immaculate Heart, Portugal would not be involved in the Second World War, which indeed happened, against all expectations.

Part three: The century of martyrs

When she wrote her *Memoirs*, Lúcia omitted the third part of the secret, putting simply an "etc." as if there were something else to say. But later, when she was a Dorothean sister, she became gravely ill and had to undergo surgery.

Fearing she might take the third part of the secret to the grave, the Bishop of Fátima, José Alves Correia da Silva, ordered her to write it down toward the end of 1943. Sister Lúcia did so in Túy on January 3, 1944, under obedience and after having received Our Lady's permission.

Lúcia wrote out the text that was made public in Fátima at the end of the concelebrated Mass at which John Paul II presided on May 13, 2000. At that Mass the Pope beatified Francisco and Jacinta. This is the complete text of the letter.

The letter

J.M.J.

The third part of the secret revealed on July 13, 1917, at the Cova da Iria, Fátima.

I am writing as an act of obedience to you, my God, who asked it of me through His Excellency the Bishop of Leiria, and your and my Most Holy Mother.

After the two parts that I have already revealed, we saw on the left of Our Lady, a little higher, an angel with a sword of fire in his left

hand; ablaze, it was sending out flames that seemed to be about to set
fire to the world; these flames were extinguished by contact with the
brilliant light which, with her right hand, Our Lady directed toward
them. The angel, pointing with his right hand toward the earth, cried
out in a loud voice: "Penance, penance, penance!"

And we saw in the immense light that is God: "something similar to
how people see themselves in a mirror when passing in front of it," a
bishop dressed in white; "we had the impression that it was the Holy
Father." Various other bishops, priests, men and women religious were
climbing a rugged mountain, at the top of which was a large cross, with
rough beams as if it were made of cork oak with the bark still on.
Before arriving at the top, the Holy Father passed through a great city,
half in ruins; he was trembling, walking with an uncertain step, broken
with pain and suffering, all the while praying for the souls of those
whose bodies were strewn along the road. When he arrived at the top
of the mountain, kneeling at the foot of the great cross, he was mur-
dered by a group of soldiers who shot at him with bullets and arrows;
thus died also, one after the other, the bishops, priests, men and women
religious, and various lay people, men and women of different classes
and positions.

Under the two arms of the cross were two angels, each holding in
his hand a crystal pitcher in which he gathered the blood of the martyrs that the angels then poured over the souls who were drawing close
to God.[23]

Túy, January 1, 1944

The history of this letter

After Sister Lúcia wrote this letter, it was kept in a safe in the bishop's
residence, by order of Bishop José Alves Correia da Silva. For greater
security, the envelope was delivered to the secret archives of the Holy
Office on April 4, 1957. Sister Lúcia was informed of this. From then on,
the letter never left Rome and was always well secured. Pius XII, already
ill and advanced in age, most likely never read it.[24]

According to the Acts of the Archives for August 17, 1959, and with
the agreement of Cardinal Alfredo Ottaviani, head of the Holy Office,
Father Paul Philippe, O.P., brought to Pope John XXIII the envelope
with the third part of the secret of Fátima. His Holiness, "after some
hesitation," said, "Let us wait. I will pray. I well let you know what I have
decided." In the end, John XXIII decided to send the sealed envelope
back to the Holy Office and not to reveal the third part of the secret.[25]

Pope Paul VI made the same decision when he was dealing with the
great crisis in the Church that occurred after the Second Vatican

Council. Paul VI read the contents with the substitute secretary of state, Angelo Dell'Acqua, on March 27, 1965, and returned the closed letter once more to the archives of the Holy Offices with the decision not to publish the text.

Pope John Paul II asked that the envelope with the third part of the secret be brought to him after the attempt on his life May 13, 1981. Cardinal Franjo Seper, prefect of the congregation, delivered two envelopes to Bishop Eduardo Martinez Somalo, substitute secretary of state, on July 18. One was white, with Sister Lúcia's original text in Portuguese, and the other was orange, with the Italian translation of the secret. On August 11, Bishop Somalo returned the two envelopes to the archives of the Holy Office.

John Paul II thought immediately of consecrating the world to the Immaculate Heart of Mary. He composed a prayer, an "act of consecration," to be recited on June 7, 1991, Pentecost, in the Basilica of Saint Mary Major, to commemorate the 1,600 years since the first Council of Constantinople and the 1,550 years since the Council of Ephesus. As we know, the Pope was still in the hospital.

He was questioned several times by the media about the contents of the third part of the secret, but he always avoided revealing it. Finally it was divulged at the beatification of Jacinta and Francisco, in the presence of Lúcia, who had been told what would happen.

The impression made on the three children

This text is too dense for commentary. However, it is good for us to understand that we are now at the heart of the message of Fátima. It was precisely at the moment when Our Lady showed the children the vision of hell that she made known the first part of the secret. The children were deeply shocked and Lúcia exclaimed: "Oh, Our Lady! Oh, Our Lady!"

It was then also that our Heavenly Mother taught the little ones the prayer: "O my Jesus, forgive us our sins, save us from the fire of hell, lead all souls to heaven, especially those who are most in need of your mercy."

The text of this prayer came to be changed by zealous priests, because they thought that Our Lady was referring to the traditional Portuguese devotion to the souls in purgatory and mentioned those who had no one to pray for them, because they were forgotten by their own.

The published text—which was even set to music—read: "O my Jesus, forgive us and save us from the fire of hell, relieve the souls in Purgatory, especially the most abandoned." It was only when Lúcia revealed the vision of hell and insisted on the genuine text that the formula taught by Mary was restored.[26]

However much people kept trying to get the children to say what had happened, they did not utter a word about it. Their faces were pale, betraying that something very serious had taken place.

The impression the vision of hell made on the three children, especially Jacinta, was indescribable. Very often, she seemed lost in thought. When she was asked what she was thinking about, she would answer: "Hell! So many people go there!" "The vision of hell had horrified her to the point that all the penances and sacrifices seemed like nothing to her, if only they could prevent some souls from falling into it."[27]

At other times, she showed immense compassion for those who were falling into hell and wondered whether, in fact, after many years, hell would come to an end. Lúcia, well instructed in the truths of faith during the family catechism sessions, cleared her doubts, explaining that hell is forever, but that only those who stubbornly persist in evil go there.

Lúcia explains the impression that the vision of hell made on the little shepherds, especially Jacinta:

> That day when we arrived at the pasture, Jacinta sat pensively on a rock.
> "Jacinta! Let's go play!"
> "I don't want to play today."
> "Why don't you want to play?"
> "Because I am thinking. That Lady told us to pray the Rosary and to make sacrifices for the conversion of sinners. Now when we pray the Rosary we must pray the whole Hail Mary and Our Father. And the sacrifices, how are we going to make them?"
> Right away Francisco came up with a good sacrifice: "Let's give our lunch to the sheep and make the sacrifice of not eating lunch!"
> In a few minutes all the contents of our knapsack was distributed among the sheep. And so we passed the day fasting like the most austere Carthusian! Jacinta stayed sitting on her rock with a pensive attitude and asked: "That Lady also said that many souls go to hell. What is hell?"
> "It's like a big deep pit of wild beasts, with an enormous fire in it—my mother explained it like that—and that's where people go who commit sins and do not confess them. They stay there and burn forever."
> "And they never come out of there? Not even after many, many years?"

"No; hell never ends. Neither does heaven. Whoever goes to heaven will never leave there, and those who go to hell won't either. Don't you see that they are eternal, that they never end?"

So that was how for the first time we made a meditation on hell and eternity. What impressed Jacinta most was eternity. Even while playing once in a while she would ask: "But look. After many, many years, hell still won't end?"

Other times [she would say]: "And those people who are there burning don't die? And they don't turn to ashes? And if people pray much for sinners, will Our Lady rescue them from there? And with sacrifices too? Poor sinners. We have to pray and make many sacrifices for them!"

Later she added: "How good that Lady is! She already promised to bring us to heaven!"[28]

From then on, Jacinta showed an immense compassion for sinners. She wanted at any cost to prevent people from condemning themselves forever to such a terrible destiny. Her cousin testifies to this:

Jacinta took this matter of making sacrifices for the conversion of sinners very much to heart, so much so that she never lost any occasion to do so. Some children from two families in Moita[29] would go begging from door to door. One day we met them as we were going along with our flock. Upon seeing them, Jacinta said to us, "Let's give our lunch to those poor little ones for the conversion of sinners."

And she ran to give it to them. That afternoon she told me she was hungry. Some holm oaks and oak trees were nearby. The acorns were still quite green, but I told her we could eat them. Francisco climbed up a holm oak tree to fill his pockets, but Jacinta remembered that we could eat the ones from the oak tree instead. Thus we could make a sacrifice by eating the bitter ones, and there, that afternoon, we tasted that delicious "repast." Jacinta made this one of her habitual sacrifices. She would gather acorns from the oaks, or olives from the olive tree.

I said to her one day: "Jacinta, don't eat that, it's too bitter."

"But I'm eating it because it is bitter, to convert sinners."

These weren't our only fasts. We agreed that whenever we met such poor children, we would give them our lunch. The poor children, happy with our offering, tried to meet us along the way. As soon as we saw them, Jacinta would run to bring them all our food for that day so contentedly that it was as if she didn't miss it.

On those days our food consisted of pine nuts, roots of campaignas ("little bells"—a type of yellow flower; in its root grows a little berry, the size of an olive), mulberries, mushrooms, and things we gathered from the roots of the pine trees, whose names I don't remember now. We had fruit if it was available on some land my parents owned. Jacinta had an insatiable thirst for making sacrifices.[30]

In the third apparition Francisco seemed to be less impressed with the vision of hell, even though it left quite an effect on him. What most captivated him was God, the Most Holy Trinity, perceived in that immense light that penetrated the deepest recesses of the soul. Afterward he said: "We were on fire in that light which is God, and we didn't burn ourselves. What is God! It cannot be put in words. This is something we could never express! But how painful it is that he is so sad! If only I could console him!"[31]

Lúcia was deeply impressed by the vision of hell. She admitted later that she would have died of fright if Our Lady had not already told her that she was going to take the children to heaven.

Our Lady's prophecy concerning the war was fulfilled to the letter, although it was a conditional prophecy depending on how people responded to her call for conversion and repentance. At nightfall on January 25, 1938, a flash filled the sky, becoming more intense and more widespread. It seemed like a great conflagration of huge proportions was taking place so far away that human eyes could not see the flames. Many people came out of their houses, greatly distressed, to see if they could find out where the fire was. Others wept, saying that it was the end of the world. The following day, the media spoke of an unusual *aurora borealis*, and scientists strove to find an explanation for the strange phenomenon.

On September 1, 1939, Hitler's troops invaded Poland with the pretense that they were responding to an attack. World War II had begun. It would claim millions of victims and wreak destruction all over the world, but especially in Europe. The end of the war gave world Communism the opportunity to seize more land, and it began to oppress more nations and people.

An explanatory letter from Sister Lúcia

On May 12, 1982, Sister Lúcia wrote a letter to the Holy Father, John Paul II, that can help us better understand what was revealed.

> The third part of the secret refers to the words of Our Lady: "If not, she [Russia] will spread her errors throughout the world, causing wars and persecutions of the Church. The good will be martyred; the Holy Father will have much to suffer; various nations will be annihilated (September 7, 1917).
>
> The third part of the secret is a symbolic revelation that refers to this part of the message, depending on whether or not we accept what the message asks of us: "If my requests are heeded, Russia will be con-

verted, and there will be peace; if not she will spread her errors throughout the world...."

Because we have not heeded this call of the message, we can see for ourselves that it has been fulfilled; Russia has indeed invaded the world with her errors. And if we have not yet seen the end of this prophecy as an accomplished fact, we can see that we are moving quickly toward it, if we do not draw back from sin, hatred, vengeance, injustice that tramples on human rights, immorality, and violence.

Let us not say that God is punishing us in this way; but rather that we ourselves are responsible for the punishment. God merely warns us and calls us back to the right road, respecting the freedom that he has given us; hence it is we who are responsible.[32]

An attempt to interpret the third part of the secret

Cardinal Sodano's interpretation of the third part of the secret, given when he spoke in the Cova da Iria, had been already presented to Sister Lúcia. "To such a proposal, she began by saying that she had been given the vision, but not its interpretation. The interpretation, she said, is not a matter for the visionary, but for the Church."[33]

Finally, however, she said that, having read the text, this interpretation corresponded to what she felt herself and that she recognized it as the correct interpretation.

If the key phrase of the first and second parts of the secret is "to save souls," in the same way, the key word of the third part of the secret is the triple cry: "Penance, penance, penance!"

Besides, Sister Lúcia said in a conversation with Cardinal Sodano, "it seemed increasingly clear that the objective of all the apparitions was to foster a constant growth in faith, hope, and charity; everything else was intended simply to lead to that."[34]

The images

In the third part of the secret, various images appear, such as an angel with a sword of fire and the light of the Mother of God. The following commentary from the Congregation for the Doctrine of the Faith explains how to understand the meaning of the secret of Fátima today:

The angel with the flaming sword on the left of the Mother of God recalls similar images in the Book of Revelation. This represents the threat of judgment which looms over the world. Today the prospect that the world might be reduced to ashes by a sea of fire no longer

seems pure fantasy: man himself, with his inventions, has forged the
flaming sword. The vision then shows the power that stands opposed to
the force of destruction—the splendor of the Mother of God and,
stemming from this in a certain way, the summons to penance. In this
way, the importance of human freedom is underlined: the future is not
in fact unchangeably set, and the image which the children saw is in no
way a film preview of a future in which nothing can be changed.
Indeed, the whole point of the vision is to bring freedom onto the scene
and to steer freedom in a positive direction. The purpose of the vision
is not to show a film of an irrevocably fixed future. Its meaning is exactly the opposite: it is meant to mobilize the forces of change in the right
direction. Therefore we must totally discount fatalistic explanations of
the "secret," such as, for example, the claim that the would-be assassin
of May 13, 1981, was merely an instrument of the divine plan guided
by Providence and could not therefore have acted freely, or similar
ideas in circulation. Rather, the vision speaks of dangers and how we
might be saved from them.

The next phrases of the text show very clearly once again the symbolic character of the vision: God remains immeasurable and is the
light that surpasses every vision of ours. Human persons appear as in a
mirror. We must always keep in mind the limits in the vision itself,
which here are indicated visually. The future appears only "in a mirror,
dimly" (1 Cor 13:12).

Site of the action

Let us now consider the individual images that follow in the text of the
secret. The place of the action is described in three symbols: a steep
mountain, a great city reduced to ruins, and finally a large, rough-hewn
cross. The mountain and city symbolize the arena of human history:
history as an arduous ascent to the summit, history as the arena of
human creativity and social harmony—but at the same time a place of
destruction, where man actually destroys the fruits of his own work.
The city can be the place of communion and progress, but also of danger and the most extreme menace. On the mountain stands the cross—
the goal and guide of history. The cross transforms destruction into salvation; it stands as a sign of history's misery but also as a promise for
history.

The personages

At this point human persons appear: the bishop dressed in white ("we
had the impression that it was the Holy Father"), other bishops, priests,
men and women religious, and men and women of different ranks and

social positions. The Pope seems to precede the others, trembling and suffering because of all the horrors around him. Not only do the houses of the city lie half in ruins, but he also makes his way among the corpses of the dead. The Church's path is thus described as a *Via Crucis*, as a journey through a time of violence, destruction, and persecution. The history of an entire century can be seen represented in this image. Just as the places of the earth are synthetically described in the two images of the mountain and the city, and are directed toward the cross, so too is time presented in a compressed way. In the vision we can recognize the last century as a century of martyrs, a century of suffering and persecution for the Church, a century of world wars and the many local wars that have filled the last fifty years and have inflicted unprecedented forms of cruelty. In the "mirror" of this vision we see passing before us the witnesses of the faith decade by decade.

To which Pope does it refer?

In the *Via Crucis* of an entire century, the figure of the Pope has a special role. In his arduous ascent of the mountain we can undoubtedly see a convergence of different popes. From Pius X to the present Pope [John Paul II], they all shared the sufferings of the century and strove to go forward through all the anguish along the path that leads to the cross. In the vision, the Pope, too, is killed along with the martyrs. When, after the attempted assassination on May 13, 1981, the Holy Father had the text of the third part of the secret brought to him, was it not inevitable that he should see in it his own fate? He had been very close to death, and he himself explained his survival in the following words: "... it was a mother's hand that guided the bullet's path, and in his throes the Pope halted at the threshold of death" (May 13, 1994). That here "a mother's hand" had deflected the fateful bullet only shows once more that there is no immutable destiny, that faith and prayer are forces that can influence history, and that in the end prayer is more powerful than bullets and faith more powerful than armies.

The blood of the martyrs

The concluding part of the secret uses images that Lucia may have seen in devotional books and that draw their inspiration from long-standing intuitions of faith. It is a consoling vision, which seeks to open a history of blood and tears to the healing power of God. Beneath the arms of the cross, angels gather up the blood of the martyrs, and with it they give life to the souls making their way to God. Here, the blood of Christ and the blood of the martyrs are considered as one: the blood of the martyrs runs down from the arms of the cross. The martyrs die in communion with the Passion of Christ, and their death becomes one with his. For the sake of the body of Christ, they complete what is still lacking in his afflictions (cf. Col 1:24). Their life has itself become a Eucharist, part of the mystery of the grain of wheat that in dying yields abundant fruit. The blood of the martyrs is the seed of Christians, said Tertullian. As from Christ's death, from his wounded side, the Church was born, so the death of the witnesses is fruitful for the future life of the Church. Therefore, the vision of the third part of the secret, so distressing at first, concludes with an image of hope: no suffering is in vain, and it is a suffering Church, a Church of martyrs, that becomes a signpost for man in his search for God. The loving arms of God welcome not only those who suffer like Lazarus, who found great solace there and mysteriously represents Christ, who wished to become for us the poor Lazarus. There is something more: from the suffering of the witnesses comes a purifying and renewing power, because their suffering is the actualization of the suffering of Christ himself and a communication in the here and now of its saving effect.

What does the secret mean?

And so we come to the final question: What is the meaning of the secret of Fátima as a whole (in its three parts)? What does it say to us? First, we must affirm with Cardinal Sodano: "... the events to which the third part of the secret of Fátima refers now seem part of the past." Insofar as individual events are described, they belong to the past. Those who expected exciting apocalyptic revelations about the end of the world or the future course of history are bound to be disappointed. Fátima does not satisfy our curiosity in this way, just as Christian faith in general cannot be reduced to an object of mere curiosity. What remains was already evident when we began our reflections on the text of the secret: the exhortation to prayer as the path of "salvation for souls" and, likewise, the summons to penance and conversion....

Another key expression of the secret ... has become justly famous: "my Immaculate Heart will triumph." What does this mean? The heart open to God, purified by contemplation of God, is stronger than guns and weapons of every kind. The *fiat* of Mary, the word of her heart, has changed the history of the world, because it brought the Savior into the world—because, thanks to her *yes*, God could become man in our world and remains so for all time. The Evil One has power in this world, as we see and experience continually; he has power because our freedom continually lets itself be led away from God. But because God himself took a human heart and has thus steered human freedom towards what is good, the freedom to choose evil no longer has the last word. From that time forth, the word that prevails is this: "In the world you face persecution. But take courage; I have conquered the world!" (Jn 16:33). The message of Fátima invites us to trust in this promise.[35]

CHAPTER 7

August: Month of Trials

THE SUFFERINGS OF THE CHILDREN

The administrator

THE PRESIDENT OF the municipality of Vila Nova de Ourém was Artur de Oliveira Santos.[1] Although he had no formal education beyond primary school, the secret Masonic lodges had promoted him to this position because he was energetic, daring, and perceptive. He had joined the lodge of Leiria when he was twenty-six years old, and later founded a "triangle" (Masonic lodge) of which he was president in the headquarters of the municipality.[2]

He founded the journal *O Ouriense* in order to spread more widely his ideas opposing the monarchy and religion. When the Republic was established on October 5, 1910, Oliveira Santos began at once to climb higher in political life. Because of the political situation, he came to occupy various positions such as president of the municipal council and even substitute for the district judge. Thus, he was both astute and feared.

The part played by this sadly famous man in the story of the apparitions cannot be underestimated. Certainly he subjected Lúcia, Jacinta, and Francisco to severe tests, anticipating the doubts that might arise later. Even though Santos did not intend it, his actions made the truth shine out more brightly.

It was certainly natural that an ambitious man would want to show himself equal to his responsibilities, and continue to merit the confidence the leaders in the political sphere had placed in him. Santos made it a point of honor to end the unusual events in Fátima, which he called superstition. Until the end of his life, however, he honestly confessed that he had failed to extract the secret from the three children.

Led by the administrator, the civil authorities saw the events in the Cova da Iria as an alarming show of religious fanaticism. They believed that the clergy had fostered it, exploiting the ignorance of the people, in order to overthrow the anti-religious regime.[3]

On their part, the clergy feared it was all a political trap that would provide a pretext for further persecutions and humiliations. That is why the pastors of the Church remained attentive, but distant and careful.

In this climate of anxiety, everyone awaited the coming Monday, August 13, the day another sign from heaven had been promised. The news of the apparitions in the Serra d'Aire had spread so rapidly that, prompted by faith or simply by curiosity, great crowds were anticipated. The good weather at that time of year encouraged such expectations.

The journey to Vila Nova de Ourém

Fátima is about twelve kilometers from Vila Nova de Ourém, a distance that takes about three hours to walk. The administrator summoned the parents of the shepherds to appear before him on Saturday, August 11, at midday.

Moved by natural timidity or, perhaps, by his easy-going nature, and wishing to avoid further complications, António Santos set out for Ourém with Lúcia. The penance involved in that journey was considerable, not only because of the normal inconvenience of such a trip, but even more because it was August and the heat beat down on them. The visionary describes this event for us with her usual good humor:

> The administration is in Vila Nova de Ourém, and so we had to travel about nine miles, quite a considerable distance for three children our size. The only way to travel at that time was either on foot or on a donkey. My uncle stated right away that he would appear but he wouldn't bring his children: "The children couldn't walk such a long distance, and they can't manage to ride on a donkey because they aren't used to it. Besides, it doesn't make sense to bring two children of that size before a court."[4]

Lúcia's parents thought differently, confused as they were by this avalanche of unexpected events.

> My father said: "I'm taking my daughter there, because I don't understand anything about these matters and I don't know what I could say."
>
> My mother actually seemed pleased and said: "Take her, take her. They can't harm a child so small. Perhaps now these men who don't want prayers or anything to do with God or Our Lady will get her to confess she lied. Then all this will end once and for all."[5]

So Lúcia had to appear before the administrator without the comforting presence of her cousins. She relates:

> [My mother] got up early, prepared breakfast for me and my father, and harnessed the donkey for riding. My father went on foot to accompany Ti Marto, who didn't have a saddle. When it came time to leave [my mother] helped me get on the donkey, saying: "Go now, and be careful not to fall." She then adjusted my father's tie and waistband— the type men wore in those days instead of a belt—saying: "Let's hope this will be resolved, that the administrators will succeed in getting the little one to say she lied, and all of this will stop once and for all! God go with you, so may it be. Good-bye, see you soon, God willing."[6]

Lúcia well remembered the difficulties of the trip: "They put me on the donkey, from which I fell three times during the journey. My father and my uncle accompanied me there."[7]

In the meantime, her two cousins remained at home in great distress, because they thought Lúcia was going to be killed. She suffered too, seeing herself abandoned. She says: "I remember thinking as we went along the way: 'How different my parents are from my aunt and uncle. They tried to defend their children and risked themselves. My parents handed me over with the greatest indifference to let them do with me whatever they wanted.'"[8]

The truth is slightly different: Lúcia's parents were convinced that the apparitions were all lies, while Manuel Pedro Marto was not. They accepted a solution that made them suffer in order to see whether the events would come to an end. We don't know any other details of the journey, but we have information about what happened in Vila Nova de Ourém from Lúcia's account:

> At the administration office, I was interrogated by the administrator in the presence of my father, my uncle, and various other gentlemen whom I didn't know. The administrator wanted to force me to reveal

the secret to him, and to promise him that I would never return to the Cova da Iria. To attain this he spared neither promises nor threats. Seeing that he wasn't succeeding, he sent me away, protesting that he would make me do it even if that meant taking my life. He strongly reprimanded my uncle for not having carried out his orders, and finally he let us go home.[9]

When they reached home, Lúcia's mother ran out to meet her husband and her daughter to find out what had happened. Perhaps she hoped that all this business of the apparitions would soon be over. António Santos, tired after the journey and annoyed by what had happened, answered briefly: "They wanted the little one to reveal the secret, but she said that she could not reveal it. They railed at Marto for not having brought the children with him, then they sent us away. I lost a day of work that I really needed. Patience!"[10]

Maria Rosa's state of mind was very different. Despite the loving care that she showed in preparing them for their journey, she had a great desire that the meeting would prove that the whole thing was a carefully thought out lie, persisted in with childish obstinacy. But the trip to Ourém had failed to achieve that, and she was greatly disappointed.

Another interrogation

The civil authorities wanted to know the secret because they hoped to find that an astute cleric was behind all this agitation. The first assault of Artur de Oliveira Santos had failed. The administrator, however, was not a man to give up at the first obstacle. Two days later, early in the morning on Monday, the day announced for the fourth apparition, he appeared at Ti Marto's house. The official ordered him to tell António Santos to bring his daughter in for a further interrogation.

Jacinta and Francisco's father had gone to his farm to gather corn, intending to go to the Cova da Iria as soon as possible. When he was already at the threshing floor, his daughter Florinda told him the administrator had just arrived. Marto returned home at once to see the administrator. Artur de Oliveira Santos began the conversation, perhaps to remove the suspicion that his presence would arouse.

"Well, Senhor Marto, do you know why I came here today? I want to go up there to the Cova da Iria, to the miracle. I want to go and see it. I'm like Saint Thomas, see and believe."

Manuel Marto said, "You do well, sir."[11]

The administrator may have been nervous and tried to make up this excuse. He had probably not expected to meet a large number of people at the houses of the little shepherds and on the way to the Cova da Iria, and that could interfere with his secret plans. Meanwhile, he began to ask for the children, saying that the time for the event was approaching but they did not seem to be starting out for the Cova da Iria, and they might arrive late. The scene in Senhor Marto's house continued to unfold as the administrator kept insisting that the children go with him.

"So the children aren't here yet? It's near the time. Better send for them and I will bring them in my car."

"It isn't necessary to call them. They know how to go themselves when it is time."[12]

Lúcia recounts her father's reaction after he was told that the administrator wanted to see his daughter:

> [My father] said that it had only been a few days since he had taken me to Vila Nova de Ourém, where the administrator had already seen and spoken to me. "Now what more does he want?"
>
> On hearing this, my mother encouraged my father to go and bring me with him: "Who knows," she said, "perhaps this time, with Jacinta and Francisco, they will get the little ones to say that they lied and all this will stop! Go there! Go there and see!"
>
> My father, urged on by my mother, took me by the hand. Passing by many people who had come to meet us, he brought me to Ti Marto's house, where the administrator was already interrogating Jacinta and Francisco.[13]

Lúcia records this second encounter with the administrator: "When I arrived, he was in a room with my cousins. He interrogated us there, making new attempts to force us to reveal the secret and to promise that we would not return to the Cova da Iria. Since he didn't succeed, he ordered my father and my uncle to bring us to the pastor's house."[14]

Meeting in the pastor's house

The intentions of the civil authorities were not clear. When the three children arrived with Ti Marto and the administrator, the latter wanted to make them get into his car. He told them that they would have a more comfortable, faster journey. He said they wouldn't be jostled and pressed by the crowds that surrounded the house and filled the roads leading to the Cova da Iria.

When the children and their families refused to accept his offer of a car ride, the administrator then said that he would wait for them at the pastor's house to ask them some further questions. With this clever trick of making the appointment at the pastor's house, near the church, Santos would gain several advantages: he would escape the vigilance of the crowds on the roads; he would win the confidence of the children and of those present; he could question them at his convenience, using promises and threats as he would do, hours later, in Ourém. Even more, he contemptibly involved the pastor in this hateful plot to remove the children from the Cova da Iria, where a great crowd awaited their arrival at the usual time of the apparition.

On the other hand, the pastor agreed to the interrogation in his house, whether to show his complete lack of interest in the apparitions, or perhaps because he hoped that the administrator would solve the whole complicated problem.

With the administrator looking on, the priest questioned Lúcia first. He wasn't calm and attentive as he had been at the first interrogation, after the June apparition. His questions were not gentle, showing clearly that the priest seemed primarily interested in washing his hands of everything that was happening. He asked Lúcia:

"Who taught you those things that you are going around saying?"

"That Lady whom I saw at the Cova da Iria."

"Anyone who goes around spreading lies that cause as much harm as the lie that you three told will be judged and go to hell if it isn't true—all the more so because many people have been deceived by you."

"If whoever lies goes to hell, then I'm not going because I don't lie. I say only what I have seen and what the Lady said to me. And as for the people who go there, only those who wish go; we don't invite anyone."[15]

The logic of the little girl's answer was so crushing that the tone of the inquiry changed. The pastor's interrogation returned to the secret, the subject that aroused the most curiosity. Lúcia answered him politely, but she also left the door open to continue the conversation later: "Look, if you like, I'll go up there and ask the Lady for permission to tell the secret, and if she allows me, I'll tell you."[16]

In a report dated October 31, 1924, addressed to the civil governor of Santarém, the administrator gave an account of what happened:

On the morning of the thirteenth, having left a unit of the National Republican Guard on duty at the council headquarters, I went to the village of Aljustrel with an official of the administration, Cândido Alho [Cândido Jorge Alho e João Lopes]. We wanted to bring the three protagonists to this town, in order to avoid a continuation of the clerical speculation that was going on around them.

I persuaded the parents of Lúcia, and of Francisco and Jacinta, and the priests, to allow the parish priest of Fátima to question the children, in order to discover something definite.... [17]

The abduction of the children

Frustrated again, the administrator tried a new plan, using the pretext that it was almost time for the apparitions. Although a few hours earlier he had wanted to force the children to promise never to return to the Cova da Iria, he now invited them to ride there in his car, with the excuse that they would arrive in time for the apparition. In their innocence, the children believed he had good faith and climbed quickly into the car. When they arrived at the main road, however, where the southern roundabout stands today with its monument to the three little shepherds, the car turned right, away from the Cova da Iria. In spite of the children's pleas, the car sped toward Vila Nova de Ourém.

When they arrived at the headquarters of the council, the administrator handed the children over to the care of his wife, Dona Idalina de Oliveira Santos. She was about thirty-two years old and known as a kind person. She treated the children well, giving them a good lunch and then sending them to play with her own children. She also gave them books and illustrated magazines to occupy them. Years later, when Lúcia was a pupil of the College of Vilar in Porto, she remembered perfectly some details of all that happened in Vila Nova de Ourém.

The administrator tried his best to woo the children with promises of gifts if they would reveal the secret, but they resisted it all. He did attain his main objective, however, which was to prevent the little shepherds from being present for the meeting with the Lady.

On the following day, the situation worsened. About 10:00 A.M., the three visionaries were brought to the headquarters of the municipal administration. Surrounded by his peers, the administrator began to submit the children to a rigorous interrogation. "But the visionaries, no matter how much they were pressured and involved in a tangled web of captious and difficult questions, did not yield an inch. They kept firmly to what they had said at first.... But as for the secret, they remained silent and firm as a rock, not telling one single word of it." [18]

After this interrogation, the administrator next took them to his house. He left them locked in a room with two well-dressed men to guard them so they couldn't escape. Later the administrator's wife came in and brought them bread and cheese for their evening meal.

Her husband came in after that, making more promises in order to try and extract the secret from them. One promise was that he would let them go see the fireworks, because it was a holiday in the town. They were still on the veranda of the house when an elderly man asked them if they would like to get away. Lúcia answered no, and with her cousins went into the room where they would spend the night.

The next day, Tuesday, August 14, "they were questioned by an old lady ... who tried to betray them into telling the secret that they were keeping so carefully,"[19] but she got nowhere with her questions. Next they went to the administration headquarters where they were questioned yet again and offered money if they would reveal the secret. The exhausting interrogations were then interrupted but not finished, and the children returned to the administrator's house, where his wife again received them warmly. They had supper and slept there Tuesday night. Thus ended the exhausting day of August 14.

On the morning of Wednesday, August 15, the feast of Our Lady's Assumption, the most tragic part of this drama took place. The children were again called to the office of the administrator and tempted with the promise of beautiful gold pieces if they would reveal the secret. Threats did not shake their resolve, so the administrator threw them into prison! Not only did the administrator bring the children to jail, putting them in the company of dangerous criminals, but he also threatened to keep them there and fry them in oil. If all this would have caused fright and anxiety to an adult, it was much worse for children between seven and ten years old, who did not understand the game in which they were victims. Despite all this, the threat of keeping them in prison was to no avail, although it must have terrified them.

Death threats

Lúcia details their experience in her *Memoirs*. They took seriously the threat that they would stay in prison until they revealed the secret, which must have exerted a terrific psychological pressure on them. She relates:

> After they had separated us, we were reunited in another room in the prison. They had told us that soon they would come take us to fry us

alive. Jacinta then went over next to a window that overlooked the cattle market. I assumed at first that she was doing this to distract herself
with the view; but before long I realized that she was crying. I went to
get her to bring her next to me and asked why she was crying:
"Because," she replied, "we are going to die without going back to see
our parents, not even our mothers!"[20]

Besides the sufferings of being thrown among hostile strangers and
threatened with a painful death—a threat the little shepherds took seriously—they also suffered from being separated from their families. In
fact, Lúcia speaks of this in her *Memoirs*:

> When we were imprisoned, what cost Jacinta the most was to feel
> abandoned by her parents. With tears running down her cheeks she
> said: "Neither your parents nor mine came to see us. We don't matter
> to them."
>   "Don't cry," Francisco told her. "Let's offer this to Jesus, for sin-
> ners."[21]

Francisco kept up his spirits and tried to encourage the homesick
Jacinta. But then they had to face the threat of being thrown into boiling
oil. A man came in and told them to leave the room and sit on a bench
outside it. Meanwhile, he gave orders to another man to prepare a cauldron. Soon after, they were told in all seriousness that the cauldron of
boiling oil was ready, and that each one of them would be thrown into it
if they did not reveal the secret.

Then a sullen guard appeared. He name is said to have been
Cândido Alho, although this is uncertain. He told them very seriously
that the cauldron was ready and called Jacinta, saying that she would be
the first to be burned. She went out quickly, without saying good-bye to
Francisco and Lúcia, convinced that the whole thing was in earnest.
Their captors were hoping that, being the youngest, she could be more
easily intimidated. They were mistaken, however; questioning her on the
way, they could not get her to say a single word.

After questioning her, they put her into another room that seemed to
belong to the prison. Meanwhile, in the administrator's office, Lúcia and
Francisco imagined that everything was taking place as they had been
told. The guard came back, announced that Jacinta was already "fried"
and took Francisco by the arm. The little boy wept bitterly as he left his
cousin alone. The men threatened him that they would boil him too, just
like Jacinta, if he did not reveal the secret. But he ignored this threat and
kept silent.

Lúcia, meanwhile, was waiting anxiously through all this, convinced that her cousins were dead. In spite of that, she did not utter a single word about the secret. Finally they gave up and allowed her to join her cousins in the room. Surprised to find them alive, she embraced them joyfully. Each had faced an insuperable dilemma, in such a way that this trial could be called a martyrdom. The three children had been ready to give their lives rather than break their promise to Our Lady.

Lúcia had been tormented by the thought: "If we don't talk, if we don't tell the secret, my cousins will die a horrible death." Jacinta and Francisco thought that they would be killed. To make things worse, they were far from their parents and had to confront a game of bluff lacking nothing in authenticity: guards, prison, escorting each child in turn to their "death." When we add to this the apparent lack of support from their families, and the doubts raised by the pastor, we can only imagine how much they suffered.

Praying the Rosary in prison

While they were awaiting what they believed would be their last moment, they did not waste time. They decided to pray the Rosary and persuaded the prisoners to join them in prayer. "Jacinta took off a medal that she had around her neck and asked a prisoner to hang it on a nail in the wall. Kneeling before that medal, we began to pray. The prisoners prayed with us, that is if they knew how to pray, but at least they remained kneeling."[22]

During the Rosary, Francisco intervened politely but courageously. He saw that one of the prisoners was kneeling with a cap on his head. Francisco went to him and said: "Sir, if you want to pray, you have to remove your cap." The poor man, without ado, gave it to him and he put it on top of his own cap on a bench.

For a little while, when they were praying the Rosary, the children forgot their critical situation. But as soon as the Rosary was over, Jacinta went back to the window and cried. She was only seven years old and in strange surroundings that were anything but friendly. The prisoners tried to console the children, but they did not really understand what it was all about. They told the children: "But all you have to do is tell the administrator the secret! What does it matter to you if the Lady doesn't want you to?"

"Never!" Jacinta replied vigorously. "I'd rather die."[23]

Lúcia then tried to encourage her.

"Jacinta, don't you want to offer this to Our Lord?" I asked her.

"I want to, but when I remember my mother, I can't help crying."

Because the most Holy Virgin has told us to also offer our prayers and sacrifices in reparation for the sins committed against the Immaculate Heart of Mary, we wanted to agree that each of us would choose one of these intentions. One would offer for sinners, another for the Holy Father, and another for the sins against the Immaculate Heart of Mary. Having agreed on this, I told Jacinta to choose the intention she wanted to offer.

[She replied:] "I offer for all of them, because I love them all."[24]

The presence of the children in the jail, sharing the same life as the criminals, awoke compassion in the hearts of these men. Perhaps one or other of them remembered his own childhood or his own little child left at home. Lúcia recalls: "Some of the prisoners played the harmonica. So they began to distract us by playing and singing. They asked me if we knew how to dance. I said we knew the fandango and the vira. Jacinta's partner was a poor thief, who, seeing her so small, picked her up and carried her as he danced."[25]

In an official interrogation of Lúcia of Jesus that took place on July 8, 1924, the visionary of Fátima, with her usual accurate memory, related the details about what happened to the three children.

When we arrived at Ourém, they locked us into a room and said that we would not be allowed to leave it as long as we refused to tell the secret that the Lady had confided to us. The next day, an elderly lady questioned us about the secret, then brought us to the administration office where we were interrogated again, and offered gold pieces if we would reveal the secret. We went back to the administrator's house where we had stayed the previous night, and in the afternoon, we were again questioned about the secret. On the sixteenth, we went again to the administration office about 10:00 A.M., but they could not get anything out of us, as had happened previously. Then the administrator ordered us to get into a car and brought us to the parish priest's house, leaving us on the veranda.[26]

The administrator's version of the facts

The report made by Artur de Oliveira Santos in 1924 contains a very different version of the events, which, not surprisingly, puts him in a good light.

On the morning of August 13, 1917, I went to get the children in Fátima. My purpose was to stop the speculation about the so-called Miracle of Fátima. At the time, the Church had not intervened in the matter, either directly or indirectly, and it was not approved until some years later.

The children came to my home, where they were received and treated as if they were one of my own, during the two days they stayed there.... The children of Fátima played with my own children as well as other boys during the two days, and many people visited them....

What is false, completely false, is that I threatened or intimidated the children, or kept them prisoners or unable to communicate with anyone, or that they suffered the slightest pressure or violence. My own family can bear witness to this, as can all the honorable people from the place, whatever their political and religious beliefs. On August 15, I brought returned the children to their parents, in Fátima, at the parish priest's house.[27]

In a document probably written around 1955, he adds:

After the children had been brought into my home where they were treated as if they were my own children, dozens of people appeared in the Largo da Loiça. They wanted to speak to the children. I did not permit them to do this because there were so many of them. However, a woman I met in the Largo begged me by all the saints to allow her only to see them, and I had to consent.

In the afternoon of the day already mentioned, the military commander, António Rodrigues de Oliveira, was talking to the children, along with some other people whom I don't remember. The children, meanwhile, were amusing themselves on the veranda, playing with other youngsters, including my own. It is not true that the children were brought to the municipal office for questioning. Neither were they threatened, imprisoned, or prevented from communicating.[28]

It is easy to understand how, in all of this, emerging utterly defeated, having acted inhumanly toward the children, the administrator concealed as much as possible. Perhaps his desire to rise to a higher political office blinded him, so that he obeyed orders without thought to the means he employed.

In a personal statement, Sister Lúcia declared that during the interrogations of those days, there were people writing. It is possible that this documentation was purposely destroyed or else is forgotten in some office. Nothing more is known about it.

A tormenting doubt

The encounter with Our Lady was to have taken place on August 13, and the children had been prevented, against their will, from going to the Cova da Iria. When that day ended, a tormenting doubt assailed them: will Our Lady appear again to us? Francisco seemed to suffer most from this.

> In prison when we saw that it was past noon and they wouldn't let us go to the Cova da Iria, Francisco said: "Maybe Our Lady will appear to us here."
>
> But the next day he showed his distress and said, almost crying: "Our Lady must be sad because we didn't go to the Cova da Iria, and she won't return anymore to appear to us. I so much loved to see her!"
>
> When Jacinta was crying in prison because she missed her mother and her family, he tried to encourage her and said: "If we don't return to see our mother, let's be patient! Let's offer it for the conversion of sinners. The worst is Our Lady will never return! This is what costs me most! But even this I offer for sinners."
>
> Afterward he asked me: "Do you think Our Lady will come back to appear to us?"
>
> "I don't know. I think she will."
>
> "I miss her so much!"
>
> The apparition at Valinhos [which occurred later, on August 19] was, therefore, a double joy for him. He felt tormented with fear she wouldn't return. Later he said: "Most likely she didn't appear to us on the thirteenth so she wouldn't have to go to the administrator's house, maybe because he is so bad." [29]

The children return home

On August 13, Ti Marto had gone to the Cova da Iria himself, thinking that his children and his niece were going there in the administrator's car. But soon the crowd heard that the administrator had abducted the three children and taken them to Ourém. The indignation of the people led them to say that they wanted to go to Ourém to demand the release of the children. The crowd shouted: "Let's go to Vila Nova de Ourém and protest! We'll do more. We'll go to the pastor because he is guilty, too. We'll see the magistrate about it!" [30]

Lúcia's uncle António da Silva was determined to go to the rectory to confront the pastor, considering him an accomplice, but the priest did not appear. Just then, the good sense and influence of Ti Marto saved the rest from a difficult situation. Marto said, "Quiet, boys, don't harm anyone. Whoever deserves punishment will get it. All this is in the power of the Most High."[31]

The administrator then tried another tactic, since his original plan had failed and he feared the anger of the crowd. He brought the children by car to the rectory. According to the official statements of Lúcia's mother and her aunt, the mother of Francisco and Jacinta, the children returned on the morning of August 15.

The parish church was crowded with people who had come for Mass for the feast of Our Lady's Assumption. When Mass was over and they all came out into the churchyard, they noticed the three children on the veranda of the rectory. Everyone wanted to go up the steps and meet them. The administrator forbade them, but António Santos and Manuel Pedro Marto disobeyed the order. Lúcia still remembers what happened:

> My father took me by the hand and went down the steps with me, bringing me to my mother, who was at the bottom of the steps with my sisters. Ti Olímpia and others embraced me, and we set out for Aljustrel with Ti Olímpia, Jacinta, and Francisco. They had come running down the steps behind me to get to their mother while Ti Marto was talking with the administrator.[32]

The administrator told Ti Marto "that the people were obsessed about seeing signs," to which he replied with a certain humor: "Then there are many people who are obsessed!" The three children had been examined by a doctor, and when he was giving them back to Ti Marto, Artur de Oliveira Santos said to them: "Now you can go to the Cova da Iria as often as you wish."[33]

The mothers of the children took care to bathe them, comb their hair, and dress them in clean clothes. Lúcia went out to Valinhos with the flock, but Jacinta and Francisco stayed home.

The administrator tries more threats

Beaten, but unconvinced, the administrator used other threats, according to a reference in Sister Lúcia's *Memoirs:* "One day three gentlemen came to speak with us. After their interrogation, which was hardly pleasant, they left, saying: 'See that you decide to tell this secret; if not, the administrator is ready is ready to stop you by taking your lives.'"[34]

Jacinta reacted to this threat with joy, saying that if it happened, it would only serve to allow them to see Our Lord and Our Lady that much sooner. Because of the threat, an aunt of Lúcia's who was married and lived in Casais tried to bring her niece to her home, since she lived outside the jurisdiction of the administrator. The little girl, however, refused to leave her own home.

Lúcia refers to all these events without bitterness. When she was asked what she, or her cousins, thought of the administrator's strategies or of the jail, she answered quite simply: "My impression was that the administrator was simply the instrument that God used to let us suffer for love of him and for the conversion of poor sinners. I suppose my cousins' impressions were the same."[35]

THE APPARITION OF OUR LADY

Events in the Cova da Iria on August 13

What was happening meanwhile in the Cova da Iria, at the end of that morning when another apparition had been promised? People had been arriving in the village of Fátima from all directions since the evening before. Everyone went to Aljustrel to see the little shepherds, speak with them, ask them questions, or ask their prayers for some problem. Lúcia relates: "In the midst of that crowd, we were like a ball in the hands of a gang of urchins. We were pulled here and there, as everyone was asking us questions without giving us time to answer anyone."[36]

The unexpected presence of the administrator put an end to this trouble, and people began to move toward the Cova da Iria, anxious to find a place where they could see everything that was happening. They were far from imagining the sinister intentions of Artur de Oliveira Santos.

An incomplete letter from a seminarian gives some information about what happened:

> When I arrived, a large crowd of people were praying and singing hymns to Our Lady around the little tree where the apparitions take place. It's a little cork oak, which has already been stripped of most of its branches.... We found a spot in the shade and stayed there quite some time. After that, more and more people began to arrive; they

crowded in everywhere, but the largest crowd extended from one side of the road to the other.

The carts kept coming in, along with people riding horses, walking, or on bicycles. It was quite a sight: carts all over the hillside, animals resting in the shade, cars jammed on the road, and bicycles piled up. By noontime, when the apparitions occurred, thousands of people had arrived ... some said 5,000 people were present.[37]

When he found the administrator had abducted the children, the seminarian left, indignant, but he returned later. On the way he met people who were leaving and he asked them what had happened.

People jammed the roads, talking about the marvelous event. I asked each group about what they had seen. Right away people surrounded me, all shouting. Everyone wanted to tell me that they had heard a thunderclap and then everyone ran away. But then they returned and saw a blue and white cloud coming down, which soon rose again and disappeared.[38]

Apparently Our Lady chose to give some sign of her maternal presence. Just as at the third apparition in July, many people began to notice a visible diminution of the sun's light, similar to a partial eclipse. A small, grayish cloud soon appeared over the holm oak, remaining for as long as the apparition usually lasted. Almost everyone saw the usual flash of lightning and heard two loud peals of thunder that shook the Cova da Iria at midday, while the usual cloud enveloped the historic tree.[39]

"The people fled. Almost everyone took off their hats, called out to Our Lady and felt happy. They said that despite the abduction of the children, Our Lady had still manifested her presence. A sort of luminous globe was also seen revolving in the clouds. After the thunder, a mist seemed to envelop the holm oak."[40]

The pastor's reaction

Soon after, the pastor of Fátima felt urged to defend himself publicly in a letter he published in the *Messenger of Leiria* on August 22. Indignantly, he refused to accept any responsibility for what had happened and declared that he had not collaborated in any way. He said that the administrator had told him nothing about his secret intentions. He thought it providential that the administrator succeeded in abducting the children without any popular resistance. The pastor explained that when a large group of angry people came to confront him at the rectory, someone had calmed them down. But he failed to mention that this peacemaker was Manuel Pedro Marto.

Then the pastor speculated about the motives the administrator had for bringing the children to the pastor's house. He wondered if the official secretly wanted to turn the people against him. In any case, the priest defended himself for being absent when the apparitions occurred. Even though the devout people of the parish wanted him there, he thought that his presence would prejudice unbelievers against the events. Finally, he himself admitted that there must have been 5,000 to 6,000 people present on August 13.[41]

Apparition of Our Lady at Valinhos

Prevented from being present in the Cova da Iria on August 13, the children had thoughts that wavered between hope and discouragement. But on August 19, Our Lady appeared to them at Valinhos. The area is just a few minutes' walk from Aljustrel, on the same side as but below Loca do Cabeço. Jacinta had stayed home that day and was replaced by João, age 11, and Francisco, who looked after the flock. Lúcia relates:

> I had gone to tend the sheep with Francisco and his brother João in a place called Valinhos. Feeling that something supernatural was approaching and enveloping us, we suspected that Our Lady had come to appear to us. We felt sorry that Jacinta wasn't there to see her, so we asked her brother João to go call her. Since he didn't want to go,[42] I offered him two coins for this, and he went running to get her.[43]

Fortunately, it was only a short distance from Valinhos to Aljustrel. When he got home, out of breath, João said that Lúcia wanted Jacinta to go to Valinhos. He admitted that Lúcia had given him a coin for going to call Jacinta, and had asked him not to tell his mother why. His mother seized him and demanded that he tell her what was going on. The boy decided to tell everything: Lúcia had said that she could see signs in the sky that Our Lady was about to appear, and she wanted Jacinta to be there, too. His mother told João to go call Jacinta, saying, "She's at her godmother's house. Then I want both of you to come back here."[44]

Olímpia wanted to accompany her daughter, but the children ran off down another road. When she asked Jacinta's godmother where the two children were, the woman replied that João had whispered a secret to

Jacinta and both of them had gone running to Valinhos. Olímpia started out also, but she met Francisco and Jacinta coming back. They said
that Our Lady had appeared to them again but that João hadn't seen
her. As Lúcia relates:

> Meanwhile Francisco and I saw the rays of light that we called light-
> ning; and Jacinta arrived. An instant later we saw Our Lady over the
> holm oak.
>
> "What do you want of me?"
>
> "I want you to continue to go to the Cova da Iria on the thirteenth
> day and continue to pray the Rosary every day. In the last month I will
> perform a miracle so that all may believe."
>
> "What do you want done with the money the people leave in the
> Cova da Iria?"
>
> "Make two litters [a sort of bier or wooden framework to carry stat-
> ues in procession]. You are to carry one with Jacinta and two more girls
> dressed in white; Francisco is to carry the other one, with three other
> boys. The money from the litters is for the feast of Our Lady of the
> Rosary, and anything left over can be put toward the chapel that is to
> be built here."[45]
>
> Lúcia then asked for the cure of some sick people. Our Lady
> answered that some of them would be cured during the year. Then,
> looking very sad, she begged: "Pray, pray very much, and make
> sacrifices for sinners, for many souls go to hell because they have no
> one who will sacrifice themselves for them."[46] As on the previous occa-
> sions, she began to ascend toward the east, like somebody returning by
> the same road to the place they had come from.
>
> On that day João also felt something extraordinary, although he
> had not seen Our Lady. When his mother asked him that night
> whether he had seen anything, he admitted that he had only heard
> Lúcia saying to Jacinta that the heavenly visitor was going away. But
> according to his mother's official statement, "he heard a noise that
> sounded like a rocket, but he saw nothing. He also said that his eyes
> hurt from looking so intently at the sky...." After the apparition,
> Jacinta told her brother that she wanted to stay there the whole after-
> noon. He told her, "No, Mother didn't want you to go with the sheep
> today, so you have to go back home.' And to keep her spirits up, he
> accompanied her there."[47]

The visible signs

This apparition at Valinhos was accompanied by flashes of lightning
and peals of thunder. The sun's light also seemed to gleam with vivid

colors, and, for the first time, a fragrant aroma could be sensed. After receiving a branch of the holm oak where the children had seen the fourth apparition, Lúcia's parents and Senhor Marto detected a pronounced aroma of incomparable perfume.[48]

Just as had happened at the Cova da Iria, the holm oak on which Our Lady appeared was stripped by the devout who took little bits of it as relics. Today, the site of this visit of the Mother of God is indicated by a marble statue of Our Lady of Fátima placed on a pedestal. It is located slightly behind the spot where, according to tradition, the holm oak stood.

The apparition took place about 4:00 in the afternoon, according to the statement of Lúcia's mother, and that day something unusual was reported. When the apparition ended, the children, who had seen, with sadness, how the pilgrims literally stripped the holm oak in the Cova da Iria, couldn't resist this time. Francisco and Jacinta were the first to cut off the branch that the Lady's dress had touched. Lúcia and João remained with the flock, while the other two, radiantly happy, went home. Jacinta brought with her the branch of the holm oak, and went to Lúcia's mother, giving her the news that Our Lady had appeared to them once more.

Maria Rosa continued to have serious doubts about the truth of the apparitions. Lúcia relates what her mother told the children:

> "Well, Jacinta, you've turned out to be quite the little liar! Imagining that Our Lady appears to you wherever you go!"
>
> "But we really did see her!" the little girl protested. Then she showed Lúcia's mother the small branch she was holding, and went on: "Look, aunt, Our Lady was standing with one foot on this branch and the other on that one."
>
> "Give that to me! Let me see it!" Jacinta offered it to her and my mother sniffed it. "But what is this scent?" She continued to sniff it. "It's not perfume ... it's not incense ... nor soap ... it's not the aroma of roses, nor anything I know ... but it's a pleasing fragrance." Then everyone wanted to smell it and we all found it very pleasant. Finally my mother put it on the table, saying: "Leave it here. Someone will come along who will know what kind of an aroma it is." But in the evening we didn't find the branch and we never knew what happened to it....

But there was no real mystery about the disappearance of the sweet-smelling branch. Hardly had Senhora Maria Rosa gone back to her household tasks than Jacinta slipped into the house and snatched it away to show to her parents.[49]

Jacinta's father testifies to this fact, but with another version. He states that when Jacinta came into the house with the branch in her hand:

> I sensed a wonderful fragrance that I could not explain. I reached for the branch, saying: "What are you bringing in, Jacinta?"
>
> "It's the small branch on which Our Lady placed her feet."
>
> I smelled it, but it was no longer fragrant.[50]

So ends the description of this detail of Our Lady's tenderness toward the three children who had, for love of her, gone through great suffering in Vila Nova de Ourém.

CHAPTER 8

The Apparition of September 13

AFTER THE UNEXPECTED apparition at Valinhos on August 19, the children were now waiting for September 13—a Thursday—for yet another encounter with Our Lady. Meanwhile, news of the happenings in the Cova da Iria spread farther and farther. More and more people believed in the apparitions and so, from one month to the next, the crowds swelled at the Cova da Iria.

We have an important statement from that time made by Dr. Carlos de Azevedo Mendes, of Torres Novas, who was then a law student at the University of Coimbra. In a letter to his brother, perhaps Father Candido de Azevedo Mendes, S.J.,[1] most likely dating from the end of October, he said:

> I talked to the pastor and then to the two little girls and the boy, questioning them separately. I first wanted to gain their trust and then, when they felt entirely at ease with me, I began to interview them.
>
> They made an extraordinary impression on me, which could truly be called sensational. I spent three hours with them, and even went to the place near the holm oak to recite the Rosary. I could not find even the smallest contradiction; they all gave the same exact account.... After I left them, the pastor showed me his report and I was amazed to see that it exactly matched my inquiry.[2]

Meanwhile the atmosphere began to change in Lúcia's home. While her mother remained incredulous, though with regret, her father began to defend his daughter, ordering silence when anyone began to bother

131

his youngest daughter or scold her. With genuine wisdom he observed: "We don't know if it's true, but neither do we know if it's a lie."[3]

The crowds coming to the children's homes grew more numerous, and many wanted to see the children. Jacinta and Francisco's parents, faced with the inconvenience of having to call the two children continually for visitors, stopped sending them out with the flock. They sent João in their place.

On the road to the Cova da Iria

Lúcia relates:

As the hour approached I set out with Jacinta and Francisco, but amidst so many people we couldn't get through. The roads were packed with people. Everyone wanted to see and speak to us, and they did so without any human respect. Many people, from simple folk to ladies and gentlemen, managed to break through the crowd around us. They prostrated themselves and threw themselves on their knees before us, asking us to present their petitions to Our Lady. Others who could not get close to us called out from afar:

"For the love of God! Ask Our Lady to cure my son who is a cripple."
Another: "Cure mine who is blind!"
Another: "Mine who is deaf!"
"To bring back my husband, my son, who went to war!"
"To convert me, a sinner."[4]

Lúcia goes on to describe this sorrowful panorama. She adds that some, so as to make themselves heard more easily or to come nearer, climbed the trees, reminiscent of the Gospel story of Zacchaeus. These pages of the faithful chronicler of the apparitions of Fátima have an evangelical flavor. In light of these accounts, we understand more readily what it was like 2,000 years ago on the roads of the Holy Land when Jesus was passing by.

Some adults had to help the three children get through the crowd. Dr. Carlos de Azevedo Mendes came on horseback to the Cova da Iria on September 8, feast of the Nativity of Our Lady. In the same letter quoted above, Mendes describes the prevailing atmosphere.

The thirteenth came, and with great anxiety I went to the place of the apparitions. Such was my frame of mind that I went to Holy Communion before going there. I very much wanted to see what would occur, and I succeeded in my attempts to get near the children. The sun was blazing so hot that the sweat poured off me, but I didn't move away.[5]

As soon as the children had set out for the Cova da Iria, Olímpia went to call on Lúcia's mother, proposing that they should both go secretly, after the children, so that nobody would see or recognize them. Maria Rosa agreed and they hurried to the Cova, not standing too near the spot of the apparitions. They stayed on the slope in order to see what was happening.

The children arrived at the holm oak and began to recite the Rosary along with the crowd, waiting for what would happen. Before long, the reflection of light let them know that the heavenly messenger was about to appear. While the children gazed at the Lady clothed in light, she began the dialogue. "While the people shouted that they saw signs, they didn't understand what the children were saying," Mendes wrote, "but they seemed to see a small cloud of smoke rising from the midst of the crowd at the base of the holm oak."[6]

The heavenly visitor

In this apparition, there were even more visible signs of Mary's presence. A great number of reliable witnesses reported seeing them.

On September 13, there were more visible signs; dozens of trustworthy people testified to having seen them.... The sun's light diminished so much at noontime that Reverend António Maria Figueiredo, professor in the seminary of Santarém, sought out the pastor of Fátima right after the apparition. Very impressed, Figueiredo told him that he had seen "stars in a region below the normal stellar space."[7]

For the first time, various witnesses like the Reverend Doctors João Quaresma, later vicar general of Leiria, and Manuel do Carmo Góis testified that they, along with a few other people, had seen clearly a globe of bright light. It moved slowly from east to west, tracing an unmistakable line in the sky before disappearing into the horizon.

Also on that day, some witnesses said that during the apparition they saw descending on the crowd from the sky a kind of shower of white flowers that disappeared on coming into contact with persons and things....[8]

Father Manuel Nunes Formigão, present for the first time in the Cova da Iria, declared: "I didn't go near the apparition area, and talked to almost no one, but I stayed on the road about 300 meters away. I barely noticed the lessening of the sunlight, which did not seem to be an important phenomenon, due perhaps to the high altitude of the hills."[9]

Mary opened the meeting with the children with a word of tenderness and motherly solicitude, as Lúcia reports:

> "Continue to pray the Rosary to obtain the end of the war. In October Our Lord will come, as well as Our Lady of Sorrows and Mount Carmel, and Saint Joseph with the Child Jesus to bless the world. God is pleased with your sacrifices, but he doesn't want you to sleep with the rope; wear it only during the day."[10]

This refers to a practice the children had begun, wearing a rough cord of rope as a form of penance. They used to wear it day and night. Lúcia explains:

> Due to either the thickness and roughness of the rope, or because sometimes we tightened it too much, this instrument sometimes made us suffer horribly. Jacinta would shed tears at times because of the great discomfort it caused her; and sometimes when I would tell her to take it off she would answer: "No! I want to offer this sacrifice to Our Lord, in reparation and for the conversion of sinners."[11]

Such penances, of course, should be submitted to the judgment of a confessor or spiritual director in order to avoid imprudent excesses. In this case, there was a health risk: the children were not getting enough sleep and their health suffered. Perhaps the children did not know about these precautions; on the other hand, it would have been difficult for them to find a priest who could advise them on these matters. So in this case Our Lady, like the best of mothers, decided to intervene, directing them spiritually. There is one more detail worth noting—the children's response: "Needless to say, we promptly obeyed her orders."[12]

Lúcia, the privileged spokesperson at these heavenly conversations, hastened to present a list of the requests recommended to her:

> "I was told to ask you for many things: the cure of some sick people, of a deaf mute."
>
> "Yes, some I will cure, but not others. In October I will perform a miracle so that everyone will believe." Then, starting to rise, she disappeared as usual.[13]

The interview with heaven was short. Someone, possibly inspired by the events at Lourdes (Bernadette had brought perfume to offer the mysterious Lady of the grotto of Massabielle) charged Lúcia with bringing Our Lady a strange present:

I offered her two letters and a bottle of perfumed water. "They gave me these, if you would like them!"

"They're not very suitable in heaven!"

Then she went away toward the east, and I told the people to turn in that direction if they wanted to see her.[14]

As the children left, the crowd followed them. Olímpia feared that she might be recognized. Seeing that the children were safe, she told Maria Rosa that they should leave quickly. They walked toward Aljustrel and returned to their own homes.

Full of longing for the Lady clothed in light, the three children returned to the reality of everyday life. Dr. Carlos de Azevedo Mendes, like many who were near the holm oak and saw nothing, felt disappointed.

The large crowd was jostling the children, everyone anxious to get near them, to ask them questions, or to touch them reverently. The little shepherds had to be saved from this. "There was a great crush," Mendes wrote. "The poor children were crying. I lifted one of them in my arms. She was obviously very timid, but she still assured me that in October the Lady would come again."[15]

After that apparition, Lúcia told Francisco that in October Our Lord would also come, and he was overjoyed.[16] The boy impatiently awaited October 13, and from time to time he would ask if there were many days left. He would say that he could hardly wait for that day, so that he could see Our Lord.

Trials of the children's families

Meanwhile, trials piled up for Lúcia's family. As if it were not enough to have their crops and fruit trees in the Cova da Iria destroyed, it became impossible for them to keep the flock that was such an asset to the family. Many visitors would come and demand to see Lúcia. When visitors arrived, the family always had to send someone to look for Lúcia and take her place watching the sheep.

> My mother found herself obliged to sell our flock, and this made no small difference to the support of the family. I was blamed for the whole thing and, at critical moments, it was all flung in my face....
>
> On her part, my mother suffered all this with heroic resignation and patience. If she scolded and punished me it was because she thought that I was lying. Sometimes, completely resigned to the trials that Our Lord sent her, she would say: "Could this be a punishment that God has sent me for my sins? If that's so, blessed be God!"[17]

The Martos' house was also constantly invaded by visitors who wanted to see and question the children. Because Jacinta was more sociable than Francisco, they questioned her constantly.

Once some very wealthy ladies went to the Martos' home and told Jacinta that if she would tell them the secret, they would give her some pieces of jewelry. Jacinta said she would never reveal it, not even if they offered her the whole world.

Even during her last illness, her mother said to her: "I will ignore you, and I won't have anything to do with you unless you tell me the secret." But her daughter replied that nothing would make her tell it. "At least you could say whether it is good or bad," her mother insisted. Jacinta answered that it was good for those who would believe. "Believe in what?" asked her mother. "In God," concluded her daughter. And she added that it was bad for those who would not believe.[18]

Meanwhile, as the date for the next apparition approached, the feverish anticipation climbed.

CHAPTER 9

A Great Miracle

THE APPARITION OF OCTOBER 13

OUR LADY'S PROMISE that she would perform a great miracle in October so that all would believe spread all over Portugal and aroused in people a great sense of expectation. Even those who feigned a certain indifference could not ignore the question in everyone's mind: Will something extraordinary happen? What will it be? Those with vivid imaginations tried to guess what might happen. Others used the occasion to make terrifying prophecies. The intolerant threatened the children, promising to avenge themselves in some way if it all turned out to be a deception.

A wave of rumors

In this atmosphere rumors spread quickly. One of the alarming rumors circulating was that the civil authorities had actually decided to plant beside the children a bomb that would detonate at the moment of the apparition. How did the three children react to these threats? They were so sure Our Lady would protect them that they were longing for the day to come so they could meet her again.

As for Lúcia, she said she felt no fear whatsoever. She talked about it with her cousins, whose reaction was: "How wonderful, if we were granted the grace to go from here to heaven with Our Lady."[1]

Only Lúcia, Francisco, and Jacinta continued to be confident, because they were certain that the Lady clothed in light would not fail to keep her promise. She would perform a great miracle that would put an end to all doubts.

Meanwhile, Lúcia's parents decided to accompany her to the Cova da Iria for the first time. "If my daughter is going to die, I want to die by her side."[2] António Santos brought his daughter by the hand to the place of the apparitions. The confusion at the Cova was so great, however, that they did not meet again until that night, at their home. Lúcia's mother, too, always so hesitant about her daughter's truthfulness, understood that the moment had come to summon all her maternal courage. "My mother," said Lúcia, "her heart torn with uncertainty as to what was going to happen, and fearing it would be the last day of my life, wanted to accompany me."[3]

The longest day

October 13 fell on the second Saturday of the month. Work on the land claimed everyone's attention because it was harvest time, but no one could resist the temptation to profit by this unique opportunity to be present at something extraordinary. That morning a heavy rain fell, which only slightly dampened the enthusiasm of the people, who came from all directions, like flooding rivers, and converged on the Cova da Iria singing and praying. The torrential showers drenched clothes and lunch baskets, and made travel on the roads more difficult. But the people did not turn back.

According to Lúcia's account, the children left home quite early, because they foresaw that only with difficulty would they make their way through the crowd of pilgrims. Some people had the strange idea of preparing special clothes for the children so they might appear well dressed. The little girls' dresses were sky blue, with a white veil, and over them a wreath of flowers, but in the end good sense prevailed, although photographs with these costumes were passed around. Lúcia says clearly, in a series of corrections to the book *Fátima* by Antero de Figueiredo: "I don't think it was true. I recall that a lady did indeed appear who wished to dress us up like that, but we didn't accept it."[4]

The crowd was estimated as being from 50,000 to 70,000 people.[5] Considering the limited means of transport available at the time and the state of the terrain at the Cova da Iria, aggravated by the continual rain, that is a significant number.

The three children made their way to the place of the apparitions, dressed, as before, like typical shepherds of the region. "On the way, the scenes of the past month, more numerous and moving, were repeated. Not even the muddy roads hindered the people from kneeling in the most humble and suppliant posture."[6]

"*I am the Lady of the Rosary*"

Eventually the children arrived at the Cova da Iria. The little that remained of the holm oak was decorated with roses and silk ribbons.[7] As soon as the children reached it, Lúcia, moved by an interior impulse, asked the people to close their umbrellas and pray the Rosary. The request seemed absurd since the rain was still drenching people to the skin. But they obeyed her at once. As soon as they started the Rosary, Our Lady began to speak.

> Soon after, we saw the flash of light and then Our Lady appeared over the holm oak.
> "What do you want of me?"
> "I want to tell you that a chapel is to be built here in my honor. I am the Lady of the Rosary. Always continue praying the Rosary every day. The war is going to end and the soldiers will soon return to their homes."

The announcement that war would end was good news for all, since it had brought suffering to so many families. Some people thought Our Lady's words meant the war would end that very day.

Lúcia took advantage of the Lady's silence to tell her the many petitions that people had entrusted to her. With the simplicity of a child of the hill country, accustomed to coming straight to the point, she added:

> "I have many things to ask you: to cure sick people, to convert some sinners, and other things."
> "Some yes; others no. They must amend their lives and ask pardon for their sins. Do not offend the Lord our God anymore, because he is already so much offended."[8]

The meeting of the three children with Our Lady had come to an end. "On October 13, the day of the last apparition ... all the people saw clearly this time, although in different degrees, the solar phenomena which we will later describe in detail."[9]

When the Blessed Mother left them, Lúcia cried out: "There goes Our Lady!" Just then Lúcia's mother perceived "the same aroma" that she had noticed coming from the branch that Jacinta brought her after the apparition at Valinhos.[10]

The mysteries of the Rosary in the light from Our Lady's hands

This time, the heavenly messenger opened her hands and had them reflect the sun. As she followed the same return journey of the previous months, she continued to project this reflection of light toward the sun.

Lúcia confessed that this was why she shouted that the people should look at the sun, although she was also moved by an interior impulse. In any case, at that moment, she was not aware of the crowd that surrounded her. The promise made in the month of July by the Lady clothed in light was about to be fulfilled.

> Our Lady disappeared in the immense distance of the firmament, and next to the sun we saw Saint Joseph with the Child Jesus, and Our Lady dressed in white with a blue mantle. Saint Joseph and the child appeared to bless the world, tracing the sign of the cross with their hands. This apparition disappeared soon after, and then we saw Our Lord and Our Lady, who seemed to me to be Our Lady of Sorrows. Our Lord seemed to bless the world in the same way as Saint Joseph had. This apparition disappeared, and I saw Our Lady again, in a form resembling Our Lady of Mount Carmel.[11]

It would seem that in this sequence of versions there is a clear reference to the Rosary—to Our Lady of the Rosary, as she identified herself. The joyful mysteries were symbolized in the first vision: Saint Joseph, the Child Jesus, and Our Lady direct our thoughts to the hidden life of Nazareth from the Annunciation to the losing and finding of the Child Jesus in the Temple.

The sorrowful mysteries are recalled next in the vision of Our Lady of Sorrows with Jesus in a red cloak. How can we not think of the scene in the praetorium with Pilate, the crown of thorns, a reed as a scepter, and a filthy cloak on our Savior's shoulders?

Finally, we can note a reference to the glorious mysteries with the vision of Our Lady of Mount Carmel, which makes us think of the life to come. Our Lady of Mount Carmel often appears—in the traditional shrines of Portugal and in other images—to the souls in purgatory to bring them to heaven.

THE MIRACLE OF THE SUN

Our Lady had promised several times that in October she would perform a miracle so that all would believe in the authenticity of the apparitions. Nothing had yet happened in the Cova da Iria that the crowd could see. The moment had come when the heavenly messenger was to fulfill her promise, however, with the miracle of the sun. In fact, while the three privileged children were contemplating these heavenly visions, unaware of everything around them, the crowd was trembling with amazement at the unique phenomenon.

Although Lúcia shouted to the crowd, "Look at the sun," neither she nor her cousins saw the miracle of the sun, nor did they know that it was going to happen. While the crowd was gazing at the miracle, the three children, in ecstasy, were contemplating the visions alluding to the mysteries of the Rosary. Other eyewitnesses described what happened in the Cova da Iria on October 13, 1917.

The miracle described by an unbeliever

Avelino de Almeida[12] is an unexpected witness to the events of that day. A journalist, he had come to the Cova da Iria to unmask and ridicule the apparitions in an article to be printed in the newspaper for which he wrote.[13] However, on October 15, two days after the events, he published a long article in the front pages of *O Século* [The Century], with a photograph of the three children, in which he described in masterly fashion what had happened.

The article was titled: "Astonishing Things! How the Sun Shone at Midday in Fátima!" The man's honesty deserves admiration: he rises above his prejudices to faithfully report the truth. Avelino de Almeida encountered on the road to the Cova da Iria an atmosphere of incredulity:

> Then a unique spectacle occurred, unbelievable to anyone who was not there. From the top of the road ... we saw the huge crowd turn toward the sun, which was at its zenith and had no clouds blocking it. The sun

seemed like a plate of dull silver, and people could look directly at it with no trouble. It didn't burn or blind. It seemed like an eclipse was occurring. Suddenly a tremendous shout broke out from the spectators, "Miracle, miracle! Marvel, marvel!"

Before the astonished eyes of the people, whose whole aspect was reminiscent of biblical times, and who, white with terror and with heads uncovered, gazed at the blue sky, the sun trembled. It made brusque movements, never before seen, beyond all cosmic laws. The sun "danced," as the peasants typically put it.

Standing on the running board of the bus from Torres Novas ... an old man turned toward the sun and recited the Credo, from beginning to end, in a loud voice. When I asked his name, he said he was João Maria Amado de Melo Ramalho da Cunha Vasconcelos. Later, I saw him speaking to the people around him who were wearing hats, begging them vehemently to remove them in the face of such an extraordinary demonstration of the existence of God. Similar scenes were repeated elsewhere. A woman, full of tears and almost choking with grief, shouted, "How pitiful! Even before so stupendous a miracle, some men still do not take off their hats!"

Immediately afterward the people asked one another if they had seen anything and what it looked like. The majority of them said they had seen the shaking, the dance of the sun. Others declared that they had seen the smiling face of the Virgin herself. Some swore that the sun had rotated on itself as if it were a wheel of fireworks, that it had come down so low that it almost burned the earth with its rays. Some said that they saw it change colors successively.

It was almost 3:00 P.M. The clouds were swept away and the sun followed its course, with its usual brilliance so no one could look at it directly.

And the little shepherds? Lúcia, the one who spoke to the Virgin, announced with theatrical gestures, as she was carried by a man who brought her from group to group, that the war was to end and our soldiers would return.... This news, however, did not make those who heard her any more happy. The heavenly sign was everything.

There was an intense curiosity to see the two little girls with their garlands of roses. Some tried to kiss the hands of the "little saints"... but what they all had desired—the sign from heaven—was enough to satisfy them and root them even more firmly in their simple faith....

The people dispersed very quickly, without difficulties, without a shadow of disorder, without any need for police supervision.... It remains for competent persons to speak objectively about the strange dance of the sun that today, in Fátima, made hosannas burst out from the hearts of the faithful and naturally impressed—as trustworthy people have assured me—freethinkers and others with no interest in religion who went to that now-famous moor.[14]

The testimony of a scientist

What really was the miracle of the sun? In order to understand better what happened in Fátima, the testimony of the scientist José Maria Proença de Almeida Garret is significant. His account complements that given by Avelino de Almeida. He began by saying that he arrived at noon and found everything at the Cova da Iria drenched by the rain. Around 1:30 P.M. he noticed a thin column of bluish smoke rise from the area where the children were. That happened three times. Shortly after that, the sun began to move as he describes:

> It was almost two o'clock. Moments before, the sun had triumphantly broken through the thick cloud cover, shining clearly and intensely. I turned toward this magnet that was attracting everyone's eyes. It could see it like a disc with a bright, well-defined rim and a sharp edge, luminous and brilliant. But it didn't hurt the eyes. Even at Fátima I heard a comparison made of the sun with a disc of dull silver, but that doesn't seem to me to be apt. Its color was more clear, active and richer, changing colors, like a pearl's luster.
>
> It was not like the moon on a clear night, for it seemed more like a living star. It seemed more like a burnished wheel cut from mother-of-pearl. This is not a banal comparison, like cheap poetry. My eyes saw it that way. It should not be confused with the sun shining through fog. (There was no fog at that time.) The sun was not opaque, diffused, or veiled. In Fátima it gave light and heat, and its beveled rim was brightly outlined. Light clouds filled the sky, with scattered patches of blue. At times the sun came out alone in rifts of clear sky. The clouds moved from west to east but did not obscure the sun. They seemed to go behind it, while the white puffs that at times slipped in front of the sun appeared in a shade of rose or a translucent blue.
>
> It was incredible that we could look at the sun for such a long time with its blazing light and burning heat, without hurting the eyes or blinding the retina. This phenomenon must have lasted about ten minutes, except for two brief interruptions when the sun gave off brighter and more dazzling rays that made us look away.
>
> The disc of the sun moved in a dizzying way. It was not the scintillation of a powerful star. It was rotating upon itself with tremendous velocity. Suddenly, a great cry was heard, like a shout of anguish from the whole crowd. The sun, still rapidly spinning, had spun out of the

sky and was rushing toward the earth. This huge, fiery mass threatened to smash into us with its weight. It made a stupendous impression.

During this solar event, which I have described in detail, the atmosphere took on varied hues of colors.... I recall that these colors did not come at the beginning, but I think appeared more at the end. Gazing at the sun, I noticed that everything around me darkened. I looked at the things around me and then looked to the extreme horizon and saw everything in the color of amethyst. The nearby objects, the sky, and the layers of the atmosphere were the same color. A small oak in front of me cast a dark purplish shadow on the ground.

Fearing that my retina would be damaged ... I turned around, closed my eyes, and covered them with my hands to keep out all the light. With my back turned, I opened my eyes and realized that the landscape and the air still had the same purple color that they had previously had.

This did not seem to be like an eclipse.... While still looking at the sun, I noticed that the atmosphere had cleared. I heard a nearby peasant exclaim with amazement, "This lady looks yellow." As a matter of fact, everything both near and far seemed bathed in the color of old yellow damask. People looked sick and jaundiced. I smiled when I saw them looking so ugly. Laughter was heard. My hand had the same yellow color....

I observed quietly and calmly, without excitement, all these phenomena that I have here described. It is up to others to explain and interpret them.[15]

Some clarifications

Gonçalo de Almeida Garrett, Professor at the University of Coimbra, and father of the man whose testimony was just presented, provides a series of clarifications in a letter dated November 3, 1917. He gave a valuable summary of the extraordinary events of October 13:

1. The phenomena lasted about eight to ten minutes.

2. The sun lost its brilliant light and looked more like the moon, for it could be looked at easily.

3. Three times over that period of time, the sun showed a rotating movement around its periphery, radiating sparks of light along its edges, like a fireworks display.

4. This rotating movement along the edges of the sun was manifested three times and interrupted three times. It was rapid and lasted eight to ten minutes, more or less.

5. Soon after that, the sun took on a violet color that soon changed to orange, shining with these colors over the earth. Then it finally returned to its normal brilliance, which was impossible to look at directly.

6. These events happened soon after noontime, when the sun was at its zenith ... when meteorological phenomena have a less intense influence on the sun. When the sun is closer to the horizon in late afternoon, more evaporation occurs, and this produces colorful sunsets.... The solar activity observed at noon in Fátima was far less likely to occur then than in the morning or afternoon, which makes these phenomena more valuable and important.[16]

The miracle seen in places far from Fátima

The pilgrims at the Cova da Iria were not the only ones to be enraptured by the miracle of the sun. The poet Afonso Lopes Vieira, who later wrote the hymn "The Thirteenth of May," witnessed this same phenomenon in São Pedro de Muel about seventeen miles away. There are also testimonies from people in the north—from Alto Minho—who followed this same event from a distance.

Years later, Pope Pius XII saw the same spectacle as he was taking his daily walk in the Vatican gardens on October 30, 1950, two days before the definition of the dogma of the Assumption of Our Lady into Heaven on November 1.[17]

A tiring afternoon

As can be imagined, when the apparition and the astonishing miracle of the sun ended, everybody wanted to talk to the visionaries. The strong arm of Dr. Carlos de Azevedo Mendes saved them from being overwhelmed. He took the children in his arms and carried them above the people's heads through the crowd.

Sister Lúcia, with her usual extraordinary memory, tells us something of what happened that afternoon, after the meeting with our Heavenly Mother.

I spent that afternoon with my cousins, as if we were some curious animals that the crowd was trying to see and observe! By that night I was extremely tired of so many questions and interrogations. Even with nightfall they did not end. Some people who had been unable to question me stayed over until the following day to wait their turn. Some even tried to talk to me that night, but I was so overcome with exhaustion that I fell to the ground to sleep. Thank God I didn't yet have human respect and self love, and because of that I was at ease in front of anyone as if they were my parents.

The next day, they continued their interrogations, or it's better to say, on the following days. Since then some people came every day to beg the protection of the Mother of Heaven at the Cova da Iria, and everyone wanted to see the visionaries to ask their questions and pray the Rosary with them.

Sometimes, I felt so tired of so much repetition and even of praying, that I looked for pretexts to excuse myself and escape. But those poor people insisted so much that I had to make an effort, and no small one, in order to satisfy them. So then I would repeat my habitual prayer in the depths of my heart: "It is for your love, my God, in reparation for the sins committed against the Immaculate Heart of Mary, for the conversion of sinners, and for the Holy Father." [18]

The visionary has yet another painful memory of that day, the unscrupulousness of people who took away "relics" of Fátima, regardless of how they went about it.

What I remember well about that day is that I arrived home without my braids that had been below my waist, and the displeasure my mother showed when she saw me with less hair than Francisco.

"But who stole them?"

"I don't know."

For in the crush of the crowd there was no lack of scissors or thieving hands. The kerchief was easy to lose, even if it hadn't been stolen. My braids had already been cut enough in the two previous months.[19]

After October 13, Francisco would say: "I loved very much to see Our Lord, but I loved more to see him in that light where we were also with him." And he would add hopefully, "A little while longer and Our Lord will take me there near him, and then I will see him forever." [20]

Thus was fulfilled Our Lady's promise of a miracle to guarantee the authenticity of the apparitions. A new chapter in the history of Fátima had now begun, or, better still, a road had opened up across the centuries.

Pilgrim statue of Our Lady of Fátima.

Francisco Marto, 1917.

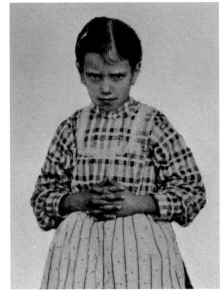

Jacinto Marto, 1917.

The Marto family house, a short walk from the Santos' house.

The Santos family home in the village of Aljustrel.

Jacinta, Lúcia, and Francisco.

Lúcia de Jesus Santos.

The visionaries Jacinta, Lúcia, and Francisco.

The Marto family at the funeral of Francisco. Back row, left to right:
Antonio, Manuel, Joseph, João, Florinda; front: Senhor and Senhora Santos.

The Santos family at the funeral of Lúcia's father António. Back row left to right: Manuel, Maria dos Anjos (holding a child), Carolina, Gloria; front: Maria Rosa Santos (seated) with Lúcia standing next to her.

The cousins Jacinta, Lúcia, and Francisco.

The three children with a group of relatives and pilgrims at the site of the apparitions at the Cova da Iria, July 13, 1917.

The immense crowd of people, estimated at 50,000 to 70,000, gathered at the Cova da Iria on October 13, 1917 for the final apparition and the promised sign: the miracle of the sun.

The small chapel on the site of the apparitions.

Sister Lúcia, a Dorothean Sister, with José Correia da Silva,
Bishop of Leiria.

On March 25, 1948, Sister Lúcia joined
the Carmel of Saint Teresa in Coimbra,
Portugal. Known as Sister Maria Lúcia de
Jesus e do Coração Imaculado, she stands
here with a group of pilgrims.

*A group of pilgrims standing before the statue of Our Lady of Fátima
at the basilica of Fátima.*

Pilgrims praying on their way to the Fátima shrine, many making the journey on their knees.

CHAPTER 10

Witnesses of the Message

THE LITTLE SHEPHERDS are the most trustworthy witnesses of the message of Fátima, not only because they were the instruments chosen to make it known, but also because they were the first to live that message fully in all its demands and beauty. Each of them, however, was called to live it according to a particular charism received from the Holy Spirit; the common note to all three was the chalice of suffering.

In the first place, they faced the opposition of good people. Many people were convinced of the truth of the apparitions and so the number of pilgrims at the Cova da Iria increased every month. But at the same time many others remained firmly convinced that the children were lying, or, judging them more kindly, thought that they were deluded by false visions.

These were difficult times. The Church suffered bitter persecution from the First Republic; churches were closed; religious demonstrations outside churches were forbidden; priests and bishops were persecuted and their material possessions destroyed. In such a climate, repercussions would inevitably follow the events in the Cova da Iria. At that time in Portugal, people distrusted one another. Some saw in the events at the Cova da Iria a clandestine reaction of the clergy opposing the fierce persecution the First Republic had launched against the Church. The Church, in turn, regarded with mistrust this outbreak of popular religiosity, fearing that behind it was an attempt to create some pretext for resuming the persecution of the Church. On this slippery ground the three children, in all simplicity and unaware of all these intrigues, had to bear witness to this explosion of the supernatural in Fátima.

Neighbors who did not believe supernatural events were occurring accused the parents of weakness and negligence in suppressing what they considered serious disturbances affecting the peace and quiet of the area. Some carried their unreasonable and untimely zeal further. Many people insulted and threatened the children as they passed them on the roads around Fátima. Someone even started a rumor that attempts would be made on the children's lives. Others qualified their threats, saying they would carry them out only if no miracle occurred in October.

HOW THE CHILDREN'S LIVES CHANGED

Difficult times for Lúcia

Within this tale of misunderstanding, Lúcia had to bear a special cross, apart from the one she shared with her two cousins: the stubborn disbelief and opposition of her family. Only her father was on her side. "About that time, my father also began to defend me, always silencing those who began to scold me. He would say: 'We don't know if it's true, but we also don't know if it's a lie.'"[1]

While her father kept an open mind about the apparitions, Lúcia's mother was convinced that her daughter had invented the whole thing. Hence, Lúcia's sorrow at her father's death was increased by the fact that she had lost her sole defender within the family.

The family was disturbed also because of the loss of the crops in the Cova da Iria, as well as the constant bustle in the house with people coming and going. This interfered with the work that Lúcia and the others needed to do to support the family.

When Lúcia complained to her cousins about the opposition she faced from her family, Francisco sought to comfort her.

> One day when I showed my unhappiness with the persecution within and outside the family that had began to escalate, he tried to encourage me, saying: "Let it go. Didn't Our Lady say that we would have much to suffer to make reparation to Our Lord and her Immaculate Heart for the many sins that offend them? They are so sad! If these sufferings can console them, then we are happy."[2]

Although Lúcia tried to conceal the trials she had to suffer because of the apparitions, she disclosed some instances. Some people did not shrink from spreading serious calumnies about her. Lúcia tells this story with a touch of humor.

> I don't know why, but a neighbor took it upon herself one day to say that some gentlemen had given me some money. I don't remember how much. Without more ado, my mother called me and asked me for it. When I told her I hadn't received any, she wanted to force me to hand it over, and for that purpose she used the broom handle.
>
> When I had the dust well shaken out of my clothes, Caroline, one of my sisters, intervened with another girl, our neighbor who was called Virginia. They said they had been there when those gentlemen questioned me, and they hadn't seen them give me anything.[3]

Her mother's illness

As mentioned in Chapter One, Lúcia's mother became seriously ill with heart problems. Lúcia was also blamed for this. She was forbidden to come near her mother, even to see her, so as not to aggravate her illness. When Lúcia ran to the Cova da Iria to beg for her mother's recovery and returned home to find her completely cured, the walls of opposition remained standing. Lúcia's smiles as she saw her mother well again quickly turned to tears.

We remember Lúcia's journey to Vila Nova de Ourém, accompanied by her father, while her uncle refused to bring his children. Lúcia was tempted to see in this a lack of parental love, as well as a certain desire on her mother's part that Lúcia would be proved a liar. The pressure continued until the end of the apparitions, in an attempt to make her declare to the pastor that it was all a lie so that he could inform the people at all the Sunday Masses, thus putting an end to the whole thing.

Before the apparitions, Lúcia was the darling of the family, pampered by all, always surrounded by children. Suddenly, to offset the joy of the encounter with heaven, she found herself alone in an uncomfortable desert.

Jacinta's conduct in trying circumstances

Supported by her family, Jacinta reacted to insults in a manner that immediately disconcerted anyone who tried to mock or scoff. Her cousin tells us:

If in her presence a child or even an older person said or did something inappropriate, she would reprimand them, saying: "Don't do that which offends God Our Lord; he is already so offended!"

If the child or adult retorted, calling her an impostor or a plaster saint or something similar—which sometimes happened—she would look at them with a certain kind of severity and go away. Perhaps this was why she didn't enjoy much popularity. If I was near her, dozens of children would quickly gather round, but if I went away, she would soon remain alone.

Nevertheless, when I was near her they seemed to enjoy her company. They would embrace her with hugs of innocent affection; they loved to sing and play with her. Sometimes they would ask me to go get her when she wasn't there. If I told them she didn't want to go because they were bad, they would promise to be good if she came, saying, "Go get her and tell her we'll be good if she comes."[4]

Jacinta's reputation for holiness

Happily, not everyone reacted this way when they met the children. Some people asked their prayers for urgent intentions, convinced that their prayers would more readily touch the heart of God.

One day a poor woman met us. Crying and kneeling before Jacinta, the woman asked her to obtain from Our Lady a cure from a terrible illness. On seeing the woman kneel before her, Jacinta was distressed and took hold of her with trembling hands to help her up. But as she wasn't able to lift her, she also knelt down with the woman and prayed three Hail Marys. Later she asked her to get up, and assured her that Our Lady would cure her. Jacinta never stopped praying every day for her, until after some time the woman returned to thank Our Lady for her cure.

Another time there was a soldier who cried like a child. He had received orders to leave for war, although his wife was sick in bed and they had three small children. He asked for either a cure for his wife or that the orders would be revoked. Jacinta invited him to pray the Rosary with her, then she said to him: "Don't cry. Our Lady is so good! She will certainly give you the grace you ask of her."

And she never forgot her soldier. At the end of the Rosary she always prayed a Hail Mary for that soldier. Some months passed, and he came back with his wife and three children to thank Our Lady for the graces received. Because of a fever he had the evening before he was supposed to leave, he had been released from military service, and his wife, he said, had been cured by a miracle of Our Lady.[5]

Endless and exhausting interrogations

The little shepherds had to face endless and sometimes rude interrogations. These often involved great suffering. They had to repeat the same things over and over again, and their interrogators often treated them as liars. Even when they were kindly treated, it was still tiring to repeat the same things time after time.

The insistent questioning went on endlessly; long lines of people wanted to meet the children at every possible opportunity. Each one, especially members of the clergy, wanted to investigate for himself, always hoping to uncover some contradiction that would confirm his suspicion that the evidence was faulty.

In general, Francisco refused to answer any question about the apparitions. He would simply lower his head, and no one could make him speak. One day, Lúcia decided to solve this mystery and asked him: "When you are asked something, why do you put your head down and refuse to answer?"

"Because I want you to answer, and Jacinta, too. I didn't hear anything. I can only say, 'Yes, I saw' [her], and then what if I say something you don't want me to?"[6]

Guided by these convictions, he behaved like this until the end of his life. In any case, he was not talkative by nature, and he never liked to talk of his most personal experiences. Whenever he had an opportunity to escape these interrogations, he did not hesitate to take it.

Strategies the children adopted to escape visitors

Dreading the endless interrogations, the children sought for ways to avoid them whenever they could. Lúcia relates:

> It would be appropriate to mention here an incident that shows how much Jacinta tried to escape from the people who were looking for her. One day we were on the way to Fátima, almost up to the main road, and we saw a group of ladies and gentlemen get out of an automobile. We didn't doubt for a minute that they were looking for us. It was too late to escape without being noticed. We went on in front of them, hoping to pass by without being recognized. The ladies came up next to us and asked if we knew the shepherds to whom Our Lady had appeared.
>
> We answered yes, we did. They asked if we knew where they lived. We gave them precise directions about how to get there, and ran to

hide ourselves in the fields among the shrubs. Jacinta was so happy with the outcome of the incident that she said: "We have to always do that when they don't recognize us."[7]

When Francisco was ill and confined to bed, Lúcia and Jacinta were keeping him company when Teresa (their sister who also died of pneumonia) came to tell them that a large group of people were coming. From the direction they were taking, it was obvious that they were looking for the three children and would surely torment them with questions. Lúcia at once thought of a way to escape them. There was still time to hide. Only Francisco, ill and in bed, could not go with the other two.

> Jacinta still managed to run behind me, and we hid in an overturned barrel next to the door that led into the courtyard. Right away we heard the noise of people going toward the house and leaving by the courtyard. They were right there near the barrel, which fortunately was turned with the open end on the opposite side. When we sensed that they had all gone away, we left our hiding place and went to Francisco, who told us all that had happened.
>
> "There were so many people and they wanted me to tell them where you were, but I didn't know myself. They wanted to see us and ask us many things. There was also a woman from Alqueidão, who wanted a cure for a sick person and the conversion of a sinner." Right away he added with that generous and practical spirit that he so often displayed: "For that woman, I'll pray; you pray for the others. There are so many."[8]

As long as Francisco was able to walk, the three of them would go to the Cova da Iria. One day, just when they were leaving Aljustrel, they were confronted by a group of people. As there were many people and the children were so small, they had the idea of putting them up on the wall running along the road so that all present could see and hear them.

> Francisco refused to let himself be put up there.... Afterward he got out of there little by little and leaned against an old wall in the front. A poor woman and a young boy, seeing that they weren't succeeding in speaking to us personally, as they wished, knelt down in front of him. They asked if he could obtain from Our Lady the cure of the father of the family, and that he would not have to go to war. (They were mother and son.) Francisco also knelt down, took off his cap, and asked if they wanted to pray the Rosary with him. They said yes and began to pray; after a little while all those people, leaving aside their curious questions knelt down also to pray. After that they accompanied us to

the Cova da Iria. On the way they prayed another Rosary with us, and at the Cova they prayed another and left satisfied. The poor woman promised to come back there to thank Our Lady for the graces she asked and obtained. She returned several times, accompanied not only by her son, but also her husband, who by then was in good health.[9]

Questioning by priests

Most of all, as the visionaries admitted, when they saw a priest approaching, they prepared themselves for one of the most costly sacrifices they could offer up to the Lord. This was because, apart from the exhausting interrogations, these interviews always had a certain note of suspicion, as if the whole thing were simply a plot to entrap the Church.

In one of these interrogations carried out by the pastor of Fátima, Jacinta behaved in such a way that it was impossible to get her to answer the questions. She lowered her head and would say only two or three words. When they left the rectory, her cousin asked her why she had behaved in such a strange fashion. Jacinta answered quite simply that she had promised not to tell anyone anything ever again.[10]

The saintly Father Cruz

But not all the priests were suspicious of the children. In fact, the little shepherds obtained help in a providential manner from three priests: Father Faustino José Jacinto Ferreira, the parish priest of Olival; the saintly Father Francisco Cruz; and later on, Father Manuel Formigão. The process of canonization has been introduced for Fathers Cruz and Formigão. Father Cruz traveled all over Portugal on his special mission. He was director of the College of Orphans in Braga and he eventually joined the Society of Jesus. Even during his lifetime he was considered to have the gifts of prophecy and of miracles, and many believers in Portugal had recourse to the saintly Father Cruz, imploring in a special way his intercession with God.

Lúcia's first meeting with Father Cruz was on the occasion of her first Communion. This priest used to travel in these districts hearing confessions and preaching. We do not know if he was in the parish of Fátima on a preaching mission. As mentioned already, humanly speaking Lúcia owed him the grace of making her First Communion at the age of six, in 1913. After asking her a few questions, Father Cruz told the pastor that he would accept the responsibility for allowing her to receive Communion so young.

Later, the children would meet him again on the occasion of the apparitions. One day the Servant of God, who was still living in Lisbon, came to question the three fortunate children as Lúcia describes:

> After his interview he asked me to go with him to show him the site where Our Lady had appeared. On the way, we walked on each side of his Reverence, who was riding a donkey so small that his feet were almost dragging on the ground. He was teaching us a litany of brief prayers, two of which Jacinta made her own and never stopped repeating: "O my Jesus, I love you! Sweet heart of Mary, be my salvation." [11]

The children gathered the precious fruit of this meeting, repeating the prayers they had learned. Later, the good priest would return frequently to this holy place.

The prayer of the three children

Sister Lúcia often refers to her cousins' prayer and tells how various people—including her own father—would ask them to pray the Rosary with them beside the holm oak. A trustworthy witness gave a statement about a visit to the Cova da Iria, in which he describes this prayer beside what remained of the blessed holm oak. Having described the lamentable state of the holm oak, Dr. Carlos de Azevedo Mendes, accompanied by the three children, described praying with them in a letter to his future wife:

> All three knelt down: Lúcia, who was in the middle, began to say the Rosary. Her recollection, the fervor with which she prayed, impressed us. The intention for the Rosary was interesting. It was for soldiers in the war. With what devotion, Prazeres, was that Rosary said!... I think I never prayed it with such attention! ...
>
> At the end I asked the children's permission to keep a little branch of basil. They all offered me a bit!... The prayer they say Our Lady taught them is simple; here it is:
>
> *O my Jesus, forgive me,*
> *save me from the fire of hell,*
> *lead all souls to heaven, especially*
> *those who are most in need.* [12]

The children have to give up being shepherds

The children enjoyed going out with the flocks. While the sheep grazed, the three amused themselves with innocent games, singing, praying, talking about the apparitions, breathing the pure mountain air, and contemplating the beautiful scenery. They were happy to be freed from tiring interviews with the people who came looking for them.

> My aunt grew tired of having to continually send for the children to satisfy the desire of the people who asked to speak to them, so she sent her son João to pasture the flock. This command cost Jacinta much, for two reasons: because she had to speak to all the people who came to look for her and, as she says, because she couldn't spend all day with me. Nevertheless she had to resign herself. And to hide herself from the people who sought her, she went with her brother into a rock cave on the slope of a hill in front of our place. A windmill was on top of it. The rock was on the east side, and was so well formed that it protected them perfectly from the rain and the heat of the sun. It was even covered by many oak and olive trees. How many prayers and sacrifices she offered there to our good God! [13]

However, this could not go on indefinitely, and the children's parents sought another solution. When Lúcia's mother decided to sell the flock, she discussed the entire situation with Olímpia. They decided the time had come to send the children to school. Our Lady's wish that they should learn to read, expressed in the apparition of June 13, began to be fulfilled.

Their desire to do penance [14]

With an intense desire to respond to the appeal that both the angel and Our Lady had addressed to them, the three children increasingly practiced corporal penances. The vision of hell in the July apparition heightened this desire. With the help of their childish imaginations, the three shepherds began to think of various ways to do penance. They did this out of love for God and their neighbor, especially for the conversion of sinners.

The idea of hunger seemed to them the sacrifice they could make most readily, and the one that cost them the most, considering the healthy appetites of normal children. They began to fast by giving away the food they had brought with them, first to the sheep and, afterward, to a group of poor children from the area.

Generosity led them to give up many things they liked. Everything served to satisfy their great desire for mortification. For example, they often denied themselves by not eating the fruit they liked so much:

> One day we were playing by the well that I already mentioned (do Arneiro). Jacinta's mother had a grape vine there. She cut some clusters and brought them to us to eat. But Jacinta never forgot her sinners. "We aren't going to eat them," she said. "We'll offer this sacrifice for sinners." Afterward she ran to bring the grapes to the other children who were playing in the street. She returned radiant with joy; she had met our poor little friends and had given the grapes to them.
>
> Another time, my aunt called us to eat some figs that she had brought home, which could really whet everyone's appetite. Jacinta sat down with us contentedly by the basket and picked up the first one to start eating; but suddenly she remembered and said: "It's true! Today we haven't made any sacrifices for sinners yet! We must make this one." She put the fig in the basket, made the offering, and left the figs there for the conversion of sinners. Jacinta frequently made these sacrifices, but don't let me recount more, otherwise I'll never finish.[15]

As time passed, they made other "discoveries." The heat of summer, up in the hills, increased their thirst. With unusual skill, Lúcia tells us all this in order to present her two cousins, already in heaven, as models, but she conceals her own part in all these mortifications behind those of her cousins. She describes a charming scene in one of her *Memoirs*.

At the height of summer they used to go to a pasture a good distance away from their homes. The intense heat made them very thirsty and gave them severe headaches. Lúcia said nothing about this, and Francisco, as was his custom, did not complain either. Jacinta, more communicative and spontaneous, let them know how she felt. Lúcia describes the scene with her usual realism:

> It was a beautiful day but the sun was blazing, and in that rocky and unproductive land, it seemed like it would scorch everything. It made us feel very thirsty, but there wasn't a drop of water to drink. At first we offered this sacrifice generously for the conversion of sinners. But after noon we couldn't resist anymore.
>
> So I suggested to my companions that I could go to a nearby house and ask for a little water. They accepted the proposal and I went to knock on the door of an elderly lady. She gave me a pitcher of water and also a little bit of bread, which I gratefully accepted, and ran to give it to my companions. I gave the pitcher to Francisco and told him to drink some: "I don't want to drink." He answered.

"Why?"

"I want to suffer for the conversion of sinners."

"Jacinta—you drink!"

"I want to offer this sacrifice for sinners too!"

Then I put the water in a hollow in the rock so the sheep could drink it and went to bring the pitcher back to its owner. The heat was getting worse by the minute. The crickets and grasshoppers joined their song with the frogs in the lake nearby and made an unbearable noise. Jacinta, dehydrated by weakness and thirst, said to me with that simplicity that was so characteristic of her: "Tell the grasshoppers and frogs to keep quiet! They give me such a headache!"

Then Francisco asked her: "Don't you want to offer this for sinners?"

The poor child, clutching her head between her little hands answered: "Yes, I want to. Let them sing." [16]

Francisco was tireless in his generosity, always with the aim of consoling Our Lord. Lúcia tells us how one day he managed to make the sacrifice of giving up a certain drink that he liked very much:

One day on the way to my house we were passing in front of my godmother's house. She had just made some honey water and called us in to give us a glass of it. We went in and Francisco was the first to whom she gave a glass to drink. He took it and without drinking passed it to Jacinta so she could drink first, with me; meanwhile he turned on his heel and disappeared.

"Where is Francisco?" my godmother asked.

"I don't know, I don't know. He was just here."

He didn't appear. Jacinta and I thanked her for the gift and went out after him where we didn't doubt for an instant he would be, sitting on the edge of the well, as I have already mentioned several times.

"Francisco, you didn't drink the honey water. My godmother called for you several times and you didn't appear!"

"When I took the cup, I suddenly remembered to make some sacrifice to console Our Lord, and while you were both drinking I ran away here." [17]

Other penances

One day they discovered a piece of rope along the road. It was the kind used to fasten wood or other loads onto farm carts, so it was thick and extremely coarse. They realized that they could wear this as a sort of penitential cord. Here is how Lúcia describes the incident:

[One day] when we went for a walk with our sheep, I found a piece of rope from a cart. I picked it up and playing, I tied it on my arm. I did not take long to realize that the cord was hurting me. So I said to my cousins: "Look, this hurts. We could tie it on as a belt and offer this sacrifice to God." The poor children quickly accepted my idea, and we then set about dividing it among the three of us. We hit it with the corner of a rock that we used as our knife on top of another stone.

Because of the thickness or roughness of the rope, or because we sometimes tightened it too much, this instrument of penance at times caused us to suffer terribly. Sometimes Jacinta shed tears because of the great discomfort it caused her, and I would tell her to take it off. She would reply: "No! I want to offer this sacrifice to Our Lord in reparation and for the conversion of sinners."[18]

We know from the advice Our Lady gave them during the September apparition that even at night the children continued to wear the rope tightly around their waists. Hence they were told: "God is pleased with your sacrifices, but he doesn't want you to sleep with the rope; wear it only during the day."[19]

This precious relic disappeared in due time. It is edifying to note the discretion of the visionaries, hiding from curious eyes everything relating to their intimate relationship with God, and behaving like perfectly normal children in the presence of others.

When she was ill, Jacinta entrusted this relic to Lúcia. "One day she gave me the rope that I've already spoken about and said to me: 'Take it away before my mother sees it. I'm not able to wear it anymore.'"[20] Lúcia then adds this comment about the rope: "This rope had three knots and also some bloodstains. I kept it hidden until I finally left my mother's house. Afterward, not knowing what to do with it, I burned it along with her brother Francisco's."[21]

While both Jacinta and Francisco were ill they sought other means of doing penance: struggling against lack of appetite, giving up things that they liked (such as fruit), saying the angel's prayer while lying prostrate until they were exhausted, never complaining about their sufferings, or renouncing the consolation of some visits. At times, without a single complaint, they put up with annoying visitors who, not noticing how ill they were, kept asking endless and wearying questions.

Our Lady's prophecy to bring this brother and sister to heaven, while Lúcia was to remain on earth to spread devotion to the Immaculate Heart of Mary, was soon to be fulfilled. At the first signs of this, the children understood what was happening, while the family of Francisco and

Jacinta cherished the hope that it was merely a passing illness. The children kept this secret carefully, since apart from anything else, they wanted to spare their family and friends the suffering it would bring. Even though they knew about the revelations of Fátima, the proximity of the children's deaths would surely prolong and intensify their families' suffering.

Vision of the devil

In the July apparition in which Our Lady showed them hell, Jacinta had been the most impressed. Lúcia also, to judge by the description she gives in her *Memoirs*, must have been horror-struck, to the point of crying out in a loud voice to Our Lady. According to the *Memoirs*, Francisco seems to have been the least impressed by the vision of hell, although it affected him considerably. He felt also an immense compassion for sinners falling into hell or in danger of being condemned. But another thought dominated him when he remembered what he had seen. "What made the deepest impression on him and what totally absorbed him was God, the Most Holy Trinity, seen in that immense light that penetrated us in our deepest soul." [22]

On one of these occasions he had a vision of the devil. Lúcia and Jacinta were strolling around in Pedreira, playing, jumping from stone to stone, or repeating words so as to hear them echo, while the sheep grazed. Francisco had moved away from them to pray by himself as was his custom. After some time, the two girls heard him shouting and calling on Our Lady. Not knowing what had happened to him, they were very upset and began to look for him, calling his name. Finding their way by the sound of his voice, they found him after some time, on his knees, still trembling with fear, as if stricken. He explained afterward, his voice smothered with fright. "It was one of those huge beasts that were in hell. It was right here throwing flames!" [23]

Francisco would advise his sister not to think so much about hell, so as not to be afraid, but to think about Our Lord and Our Lady instead. So the two girls did not miss the chance to remark that he was the one who ended up being terrified.

Francisco, trusted friend of Jesus in the tabernacle

Although he was enrolled in the primary school, Francisco was convinced that for him there was no point in learning to read because he would shortly be going to heaven as Our Lady had promised him on June 13. Stricken by pneumonia, he spent the time of his illness in his parents' house; it seemed, however, that he would recover because of his strong constitution. At this time he gave a wonderful example that we can still learn from.

The rumor circulated that everyone in the families of the little shepherds was going to die. Fortunately, that was not true. After his first attack of influenza in October 1918, Francisco became seriously ill on December 23, 1918, and was confined to bed. He had contracted bronchial pneumonia, a complication of the influenza that spread all over the world. From the beginning of October, he was never well again.

His home became a hospital because, except for his father, everyone else was ill and in bed, even his mother, Olímpia de Jesus. With the help of some kind neighbors, the distraught Ti Marto looked after the family. After two weeks, at the beginning of January, Francisco got up, but in a state of increasing weakness.

Jacinta went to school every day, but she loved to visit the Blessed Sacrament during the breaks or at recreation time. Possibly Lúcia did likewise, accompanying her cousin. However, with her usual skill, she never talks about herself.

Between October—when the first symptoms of his illness appeared —and December, when he had to return to bed, Francisco accompanied his sister and Lúcia to the school near the parish church, about a kilometer from Aljustrel.

One day, Lúcia's sister Teresa came looking for her to tell her about the suffering of a poor mother whose son had been unjustly accused of a crime and imprisoned. If he could not prove his innocence, he would be deported or, at least, condemned to spend many years in prison. Lúcia told her cousins about this distressing problem while they were on their way to school. Francisco listened in silence, and when they neared the parish church, he said:

> "Look, while you go to school, I'll stay here with the hidden Jesus and I'll ask him for that grace."
>
> When school was over, I returned to church to call him and asked: "Did you ask Our Lord for that grace?"
>
> "Yes, I asked. Tell your Teresa that in a few days he'll come home."
>
> A few days later the poor young man was home, on the thirteenth. He was there with his whole family to thank Our Lady for the grace received.[24]

Francisco's love for the Blessed Sacrament in the tabernacle led him to make generous sacrifices so that he wouldn't miss a meeting with Jesus there. One day as they were leaving the house, Lúcia noticed that Francisco was walking very slowly, as if it cost him a great deal. Worried, she asked him what was the matter.

"My head hurts so much, and I feel like I'm going to fall."

"So then don't come; stay home."

"No. I won't stay home! I want to stay in church with the hidden Jesus while you go to school." [25]

Francisco's love of the truth

Francisco took great pains to be truthful, and he wanted everyone around him to do the same. Various episodes from his life demonstrate this concern. Lúcia recounts:

> One day they asked me if Our Lady had commanded us to pray for sinners. I answered no. As soon as he could, while the people were questioning Jacinta, Francisco called me and said: "You just lied. How can you say that Our Lady didn't tell us to pray for sinners? Didn't she tell us to pray for them?"
>
> "For sinners, no. She told us to pray for peace, and for the war to end. For sinners she told us to make sacrifices."
>
> "Ah! It's true. I was beginning to think you had lied." [26]

The gift of prophecy

The Lord deigned to endow Francisco and Jacinta with the gift of prophecy. We know quite well that the original meaning of the word "prophet" is messenger or herald, someone who speaks in the name of another. It is in this sense that Vatican II tells us that the People of God are a prophetic people.

To prove the authenticity of their mission, however, those who claimed to speak in the name of God sometimes predicted future events they could only have known by divine revelation. A prophet gradually came to be identified as someone who foretells future happenings that could only be known through a revelation from God. It is in this sense that we speak of Jacinta and Francisco's gift of prophecy.

When Francisco was asked to pray for an intention, he would be able to say what was going to happen, although it was humanly impossible to explain the source of his information. This happened, for example, in the case of the boy who was about to be deported or imprisoned because of a false accusation. After spending hours before the Blessed Sacrament, Francisco announced with assurance what was going to happen, and in fact it did.

Jacinta was also favored with the gift of prophecy, as Lúcia tells us. One day when her cousin was visiting her, she found her at home, sitting on her bed, wrapped in thought. When Lúcia asked her why she was so pensive, Jacinta answered: "In the war that is coming, so many people have to die!... Many houses will be destroyed, many priests will die. Look, I'm going to heaven. And you, when you see on that night the light that the Lady told us would come before, you flee there, too." [27] This was not the only time that Jacinta surprised her cousin by thinking so deeply about the effects of the war.

Jacinta also foretold the course of her illness and death. She declared that the operation she was to have in the Dona Estafânia Hospital would be to no purpose, which, in fact, turned out to be true.

Our Lady's prophecies are fulfilled

At a certain point, the children's way of suffering began to move in different directions. During the apparition in June, Our Lady had foretold that she would soon bring Francisco and Jacinta to heaven: "I will take Jacinta and Francisco soon." [28]

The promise was to be fulfilled soon after the apparitions in an unexpected way. The year 1918 was marked by the end of World War I and a deadly epidemic. In every village of Portugal, people remember the many lives cut down by this influenza. In the parish of Fátima alone, 118 people died. To add to people's distress, few effective means were available to fight the illness. It was a question of fighting an unknown enemy.

Jacinta and Francisco became ill with the influenza at nearly the same time, at the end of October 1918. This epidemic, known as the Spanish influenza, took many millions of lives around the world. It killed more than 100,000 people in Portugal. This strain of flu attacked children and young people, those who are usually able to resist because of their stronger constitutions. Many people who contracted the disease died from bacterial pneumonia, which was an effect of the influenza.

In the Marto household, the whole family caught it, except for the father, Manuel Pedro, who devoted himself completely to looking after them all. Remembering Our Lady's prophecy, Jacinta and Francisco had no illusions about their destiny. They realized that this was the sign that their earthly pilgrimage was soon to end. For their part, they profited from this time of grace to live out the Lady's message. The epidemic also claimed the lives of two of their sisters, Teresa and Florinda.

In Lúcia's home, despite the extraordinary dedication of her mother, father, and the children, who hurried from house to house to help those who were ill, no one contracted the disease.

FRANCISCO'S ILLNESS AND DEATH

In God's mysterious designs, Jacinta's brother was the first to leave to meet the Lady of the Cova da Iria in heaven. In compliance with Our Lady's words, Francisco prayed the Rosary many times. According to his mother, when he had to stay in bed, and no one was with him, he always had his beads in his hands and would pray the Rosary eight or more times a day. Eventually he would not have the strength to pray even one Rosary.

Francisco's sorrow at being unable to pray a full Rosary

During the short time when he could still walk, Francisco would complain to his mother that he could no longer recite the whole Rosary—he got tired in the middle—such was his extreme weakness. His good mother tried to console him, advising him to say the Our Father and the Hail Mary mentally, and telling him that Our Lady would still accept his prayer with the same pleasure.

Sometimes, when he was feeling better and he would take a walk, he managed to visit the Cova da Iria. As Lucia relates, "He would often tell his mother not to forget the prayer that the Most Holy Virgin had taught the three of them, for he himself never forgot to say it."[29] When Senhora Olímpia confessed that she had forgotten to pray it several times, her son told her that she could pray it when she was walking along the roads in the village.

Lucia recalls, "If anyone ever said that he most certainly would regain his health, Francisco responded right away with a no. He said this with a mysterious air, and a solemn tone of voice."[30] He knew quite well where he was going.

It even happened that his godmother, Teresa de Jesus,[31] had promised in his presence to make an offering of his weight in wheat if Our Lady made him better. Francisco declared at once that it was useless to make such a promise because she would never obtain his cure.

Strong and discreet in suffering

Despite his illness, Francisco always appeared joyful and happy. Only God knows what this smiling good humor cost him. Normally, he never spoke in confidence about his interior life except to his cousin and his sister. Lúcia declares:

> Francisco didn't speak much. He usually did what he saw us doing, and on rare occasions he would suggest something [we could do]. During his illness he suffered with heroic patience, without letting out a groan or the slightest complaint. I asked him one day shortly before he died: "Francisco, are you suffering a lot?"
> "Yes, but I suffer everything for the love of Our Lord and Our Lady."[32]

At other times he would say: "Quite a bit, but it doesn't matter. I'm suffering to console Our Lord; and in a little while I'll go to heaven."[33]

This same prudence led him to give the rope with which he had done so much penance to his cousin. Even in his illness, he never missed a chance to make a sacrifice. "He took everything his mother brought him, and I never could tell if there was something he didn't like."[34] In the plans of God, the influenza from which the two children suffered would be the path bringing them to heaven.

Reduced to inactivity by his illness, and limited in his ability to pray, Francisco strove to be the least possible trouble to others and always tried to spare his family any suffering. Hiding the weight of his cross and thinking of others, he wanted to do good to all who visited him.

"During his illness children would come and go from his room with the greatest freedom; they would speak to him through the window and ask him if he was better, etc."[35]

A mysterious attraction drew them to their friend, even at the risk of catching pneumonia themselves. Nevertheless, he liked to be alone in order to continue in silence the contemplative prayer to which he had so often given himself while minding the flocks.

"If he was asked if he wanted some children to keep him company, he would say no, he would rather be alone. 'I only like it,' he would sometimes say, 'when you are here, and Jacinta too.'"[36] Naturally, with them he could speak freely about the wonderful things they had experienced together during Our Lady's visits.

Even adults quickly realized how they benefited from being in Francisco's presence.

> When adults visited him he would remain silent or answer whatever they asked him with few words. The people who visited him, whether they were neighbors or from a distance, would sit next to his bed, sometimes for a long time, and say: "I don't know what there is about Francisco, but it feels so good to be here!"
>
> One day after having spent a good bit of time in Francisco's room, some neighbors commented: "It's a mystery that's hard to understand. They are children like any others, they don't say anything to us, yet being near them one feels that there's something different from the other children."
>
> One woman named Romana, a neighbor of my aunt, said that entering Francisco's room felt like going into a church. This woman never gave any indication of believing in the happenings.[37]

People were so convinced of Francisco's holiness that they entrusted urgent intentions to him in the hope that his prayers would obtain an answer from heaven. The following example illustrates this confidence in his intercession, as Lúcia relates:

> One day a woman named Mariana of Casa Velha went to Francisco's room. She was upset because her husband had thrown her son out of the house. She asked for the grace of reconciliation between father and son. Francisco responded to her: "Be at peace. I am going to heaven soon and when I get there I'll ask that grace of Our Lady."
>
> I don't remember well how many days were left before he went to heaven; but I do remember that in the afternoon of the day Francisco died, the son went a second time to ask pardon from his father. The father had refused him the first time because the son didn't want to accept the conditions imposed. But now he accepted all that his father demanded, and peace was re-established in that home.[38]

Consoling the Lord

Francisco's constant desire was to console Our Lord for the many sins by which he is offended. During the apparitions, the Lord's sad expression greatly impressed the boy. When Jacinta and Lucia had helped him to examine his conscience for his last confession, he told them that perhaps it was because of his sins that Our Lord looked sad. And Francisco declared at once his intention never to sin again.

His love for the Holy Eucharist

From the time of the angel's apparitions, Francisco developed a deep devotion to the Eucharist. As long as his health permitted, he spent long hours before the tabernacle.

> Sometimes on my way to school, when we arrived in Fátima, he would say to me: "Look, you go to school. I'll stay here in church next to the hidden Jesus. It doesn't pay for me to learn to read; from here I'll soon be going to heaven. When you return, come here to call me."
>
> At that time the Blessed Sacrament was on the left side near the entrance to the church because of repairs. Francisco stayed between the baptismal font and the altar, and I found him there when I returned.
>
> Later, after he got sick, he would tell me sometimes when I passed by his house on the way to school: "Go to the church and give my love to the hidden Jesus. What makes me suffer most is the pain of not being able to go there and stay a little bit with the hidden Jesus." [39]
>
> Francisco longed to receive Holy Communion. Once when Lúcia was going to the church, Francisco did not want to miss the chance of trying once more to obtain his desire. He asked his cousin: "Please ask the pastor to give me Holy Communion."
>
> Francisco wanted this so much that, even when he had already received an affirmative answer to his request, he still asked Lúcia when she came to the house: "Did you ask the hidden Jesus to have the pastor give me Communion?" [40]
>
> When Lúcia told him that she had done so, he promised to pray for her in heaven.

Francisco's first Communion

Though Francisco had a great desire to receive Holy Communion, he had not yet completed his twelfth year—the normal age for children to receive Communion in those days, even after Saint Pius X's Decree *Quam singulari*, which lowered the age.

Unexpectedly, Francisco's health deteriorated considerably. The pneumonia was relentless.

> A deep expectoration that he could not rid himself of, a constantly rising temperature, a loss of appetite, increasing weakness, complete

exhaustion, all these symptoms left no doubt. The exile of the little shepherd boy was coming to a close.

"Father, before I die, I want to receive Our Lord," he said in a weak voice.

"I'll take care of that immediately," answered Ti Marto. His heart was broken not only because he knew his son was dying, but also because he feared that the pastor would once more refuse to bring the "hidden Jesus" to Francisco. So Ti Marto set out for the church, sad and utterly dejected.

At that time, Father Moreira from Atouguia was substituting for Father Marques Ferreira, and he willingly agreed to bring Holy Communion to the little boy. "As we were going home we prayed the Rosary. I recall quite clearly that I did not have a rosary in my jacket pocket and I had to count the Hail Marys on my fingers."[41]

The father's fears were well founded. The pastor had several times already refused to let Francisco make his first Communion, because, timid as he was with strangers, the little boy would get mixed up and couldn't answer the catechism questions without making mistakes. But before receiving Communion, Francisco would make his last confession.

Francisco's last confession

The Lord had granted Francisco a delicate conscience. Several times he had shown this at the time of the apparitions, whether by refusing to bring the sheep to land belonging to his godmother without her express permission, or by alerting his sister or his cousin to some phrase of theirs that seemed to him not to be entirely true.

The following episode should be situated in that context. It took place on the morning of April 2, before Francisco's confession in preparation for receiving Viaticum.

One day, very early in the morning, his sister Teresa came to call me: "Come right away. Francisco is very sick and he says he wants to tell you something!"

I got dressed quickly and went over there. He asked his mother and brothers and sisters to leave the room, saying that he wanted to ask me about something secret. They left and he said to me: "I'm going to go to confession, receive Communion, and then die. I want you to tell me if you ever saw me commit some sin, and then go ask Jacinta if she saw me commit any."

"You disobeyed your mother sometimes," I told him, "when she told you to stay home but you ran off to be with me and to hide."

"It's true! I remember that. Now go ask Jacinta if she remembers anything else."

I went out to Jacinta and after thinking a little she answered me: "Well, tell him that even after Our Lady appeared to us, he stole a coin from father to buy a music box from José Marto from Casa Velha; and when the boys from Aljustrel threw rocks at the boys from Boleiros, he threw some too."

When I gave him this message from his sister, he answered: "I've already confessed those, but I'll confess them again. Maybe it's because of these sins that Our Lord is so sad! But even if I don't die yet, I will never commit them again. Now I am very sorry for them."

Joining his hands he prayed: "O my Jesus, forgive us, save us from the fire of hell, bring all souls to heaven, especially those who are in most need."

Then he said: "Look, you also ask Our Lord to forgive me my sins."

"I'll ask, yes; be at peace. If Our Lord hadn't already forgiven them, Our Lady wouldn't have told Jacinta just the other day that she was coming very soon to take you to heaven. Now I'm going to Mass, and there I'll pray to the hidden Jesus for you."

"Then please ask him to have the pastor bring me Holy Communion."[42]

On April 2, the priest came to hear Francisco's confession. By then the little boy was much worse. But the following morning he had the great joy of receiving his first Holy Communion, which was also his Viaticum. We can imagine how happy he was, he who had spent so many hours in prayer before the tabernacle in the parish church, keeping company with the "Hidden God." After receiving Holy Communion, he said to Jacinta: "Today I'm happier than you because I have the Hidden Jesus within my heart. I'm going to heaven, but when I'm there I'll pray very much to Our Lord and Our Lady to bring you both there soon."[43]

Father Moreira promised to return the following morning and bring Francisco Holy Communion a second time, but the little boy died that night.

A holy death

Francisco died on April 4, 1919. During that day, which seemed endless, he asked now and again for water and milk. When night came, his state of health worsened. But when his mother asked him how he was feeling, he answered that he wasn't any worse and that he had no pain. Perhaps he did not want to make his mother suffer, or else Our Lady wanted to grant him a death without pain.

On this last day of his life, a Friday, Jacinta and Lúcia spent the whole time in his room. Only the three of them knew that his departure for heaven was approaching. As he was too weak to recite vocal prayers, he asked them to pray the Rosary for him.

He thought of heaven, as we all do, in terms of this life's experiences. He would say that he was going to miss Lúcia in heaven and he wanted Our Lady to bring her there also. As for his sister, he knew that he would have to wait only a little while before she joined him in heaven.

When night came, Lúcia bade him good-bye. Her voice choking with emotion, she said:

"Francisco, good-bye! If you go to heaven tonight don't forget me, do you hear?"

It cost him a lot to answer: "I won't forget you; be at peace." Grasping my right hand he squeezed it tightly for a bit, while looking at me with tears in his eyes.

"Do you want anything else?" I asked him as tears ran down my cheeks too.

"No," he answered in a fading voice.

Since the scene was becoming too moving, my aunt told me to leave the room.

"So then, good-bye, Francisco! Until we meet in heaven!"

"Good-bye, until heaven!"[44]

Francisco was only waiting for this farewell. That same night, April 4, at about 10:00 P.M., Our Lady kept her promise and came to bring him to heaven.

He had completed ten years, nine months and twenty-four days since he was born on June 11, 1908, at 10:00 P.M. His last words were addressed to his godmother. When he saw her at the door, a few instants before drawing his last breath, he asked her to give him her blessing and to forgive him for any trouble he had caused her. It is said that, at the last moment, he exclaimed that he saw "a very beautiful light."[45]

He was buried the following day in the parish cemetery of Fátima, to the inconsolable grief of his family and of all who had known him. Francisco had a simple funeral cortege, headed by the cross followed by men in green cloaks. Behind them walked the priest, in surplice and black stole, immediately in front of the coffin. It was carried by four boys in white cloaks. A small crowd followed. The priest led the Rosary, which Francisco could no longer answer, while Lúcia wept in the middle of the crowd. Jacinta had stayed at home crying because her illness no longer permitted her to leave her room.

In the little parish cemetery—now greatly enlarged—Francisco was buried in an unmarked grave. Only a cross like all the others indicated that here was buried the body of a child of God.

However, Lúcia with the keenness that came from friendship and her ability to observe things closely, engraved the place in her memory. As long as she remained in Aljustrel, she visited her cousin's grave daily.

On March 13, 1952, the official recognition of the mortal remains took place in the presence of the religious and civil authorities. The remains were then transposed to the basilica of Fátima, to the first chapel on the right side, where they await the glory of the final resurrection.

In front of the basilica, two large photographs of Francisco and Jacinta were uncovered when John Paul II proclaimed them blessed on May 13, 2000. Enthusiastic applause of approval came from the million or so faithful who were at the Cova da Iria.

JACINTA'S ILLNESS AND DEATH

Jacinta became ill with influenza in October 1918, exactly a year after the apparitions had ended. She began by having severe headaches, which forced her to stay in bed. A few days later Francisco also got sick. In a visit from Our Lady, when she told them that Francisco would soon be going to heaven, she added that Jacinta would stay on earth a little longer to suffer and convert sinners. Meanwhile, throughout the painful Calvary of her illness, Jacinta showed clearly the richness of her interior life and drew people to God.

Love for the Holy Eucharist

One of the most marked features of Jacinta's spiritual life was her love for the Blessed Eucharist, now more evident than ever as her health deteriorated and her illness became irreversible. The meeting with the angel who asked the children to make reparation for sins committed against the Real Presence of Christ in the Eucharist marked the beginning of Jacinta's abiding love of the Holy Eucharist. This was reinforced by the Holy Communion that he gave them during the third apparition at Loca do Cabeço. She had grasped an essential truth about the interior life: a personal relationship with Jesus Christ, present in the Sacrament of Love. With all the simplicity of a child, the little visionary expressed her devotion when Lúcia was going to school and would pass by the parish church. "When I passed by one day on my way to school, Jacinta said to me: 'Tell the hidden Jesus that I like him very much, and that I love him very much.' Other times she would say: 'Tell Jesus I miss him a lot.'"[46]

It was the heart of a child expressing itself in the language of a contemplative. Jacinta used every opportunity to express her love for the sacred humanity of Jesus and his real presence in the Eucharist. Fortunately, Lúcia's preserved in her *Memoirs* some facts about this aspect of Jacinta's spirituality:

> One day they gave me a holy card of the Sacred Heart of Jesus, an attractive one, as people are able to make. I brought it to Jacinta: "Would you like this holy card?"
>
> She took it and looked at it attentively and said:
>
> "It's so ugly! It doesn't look anything like Our Lord who is so beautiful! But I want it; it's still him."
>
> And she always kept it with her. At night and during her illness she kept it under the pillow until it fell apart. She would often kiss it and say: "I kiss him on the heart, that's what I like the most. Who will give me one of the Heart of Mary too! Don't you have one? I would like to have them both together."
>
> She would also be deeply moved at the sight of any symbol or holy card that made her think of the Holy Eucharist.
>
> On another occasion, I brought her a holy card that had the sacred chalice with a host. She took it, kissed it, and, radiant with joy, said: "It's the hidden Jesus! I love him so much. Who will let me receive him in church! In heaven don't they go to Communion? If they do, then I'll go to Communion every day. If only the angel were to come to the hospital to bring me Holy Communion again! How happy I would be!"
>
> She understood perfectly that each person who goes to Communion is transformed into a living tabernacle for as long as the sacred species remains. Sometimes when I returned from church and went to her house, she would ask me: "Did you go to Communion?"
>
> If I answered yes, she said: "Come here close to me because you have the hidden Jesus in your heart."
>
> At other times she would say to me: "I don't know how it is! But I feel Our Lord within me. I understand what he is saying to me, even though I don't see or hear him; but it is so good to be with him!"
>
> Her desire to make reparation for offenses to the Sacred Hearts of Jesus and Mary was always with her.

On another occasion she said: "See, do you know this? Even though Our Lady said not to offend Our Lord anymore because he is already so offended, Our Lord is sad because no one pays any attention; they continue to commit the same sins."[47]

Jacinta's love for the Immaculate Heart of Mary

After so many meetings with Our Lady, Jacinta's heart became hers once for all. The Lord sent Jacinta special graces that led her to this intimacy with him and with Our Lady. Lúcia recalls: "One day during her illness she said: 'I really like to tell Jesus I love him! When I tell him many times, it seems like I have a fire within my heart, but it doesn't burn me.' Another time she said: 'I love Our Lord and Our Lady so much that I never get tired of telling them.'"[48]

Our Lady treated Jacinta with great tenderness, especially during her illness, appearing to her several times and making new appeals to her generosity. Jacinta answered Our Lady's requests with unselfish generosity and urged her cousin to do likewise.

Searching in the archives of her loving heart for memories of her cousin, Lúcia wrote in her *Memoirs:*

> Shortly before going to the hospital she said to me: "It won't be long before I go to heaven. You stay here to tell everyone that God wants to establish devotion to the Immaculate Heart of Mary in the world. When you are to say this, don't hide yourself. Tell everyone that God grants us graces through the Immaculate Heart of Mary; that they must ask these graces through her; that the Heart of Jesus wants that the Immaculate Heart of Mary be venerated alongside his; that they should ask peace of the Immaculate Heart of Mary, and God will grant it. If I could only put in the hearts of everyone the fire that I have burning within my heart that makes me love the hearts of Jesus and Mary so much!"[49]

Love for the Holy Father

Divine Providence so arranged it that the three little shepherds developed a great love for the Holy Father, even though they had never seen him in person and probably not even a photograph. This devotion began with a casual event. Two priests who were visiting them suggested to the children that they should pray very much for the Holy Father.

They explained who he was and how important was his role in the Church.

> Jacinta asked who the Holy Father was, and the good priests explained to us who he was and how he needed many prayers.
>
> [Then Jacinta asked:] "Is he the same one I saw crying, whom the Lady spoke of in the secret?"
>
> Jacinta had a great love for the Holy Father, and when she offered her sacrifices to Jesus she would always add: "and for the Holy Father." When she finished praying the Rosary she always added three Hail Marys for the Holy Father. Sometimes she would say: "How I would love to see the Holy Father! So many people come here but the Holy Father never comes."[50]
>
> In her childlike innocence, she thought the Holy Father could make that trip like other people.[51]

Her hope was increased when she heard Lúcia's mother saying that her daughter would certainly have to go to Rome to be questioned by His Holiness the Pope. As can be imagined, Lúcia was radiant with joy, while her cousins prepared to offer up to the Lord the sacrifice of not going with her.

One day they were spending their siesta time by the Arneiro well, in the farmyard of Lúcia's parents. While Lúcia and Francisco went to look for wild honey in a bramble patch, Jacinta called her cousin and asked her if she had seen the Holy Father.

When Lúcia said no, Jacinta said: "I don't know how, but I saw the Holy Father in a very big house, kneeling by a table with his face in his hands, crying. Many people were outside the house, with some throwing stones at him while others cursed him and said many terrible things to him. Poor Holy Father! We have to pray a lot for him."[52]

Who was the Holy Father shown in this vision? Was it Pius XII, against whom an international campaign was launched when he consecrated the world to the Immaculate Heart of Mary? Paul VI, who suffered from the crisis in the Church after the Second Vatican Council? John Paul II, victim of an assassination attempt?

Another time, the children were on their way to Loca do Cabeço to prostrate themselves on the ground and recite the angel's prayers. After a short time, Jacinta called her cousin and asked: "Don't you see all those roads, so many highways and fields full of people, crying out with hunger that they have nothing to eat? And the Holy Father in a church, praying before the Immaculate Heart of Mary? And so many people praying with him?"[53]

Today, with the revelation of the third part of the secret confided to the three children, we can better understand the response that devotion to the Holy Father aroused in their hearts.

Discreet in her sacrifices

With great delicacy—unusual in a child of eight—Jacinta hid her intense sufferings as far as she possibly could, so as not to cause pain to her parents. The evening before she became very ill she confided to her cousin: "My head aches so much and I am so thirsty! But I don't want to drink, so that I can suffer for sinners."[54]

Other times, she told Lúcia: "I feel so much pain in my chest! But I'm not going to say anything to my mother; I want to suffer for Our Lord in reparation for the sins committed against the Immaculate Heart of Mary, for the Holy Father, and for the conversion of sinners."[55] These were her constant intentions in everything she did.

Confined to bed by a disease that would prove terminal, Jacinta discovered new ways of mortifying herself. In her conversations with Lúcia, perhaps with the aim of encouraging her to be generous also, she asked once: "How many sacrifices did you offer to Our Lord last night?"

"Three: I got up three times to recite the prayers of the angel."

"Well, I offered him many, many sacrifices; I don't know how many there were because I had a lot of pain and I didn't complain."[56]

Here is another example of this kind, recounted, as always, by her confidant: "Another time, one morning, I found her looking very sick and I asked her if she was feeling worse. 'Last night,' she answered, 'I had a lot of pain and I wanted to offer to the Lord the sacrifice of not turning over in bed, which is why I didn't sleep at all.'"[57]

The angel had recommended: "In everything you can, offer to God a sacrifice as an act of reparation for sins by which he is offended, and humbly beg God for the conversion of sinners." This phrase was indelibly engraved in Jacinta's mind, and in everything she sought an opportunity to make a sacrifice.

"Whenever I went to her room first she would say: 'Now go see Francisco; I'll make the sacrifice of staying here alone.'"[58]

And on another occasion: "One day when I went near her she asked me: 'Have you already made many sacrifices today? I made many. My

mother went out and I wanted to visit Francisco so many times but I did
not go.'"[59]

She was determined not to lose any opportunity of doing penance.
Every example cited in the *Memoirs* is a fragrant flower that moves us to
be generous also in offering up to God the difficulties of our daily lives.

> One day her mother brought her a cup of milk and told her to drink it.
>
> "I don't want any, mother," she answered, pushing away the cup
> with her little hand.
>
> My aunt insisted a little and then left the room, saying: "I don't
> know how to make her take something, she has so little appetite!"
>
> As soon as we were alone I asked her: "How can you disobey your
> mother like that and not offer this sacrifice to Our Lord?"
>
> On hearing this, she shed a few tears that I had the joy of wiping
> away, and she said: "I didn't remember this time!" She called her
> mother, asked her forgiveness, and said that she would take as much as
> her mother wanted her to.
>
> Her mother brought her the cup of milk and she drank it without
> showing how much it repulsed her. She told me later: "If you only
> knew how much it cost me to drink it!"[60]

Lúcia relates a similar incident about Jacinta:

> Her mother knew how much the milk repulsed her, so one day she
> brought her a tasty bunch of grapes with the cup of milk.
>
> "Jacinta," she said, "take this. If you can't drink the milk, leave it
> and eat the grapes."
>
> "No mother, I don't want the grapes. Take them away. Leave me
> the milk and I'll drink it."
>
> Without showing the least repugnance, she drank it. My aunt left
> the room, happy because she thought her little daughter was getting
> over her lack of appetite. Afterward Jacinta turned to me and said: "I
> wanted those grapes so badly and it cost me a lot to drink the milk! But
> I want to offer this sacrifice to the Lord."[61]

Meanwhile, the sacrifice did not grow any easier for being repeated.
So that we would have no doubts on that score, she herself confessed:
"Each time it costs me more to drink the milk and broth, but I don't say
anything. I take everything for the love of Our Lord and the Immaculate
Heart of Mary, our dear Mother in heaven."[62]

Like Francisco, Jacinta also wanted to hide the piece of rope she
used for penance, so she gave it to Lúcia for safekeeping. When she was
handing it to Lúcia, she seemed to have a slight hope that she might use
it again. Lúcia recalls: "A few days after falling ill, she gave me the rope

she had been using, saying: 'Keep it for me, I am afraid my mother might see it. If I get better, I want it back again!'"[63]

Besides these physical penances, Jacinta had to face the pain of letting go of things as death approached. She loved the world she lived in: flowers, singing birds, and the lovely landscapes of her own country. The limitations of her illness entailed a gradual withdrawal from all this. Here is one example among the many recorded by Lúcia:

> I used to like to go to Cabeço whenever I could, to pray in our favorite cave. Since Jacinta loved flowers so much, on my return home I would gather on the hill a bunch of irises and peonies when they were in bloom, and bring them to her saying: "Take them! They're from Cabeço." She would take them and sometimes with tears streaming down her cheeks she would say: "I'll never go back there! Nor to Valinhos, and not even to the Cova da Iria! I miss them so much!"
>
> "But what does that matter, if you go to heaven to see Our Lord and Our Lady?"
>
> "That's right!" she would respond. And she would happily pick petals from her bunch of flowers, counting them one by one.[64]

Jacinta's docility

Jacinta had such a great desire to sacrifice herself that she was not convinced that it was enough to carry the heavy cross of her illness with patience and resignation. But the disease was inexorably taking complete control. Another confidential admission made to her cousin shows the beauty of her soul. "When I'm alone I get out of bed to pray the prayers of the angel. But now I can't reach the floor with my head because I fall over, so I pray only on my knees."[65]

She needed the prudent advice of a priest, the pastor of Olival, to dissuade her from this particular sacrifice. She followed this suggestion with docility, seeing in it the will of God.

On the way to heaven

Naturally, the family hoped that the children would recover, especially Jacinta, because it seemed at one point that the worst was over for her. But the two visionaries knew that any improvement in their condition was only temporary. Lúcia records how Our Lady visited the sick children at home.

Jacinta recuperated somewhat in the meantime. She could even get up and then would spend the days sitting on Francisco's bed. One day she called for me, saying that I should come to her quickly. I went running over.

"Our Lady came to us and said she was coming very soon to take Francisco to heaven. She also asked me if I wanted to convert more sinners. I said yes. She told me I would go to a hospital, and there I would suffer a lot; that I would suffer for the conversion of sinners, in reparation for sins against the Immaculate Heart of Mary, and for the love of Jesus. I asked her if you would be coming with me. She said no. This is what cost me the most. She said that my mother would bring me and afterward I would be all alone!"[66]

The solitude of the cross

Jacinta found it very hard to be separated from her cousin, who was her confidant. To whom could she talk intimately about their spiritual experiences if not Lúcia? As a rule the crosses we imagine are greater than those we really bear, and so Jacinta suffered when she tried to imagine what the hospital would be like. She would say, "It could be that the hospital is a big house, very dark, where you can't see anything; and I will be there to suffer all alone!"[67] Once more, her desire to make reparation and to convert sinners proved greater than the suffering it cost her.

Our Lady announces Jacinta's future

Jacinta received more visits from Our Lady, who again appealed to her generosity. According to Lúcia's testimony, Our Lady visited Jacinta at home four times. She showed Jacinta the next steps she would have to take here on earth before departing for heaven. This news caused her both suffering and joy. She felt happy to know that she would soon contemplate in heaven the Lady clothed in light, whom she had seen in the Cova da Iria between May and October. She suffered, however, at the separation from her loved ones, and she imagined the loneliness she would experience. Once more, her cousin Lúcia, in her praiseworthy task as chronicler, tells us of all these events:

The most Holy Virgin deigned to visit Jacinta again, to tell her of new crosses and sacrifices. She gave me the news and said: "She told me I will go to Lisbon to another hospital; that I won't return to see you or my parents; and that after suffering a lot I will die alone. But she said not to be afraid because she will come to get me and will take me to heaven."

And crying, she hugged me and said: "I'll never see you again. You will not come to visit me there. Oh, please pray for me very much because I'll die alone."[68]

The little girl was climbing her own personal Calvary. Lúcia gives us more details relating to Jacinta's final sufferings and death:

> She suffered horribly right up to the day that she went to Lisbon. She hugged me and sobbed: "I will never see you again! Nor my mother, nor my brothers, nor my father! I will never see anyone again! And afterward I will die alone!"
>
> "Don't think about this," I told her one day.
>
> "I want to think about it because the more I think the more I suffer, and I want to suffer for love of Our Lord and for sinners. After that it doesn't matter to me, because Our Lady will come there to take me to heaven."
>
> Sometimes she would kiss a crucifix, and embracing it she would say: "O my Jesus, I love you and I want to suffer very much for your love."
>
> Other times she would say: "O my Jesus, now you can convert many sinners, because this sacrifice is very big!"
>
> Sometimes she asked me: "Am I going to die without the hidden Jesus? If only Our Lady will bring him to me when she comes to get me!"
>
> I asked her one time: "What are you going to do in heaven?"
>
> "I am going to love Jesus and the Immaculate Heart of Mary very much, and ask many things for you, for sinners, for the Holy Father, for my parents, my brothers, my sisters, and for all those people who have asked me to pray for them."
>
> When her mother looked sad seeing her so sick, Jacinta would say: "Don't be upset, Mother; I'm going to heaven. There I will pray very much for you."
>
> Other times she would say: "Don't cry. I'm all right."
>
> If they asked her if she needed anything she would say: "Thank you very much, I don't need anything." When they left she would say: "I'm so thirsty but I don't want to drink anything. I'm offering it to Jesus for sinners."
>
> One day when my aunt was asking me some questions, Jacinta called me and said: "I don't want you to say anything to anyone about my suffering, not even my mother, because I don't want her to be upset."
>
> One day I found her embracing an image of Our Lady and saying to her, "O my dearest Mother of Heaven, so I have to die all alone?"

The poor child seemed frightened at the idea of dying alone. To encourage her, I would tell her: "What difference does it make if you die alone, as long as Our Lady comes to take you?"

"It's true! It doesn't matter to me at all. I don't know why, but sometimes I don't remember that she is coming to get me. I only think that I'll die without you being near me."[69]

Jacinta's sorrow at Francisco's death

The period of time after her brother's death was very sad for Jacinta. She still had the courage to give him a few messages before Francisco died. "Give all my love to Our Lord and Our Lady, and tell them I'll suffer as much as they want for the conversion of sinners and in reparation to the Immaculate Heart of Mary."[70]

Humanly speaking, however, she felt this blow deeply, in spite of all her good will. "Jacinta suffered a lot at the death of her brother. She spent a lot of time thinking, and if anyone asked her what she was thinking about, she would answer: 'Francisco. How I want to see him!' And her eyes filled with tears."[71]

Favors obtained by Jacinta during her lifetime

In her *Memoirs*, Sister Lúcia refers to certain favors that people attributed to Jacinta's intercession even during her lifetime.

The conversion of a woman

The three children were sometimes insulted and ill-treated by a neighbor who ridiculed them whenever she met them. On one occasion, however, she had just paid a visit to the tavern and was especially insulting. Without the slightest complaint, Jacinta merely said, when the poor woman had left them in peace:

"We have to pray to Our Lady and offer her sacrifices for the conversion of this woman. She says many sinful things and if she doesn't go to confession, she'll go to hell."

Some days passed and we were running by the front door of this woman's house. Suddenly Jacinta stopped in her tracks, turned around and asked: "Listen, is tomorrow the day we are going to see the Lady?"

"Yes, it is."

"Then let's not play anymore. Let's make this sacrifice for the conversion of sinners."

Without thinking that someone might see her, she lifted her little
hands to heaven and made the offering. The woman was watching
attentively through the shutters of her house. She later told my mother
that she had been so impressed by what Jacinta did that she didn't need
any other proof to believe in the truth of the apparitions. From that
time on not only did she never insult us, but she continually asked us to
pray to Our Lady for her, that her sins would be forgiven.[72]

Cure of hiccups

Reading about the following incident that Lúcia recounts, we can
understand better what it was like when Jesus passed through towns and
villages during his earthly life:

> The first time that the good Senhora Emilia came to get me to bring
> me to Olival, to the house of Senhor Vigario, Jacinta came with me. It
> was already night when we arrived in the village where this good
> widow lived. In spite of that, the news of our arrival spread quickly,
> and we were soon surrounded by innumerable people. They wanted to
> see us, question us, ask for graces, etc.
>
> There was a devout woman who used to recite the Rosary in her
> house, together with others from the small village who wanted to join
> her. So she came there to ask us if we would like to join her in praying
> the Rosary in her house. We wanted to excuse ourselves, saying that we
> were going to recite it with Senhora Emilia. But this woman was so
> insistent that we had no other choice but to give in. When word spread
> that we were going there, people crowded into the house of the good
> woman....
>
> Along the way a young woman about twenty came to meet us, cry-
> ing. She knelt down and begged us to come to her house to pray at least
> one Hail Mary for her father. For over three years he had been unable
> to sleep because of continual hiccups. It was impossible to refuse this
> heart-rending request.
>
> I helped the young woman to get up. Because it was already quite
> late and we were finding our way by the light of lanterns, I told Jacinta
> to go with her, and I would go to pray the Rosary with the people, and
> call for her on my way back. She agreed.
>
> When I returned, I too entered that house. I found Jacinta sitting
> on a chair, facing a man who was also sitting down. He wasn't very old,
> but he looked quite emaciated, and he was sobbing. I assumed that the
> people gathered around him were members of his family. When she
> saw me, Jacinta got up and said good-bye, promising she would not for-
> get him in her prayers. Then we went to Senhora Emilia's house.
>
> The next day, we left early in the morning for Olival, and only
> returned three days later. Upon arriving at the house of Senhora

Emilia, the same young woman came there with her father. He looked much better and no longer had that extremely nervous and weak appearance. They came to thank us for the grace they received, saying that the hiccups no longer bothered him. Every time I passed by there, this good family always came to thank me. They said that he was completely cured and never again had even the slightest symptom of hiccups.[73]

Return of a prodigal son

The other favor was received by one of my aunts named Vitoria, who was married and lived in Fátima. She had a son who was quite a prodigal. I don't know why, but he had abandoned his family home and no one knew what had happened to him.

Upset over this, my aunt came to Aljustrel one day to ask me if I would pray to Our Lady for her son. Not finding me, she asked Jacinta instead, and she promised to pray for him. A few days later he appeared suddenly and returned home to ask his parents' forgiveness. Then he went to Aljustrel to tell his sad story.

He said that after he had spent all he had stolen from his parents, he wandered around for a while as a vagrant until ... he was thrown into jail in Torres Novas. After staying there some time he managed to escape one night, fleeing under cover of darkness between unfamiliar hills and a pine forest.

Realizing he was completely lost, and torn between the fear of being captured and the darkness of a dense and stormy night, he took recourse in prayer. Some minutes passed, he affirmed, and then Jacinta appeared to him. She took him by the hand and led him to the paved road that leads from Alqueidão to Reguengo, and then made a sign for him to continue along that way. When morning dawned, he found himself on the road to Boleiros. Realizing where he was, he was deeply moved and went home to his parents' house.

He maintained that it was Jacinta who had appeared to him. I asked Jacinta if she had been his guide. She told me no, saying she did not even know where the hills and pine forest were that he had been lost in.

"I only prayed and begged Our Lady very much for him because I felt so bad for Aunt Vitoria. That was how she answered me."

"So then how did this happen?"

"I don't know, God knows."[74]

From Aljustrel to the hospital in Ourém

From July 1, 1919, three months after Francisco's death, until August 31, Jacinta was a patient in the Hospital of Saint Augustine in Vila Nova de Ourém. But her condition did not improve. Against all expectations, the painful treatment did her no good whatever. When her mother visited her, Jacinta told her she wanted to see her cousin. She was absolutely delighted when, after some time, she saw Lúcia at her bedside. Jacinta asked her mother to leave them by themselves for a while. Lúcia took this opportunity to ask her if she was suffering much. She responded: "Yes, I am suffering, but I offer everything for sinners and in reparation to the Immaculate Heart of Mary."[75]

Return home from the hospital

Since her hospitalization proved ineffective, Jacinta returned to her parents' home in Aljustrel, and in this loving environment, she recovered slightly. She had a large open wound in her chest that had to be dressed daily, causing her great suffering. Yet she never complained, nor did her face ever show the slightest annoyance. Despite her weakness, she kept on praying.

She was not spared the endless interrogations, and now, confined to bed, she could no longer escape. But she did not waste this opportunity of continuing her mission. "I am offering this sacrifice, too, for the conversion of sinners,"[76] she said with resignation.

Perhaps because all the questions revived the memories of the places where she had received so many graces, she sometimes confided in her cousin. "'How I would love to go to Cabeço and pray a Rosary in that place. But I can't go anymore. When you go to the Cova da Iria, pray for me. I surely will never go there again,' she said, with tears running down her cheeks."[77]

Jacinta leaves for the Dona Estefânia Hospital in Lisbon

Meanwhile, Dr. Eurico Fernandes Lisboa, a distinguished doctor in the capital and a native of Viana do Castelo, came to Fátima. He examined Jacinta and decided to move her to the Dona Estefânia Hospital for Children in Lisbon. He was convinced that an operation would cure her pleurisy and save her life.

On January 21, 1920, as Our Lady had predicted, Jacinta was brought to Lisbon. Her mother and her brother António accompanied her. They arrived at the Rossio railway station, and both had a white handkerchief that they waved from time to time. This was the sign they had arranged with some women who were to meet them, but there must have been some mistake because no one appeared. To add to the pain of having to bring her daughter such a long distance, Jacinta's mother now found herself abandoned with a sick child in a strange city.

António knew nothing about Lisbon either, so he could not help her. But he could read and ask for information. He returned shortly with two women who said they were friends of the Baron of Alvaiázere. Unfortunately they had no room in their homes for the mother and child and could only help them to find somewhere to stay.

The real difficulty began precisely here, when they were looking for lodgings for the sick child, because the hospital had no vacancies just then. With the help of some friends, Father Manuel Formigão undertook to find them lodgings.

They approached the best families in Lisbon, but all refused to take her. Fear of contagion, the extra work involved, interruption of their daily routine, or even fear of the persecution recently aroused by the apparitions could have been reasons for refusing.

After a long and exhausting search, a good woman took them in for a week. Then they were finally received into the orphanage of Our Lady of Miracles, in Rua da Estrela, founded and managed by Mother Godinho. Jacinta came to have great confidence in her. Furthermore, the atmosphere in this house, almost like a family, took her away from the anonymous environment of the hospital.[78]

This house was next to the Chapel of the Miracles and had a choir stall from which a person could see the tabernacle and participate in the daily Mass celebrated there. Jacinta was overjoyed when she found out about this shortly after she arrived. It was hard for her to express how much it meant to her to live under the same roof as Jesus in the Blessed Sacrament.[79] In fact, as long as she remained there, Jacinta could receive Holy Communion every day, carried in her mother's arms or, after Olímpia had returned home, by the superior.

One day, Jacinta asked her mother if she could go to confession. Her mother brought her to the nearby Church of Estrela. When they returned, Jacinta told her mother the priest had been very, very good to her and asked her many questions.

Jacinta showed her love for the Blessed Sacrament by praying in the chapel as much as she was able to. She sat in a little chair, because she could no longer kneel, and fixed her eyes on the tabernacle, praying and meditating.

It seems that Our Lady visited Jacinta in the orphanage several times. On one occasion Jacinta asked her godmother—as she called the lady who took her in—not to sit on a certain chair in her room because she said that Our Lady had occupied it. Before being taken to the hospital, Jacinta said that Our Lady had appeared, assuring her that she would die; as a result, Jacinta felt the surgery would be of no use.

She sent word to Lúcia that Our Lady "had come to see her there; she had told her the day and hour of her death"[80] and reminded her cousin to be very good.

Her mother went to see her several times. And one day Jacinta also had the pleasant surprise of a visit from her father. He could only stay a short time because many people were sick in the family and they had to be cared for.

On February 2, 1920, she was admitted to the Dona Estafânia Hospital to undergo the operation in which the doctors put so much hope. She immediately felt the coldness and anonymity of the hospital. The operation took place on February 10. Although it was successful, it did not have the hoped-for result.

Jacinta was so weakened that she could not be completely anesthetized. She found the procedure embarrassing and cried when they removed her clothes. The operation began, and Dr. Castro Freire removed two infected ribs from her left side.

Leonor da Assunção, a retired nurse who was not practicing her religion, knew Jacinta while she was in the hospital. The nurse told her colleague, Mariana Reto Mendes, that Jacinta had ribs removed and wore a dressing with a drain, the latter with a Dakin solution. Mariana commented that this kind of treatment burns a lot and is quite painful. Leonor said that Jacinta never complained, but endured everything without any sign of suffering.

Our Lady must have continued to appear to Jacinta in the hospital, according to the testimony of the lady who took her into her house. When anyone stood in a certain place beside the bed, Jacinta would tell them to move because Our Lady had been there.

Jacinta declared that Our Lady had told her that the sin that sends most people to hell is the sin of the flesh, that we must avoid luxury, that we must stop sinning, and that we must do much penance.

It was just a few days before Jacinta would go to heaven. She was asked, therefore, if she would like to see her mother once more. She answered in all simplicity that her family would not live much longer

and that soon they would all meet in heaven. She spoke of a last apparition of Our Lady, adding that it would not be to her because she was
going to die very soon.[81]

On February 16, four days before her death, Jacinta was complaining of great pain. Mother Godinho encouraged her to bear her sufferings patiently because that would please God. The next morning Jacinta
said to her: "See, godmother! I'm not complaining anymore! Our Lady
appeared to me again, saying that she would come for me soon and I
won't suffer anymore!"[82] And, in fact, from that day until her death, she
never again complained or showed any sign of suffering.

Peaceful death

At 6:00 P.M. of Friday, February 20, Jacinta called the nurse, Aurora
Gomes, of whom she was very fond. She told her that she was going to
die and wanted to receive the last sacraments, although she had been to
confession and received Communion before coming to the hospital.

She made her confession to the parish priest of Anjos, Father
Pereira dos Reis,[83] on the day of her death, at 6:00 in the evening. He
promised to bring her Holy Communion the next morning, but Jacinta
died at 10:30 P.M. The nurse had to leave the room for a few moments
but returned in time to see Jacinta draw her last breath. She died on the
first Friday of Lent. She was only nineteen days short of her tenth birth-
day. For her the great Easter of heaven had begun. But the time she
spent in the hospital was, without doubt, the most painful part of her
way of the cross.

Jacinta's funeral

Immediately after closing her eyes to the light of this world, Jacinta's
face became rosy again, and a heavenly smile lit up her lips. After her
death, someone suggested that she be transported and buried in her
hometown.

But the first plan was to bury her in Lisbon, and a day was settled,
February 22, the first Sunday of Lent, for her burial in one of the city's
cemeteries. A public fund was opened at once to defray the funeral
expenses.

Informed the following morning of the death of the child whose
affection he had won, Dr. Eurico Lisboa set about solving the problems

involved. He invited Dona Amélia de Sande e Castro, his patient in his work as an ophthalmologist, to ask the Marchioness of Rio Maior and the Marchioness of Lavradio, her cousins, to provide a burial garment for Jacinta.

Jacinta had expressed a wish to be clothed in blue and white, like Our Lady. The Marchioness of Rio Maior offered a white first Communion dress that was used for poor children of the parish; the Marchioness of Lavradio offered white garments and money for a blue sash in which the little body of the visionary would be buried. Jacinta's body was placed in a white coffin. This good doctor thought that, if the apparitions at Fátima were ever fully accepted as worthy of belief, it would be convenient to bury Jacinta's body in a place where it could be easily identified.

A wake was held in the Church of the Angels while the legal formalities for the burial were being completed. The body was placed in one of the rooms attached to the church. Later it was moved to the mortuary belonging to the Confraternity of the Blessed Sacrament, above the sacristy of the same parish. An incalculable number of people attended the wake.

On June 11, 1934, António Rebelo de Almeida made the following statement:

> I seemed to be seeing an angel. Lying in the coffin, she looked almost alive, with rosy lips and face; she was very beautiful. I have seen many corpses of both children and adults, but never like this.
>
> The pleasant aroma that came from the body has no natural explanation, no matter what anybody says. The most incredulous person could no longer doubt.... The little girl had been dead for three and a half days and the fragrance from her body was like a bouquet made up of a great variety of flowers.
>
> The number of visitors who wanted to see the child was very great.... I did not allow anyone to remove pieces of clothing as relics. On that point I was adamant. When people arrived in front of the coffin, they showed enthusiasm, admiration, and excitement.[84]

A large crowd of people mobbed the coffin because everyone wanted to touch the child's clothes with religious objects—rosaries, holy cards, etc.—and even to take away a relic, if possible. The parish priest was concerned that all this would turn into a public cult. Besides, he did not want to annoy the cardinal patriarch—who was already skeptical about the apparitions in the Cova da Iria. Furthermore, the public health authorities could raise serious issues, which, in fact, they later did, since the country was still ravaged by the influenza epidemic. Hence, the priest ordered the people to leave, but they ignored his orders, which gave rise to bad feelings and unfavorable comments.

The funeral was scheduled to take place in Lisbon, but then the Baron of Alvaiázere offered a vault belonging to him in the cemetery of Vila Nova de Ourém. The preparation of the vault took about two days. On February 23, the coffin was brought back to the Church of the Angels. However, before it was finally closed, many groups of people who wanted to see Jacinta's body for the last time were allowed to do so. Only small groups were permitted, to avoid disorder. This pilgrimage continued all day. People filed past the coffin with great respect and real devotion, remarking on the rosy complexion of Jacinta's face. Finally António Rebelo de Almeida gathered together some people to identify the remains of the little visionary, before enclosing them in a lead casket. To everyone's amazement, the child's body had the same pleasant fragrance that had been perceived just after her death.

The next day, Tuesday, at 11:00 A.M., the lead casket was sealed and the coffin closed. That same afternoon, it was brought to the Rossio railway station, accompanied by many people who walked there despite the rain. It was placed in a railway carriage traveling to Chão de Maçãs, and from there a vehicle would carry it to Ourém.

As handkerchiefs waved in farewell, the train moved off toward the north. Jacinta's body was brought to Vila Nova de Ourém, where it was buried in the vault belonging to the Baron of Alvaiázere.

Jacinta's parents were devastated by her death. Ti Marto had only managed one quick visit to Jacinta, and he hoped to see her back home in good health because he had been told the operation was successful. Coming so soon after the death of their son Francisco, Jacinta's death was a bitter blow to him and his wife.

Some years later, on September 12, 1935, by order of Bishop José Alves Correia da Silva, Jacinta's coffin was brought to the cemetery in Fátima. A new vault had been built for her and Francisco so they would rest together and be nearer their family. Before the departure, the coffin was opened, and to the great amazement of everyone present, the child's face appeared perfectly incorrupt. A photograph was taken and sent to Sister Lucia.

Jacinta's remains were brought by car to Fátima, covered with rich silk quilts, and placed beside Francisco's coffin. Both were carried to the sanctuary and then into the confessional chapel, where the Archbishop of Évora, Manuel Mendes da Conceição Santos, celebrated Mass. When Mass was over, the mortal remains of the brother and sister were brought to the cemetery of Fátima. Jacinta's casket and the coffin with the bones of Francisco were sealed and locked into the shelves of the vault.

On March 13, 1952, upon the completion of the basilica in Fátima, Jacinta's mortal remains were brought to the first chapel on the left, near the high altar. On the other side rest the remains of Francisco, brought there on the same day.

To mark Jacinta's stay in the Dona Estefânia Hospital, a small statue of her was placed in the hospital corridor, along with a plaque near the area where she was bedridden. (Today what was once the infirmary has become a spacious corridor where the hospital administration functions.) A statue of the Immaculate Heart of Mary stands in Jacinta's honor in the garden. Since Jacinta's death, people have continued to place flowers in these two places, along with their prayer petitions.

CHAPTER 11

Lúcia's Journey

LÚCIA'S LIFE AFTER THE APPARITIONS

WITH JACINTA'S DEATH, only Lúcia remained in Aljustrel. With whom could she exchange confidences now? How was she going to carry out the mission Our Lady had entrusted to her to spread devotion to the Immaculate Heart?

Lúcia was also tormented by the endless interrogations and was in real danger of falling victim to the epidemic. The people nearest to her, unaware of Our Lady's promise to keep her in the world for some time longer, were afraid to lose the only living witness to the great happenings in Fátima. In addition, some people feared that she would continue to be persecuted or might even become the victim of kidnapping or an attempt on her life. People were genuinely concerned to find a place where Lúcia would be safe and could lead a peaceful life.

While she remained in Fátima, the little visionary was not preserved from suffering, especially of a moral nature. Lúcia was going through the difficult time of pre-adolescence, which led her to keep her doubts, uncertainties, and difficulties to herself. Meanwhile, external events added to her sorrows.

The death of António Santos

We have already mentioned how much Lúcia suffered over her father's death, especially because of the bonds of affection uniting them. Her sorrow was compounded by the fact that he had been the one person in her family who defended her when everyone else doubted the apparitions. From the beginning, António Santos believed in the sincerity of his youngest daughter.

With the marriage of Lúcia's sisters, the house was becoming emptier. The father's absence deepened this void because he had always brought joy and happiness into the home.

The pastor leaves Fátima

Lúcia also suffered considerably because the pastor left Fátima. Some people thought he did this because of the problems that the events in the Cova da Iria had caused him.

> The good priest grew more and more displeased and perplexed with regard to the apparitions, until one day he finally left the town. The news spread that His Reverence had left because of me, because he did not want to assume any responsibility for the events. Since he was a zealous pastor, greatly loved by the people, I suffered a lot because of this. Some pious women when meeting me would vent their disgust by insulting me, and sometimes they would send me away with a few slaps or kicks.[1]

Ill treatment

Some people maintained their aggressive attitude. Lúcia explained what sometimes happened when she was away from home: "On these trips I didn't always meet with esteem or kindness. On one side there were people who admired me and thought I was a saint, but there were always others who insulted me and called me a hypocrite, a visionary, and a witch."[2]

The questioning continues

People sought her out everywhere and exhausted her with questions. These interminable interrogations brought her more suffering every day.

After the miracle of the sun on October 13, curiosity had grown even greater. Anybody who went to the Cova da Iria tried to speak with Lúcia. Of course, people were motivated by genuine devotion as well as mere curiosity. During visits to the Cova da Iria, it was inevitable that questions would arise, since information about the events at Fátima was scanty at the time.

The death of Lúcia's cousins

Francisco and Jacinta's illnesses had caused Lúcia a great deal of suffering, not only because of her love for them, but also because she knew that they would die. After their deaths, Lúcia must have experienced great interior conflict and anxiety. From then on she had no one in whom to confide, no one to go to for counsel and advice. In addition, she could not visit Jacinta's tomb, because it was in the vault belonging to Baron Alvaiázere in Vila Nova de Ourém. She could visit only Francisco's grave in the Fátima cemetery.

At the pastor's house

With great charity, the pastor of Olival, Father Faustina José Jacinto Ferreira, sent a message to Lúcia's mother, asking her to allow her daughter to spend some days at his house to keep his sister company. Lúcia's mother gave her consent. Accompanied by a woman, Lúcia made the trip and spent a few days in the parish of Olival. The priest's thoughtfulness in this regard benefited Lúcia. He was practically the first spiritual director who seriously set out to help Lúcia and lead her to holiness. But in this respect, Lúcia made a judicious observation, indicating the priest had another reason for wanting to speak with her at length:

> At that time, I believed it to be like that. Today it seems to me that the reason must have been something else: so as to be better able to study the happenings, to observe my behavior closely, and to be able to speak with me at length, etc., in order to form a more certain and sure judgment, as far as possible.[3]

Lúcia leaves Fátima

It was becoming more difficult for Lúcia to remain in Fátima. The curious crowds only seemed to increase. Some people were alarmed at all this and asked Lúcia's mother to allow her to go away for a time to a place where she would be safe and well supervised. Lúcia's father had always categorically refused to allow her to leave home. But now that he had died, the decision rested with her mother. Although she would find Lúcia's absence difficult, Maria Rosa gave her consent.

Lúcia was sent away to rest, and no one was told where she was going. With the help of Father Formigão, Lúcia went to Lisbon from July 7 until August 6, 1920. Her mother felt deeply the separation from Lúcia, but she believed it would be the best thing for her daughter. She probably hoped that her daughter would regain her health, and that she would be freed from the inconvenient visitors who upset the family's life. Maria Rosa probably also cherished a secret hope that Lúcia's absence would finally put a stop to this unending stream of people to the Cova da Iria.

While Lúcia was in Lisbon, she was under the care of Dona Assunção Avelar. Lúcia was enrolled as a pupil in a private school. But word of her presence there began to spread. Dona Assunção Avelar, who had taken her into her home, was warned that the civil authorities were searching for the house where Lúcia was staying. Naturally, the kind lady was afraid, especially because she was a monarchist, who were still being persecuted at the time. Her fear of reprisals by the political authorities cut short Lúcia's stay in Lisbon.[4]

In Santarém

As the intent of the authorities became clear, Father Formigão's sister went immediately to Dona Assunção Avelar's house and took Lúcia with her to Santarém on the first night train. Father Formigão lived with his mother and sister. Lúcia was hidden in this house, never leaving it for any reason and never approaching the windows. The priest brought her Holy Communion secretly, under the pretext of celebrating Mass in one of the churches of the town.

After some days, it seemed that the danger of being pursued in Lisbon had passed, and she went to Mass in the Church of Santo Milagre. But people recognized her at once. Meanwhile, in Fátima, people were very worried about her, not knowing where she was. So she returned to Aljustrel on August 12, 1920. She had been away a little over a month.

In search of peace and quiet

The problem of getting Lúcia away from Fátima still remained to be solved. The solution came about through the farsightedness of the Bishop of Leiria, José Alves Correia da Silva, who had been installed as the diocesan bishop on August 5, 1920. He soon set out to solve this problem, seeking some arrangement that would not only take Lúcia away from Fátima but would also provide for her human, intellectual, and spiritual development. The bishop's plans for her were made with the greatest kindness and respect for her freedom. He wanted her to go to a boarding school in Porto. He did not impose his will on her but made a friendly suggestion in a meeting he had with Lúcia on June 13, 1921. The journey to meet the bishop was entrusted to Dona Gilda, who brought Lúcia there in her own carriage.

Lúcia dined and spent the night in Dona Gilda's house. While they were at supper, Dona Gilda asked Lúcia if she would like to assist at the Mass the bishop would celebrate in the cathedral the next morning. Lúcia said yes, so Dona Gilda asked if she would like to go to confession before the Mass, and if she would like to make her confession to the bishop. Lúcia said she preferred not to confess to the bishop because she would be shy; she would rather make her confession to the other priest who was there.

> Early in the morning the next day, we went to the cathedral. We went toward the high altar, and we saw there was a confessional to the left. A priest was hearing confessions. And when the person who was there finished, Senhora Dona Gilda got up to go to confession. I stayed there waiting, and when she left, I went to kneel down on the other side to go to confession. When I finished I went back to kneel next to Dona Gilda and was surprised to see the bishop leave the confessional. I turned to Dona Gilda and asked: "So, then, he was the bishop?"
>
> "Yes, it was," she answered. "Did you like him?"
>
> "Yes, I did," I replied.[5]

They received Holy Communion at the Mass, had breakfast in Dona Gilda's house, and then went to the bishop's residence. During their meeting, the bishop suggested that Lúcia go to school in Porto. In a spirit of obedience, Lúcia agreed. But first Gilda brought Lúcia back to Aljustrel to prepare for the trip.

The bishop's motives for sending Lúcia to Porto came out of his concern for her. She was the only visionary still alive, and he wanted to take her away from the unpleasant and sometimes ill-intentioned inter-rogations she still endured. Lúcia's mother, concerned that her daughter should choose this freely, would occasionally ask her: "Are you sad? Don't you want to leave for Porto? We didn't sign anything, so if you don't want to, don't go!"[6] In all sincerity, her daughter answered that she would rather go to Lisbon or to Santarém—she would be nearer her mother in either place—but that the bishop wanted her to go to Porto. So she would offer to the Lord the sacrifice of being so far away.

Her mother wanted to accompany Lúcia to Leiria, and from there she would set out for Porto by train. At 2:00 A.M. on the morning of June 16, 1921, the fourteen-year-old Lúcia left Aljustrel for Leiria. She walked, accompanied by her mother and Senhor Manuel Correia, who was going there to work. They went by the Cova da Iria so Lúcia could bid farewell and pray a Rosary there. Even today it is with emotion that we read the description of the journey that Lúcia gives in the sixth *Memoir*.[7] They arrived in Leiria at 9:00 A.M., after seven hours on the road.

In Fátima the evening before, Lúcia had visited all the family fields, firmly convinced that she would never see them again: the Cabeço, the rock, and Valinhos. She went to the parish church and once again visit-ed the cemetery and the graves of her father and Francisco.

Before Lúcia went to the home of her aunt and uncle, where her mother would stay for a few days, Maria Rosa went to a shop and bought a little traveling bag in which her daughter could put the few things she was bringing with her. She also bought some clothing, exercise books, school books, and other necessities.

Lúcia tells us in all simplicity:

> I still have that suitcase, which has accompanied me all my life. It's the one I carried with my few things when going on vacations. I brought it to Spain, when I went to be a religious; I took it to the beach every year, when on doctor's orders I went to bathe in the ocean. I took it to Portugal when I returned in 1946, and to Carmel when I transferred with permission of my superiors. In this suitcase I keep a few personal things that I treasure. I made a gray cotton cover for it so it wouldn't get ruined, and I brought it to Fátima the times I went there. It is a remembrance of my dear mother.[8]

Some doubt about the genuineness of the apparitions still tormented her mother when Lúcia departed from Leiria for Porto: "Go, daughter, and if it's true that you saw Our Lady she will take care of you. I entrust you to her, but if you lied, I don't know what will become of you."[9]

At 2:00 P.M., leaving her mother in tears, Lúcia set out for the College of Vilar, run by the Dorothean Sisters in Porto. She arrived the next morning. Both the reason behind the decision to go to Porto and the attitude that she should take from now on were explained to her:

> Precisely because in Porto I didn't know anyone … it was fitting that I go there. To avoid being recognized I would change my name, and I would not say where I was from or whose daughter I was, nor would I speak about any other person in my family. Only the lady to whom the bishop entrusted me, and the superior of the school where I would go would know who I was—no one else. So then people wouldn't start to go there to find me, wanting to speak to me, to disturb me and take the time I had to devote to study.[10]

Her mother visited Lúcia once a year while she was in Porto. In the last year that she lived there, Bishop José Alves Correia da Silva invited Lúcia and her mother to spend a few days in the Quinta da Formigueira in Braga, where he gave Lúcia the sacrament of Confirmation. Her mother was very happy to be present.

Lúcia is now called Maria das Dores

In the school Lúcia was known as Maria das Dores. She received an excellent education—human, professional, and spiritual—and she completed her primary education and learned needlework. At this time her physical appearance was described in this way:

> High and broad head, large and lively brown eyes. Thin eyebrows, flat nose, large mouth, thick lips, a round chin. The face has something supernatural. The hair auburn and fine. Small stature but tall for her age. Strong features but a friendly face. An air of seriousness and innocence. Lively and intelligent, but modest and without pretensions. Rough hands from work and of normal size.[11]

In Braga, wondering about her vocation

During this time Lúcia went to Braga, where the bishop had an estate[12] and used to spend his holidays. Lúcia lived in Braga for a while, going to the Bom Jesus do Monte, where the Pestana family of Porto welcomed her into their home. The rural environment to which Lúcia refers in the sixth *Memoir* was disappearing because of the increasing urbanization of the area, except for the bishop's house and the land around it.

It was there that Lúcia met her mother and told her of the possibility that she might enter religious life. Lúcia tells how this came about on one of her mother's yearly visits to the College of Vilar. Lúcia took advantage of the opportunity to ask her mother's permission to become a religious. She replied:

> "My daughter, I don't know anything about that kind of life. I will ask the bishop."
>
> She went downstairs to look for the bishop, who was sitting on a bench in front of the porch, reading in the shade of the trellised vines. As soon as the bishop saw her, he called her and had her sit next to him on the bench. I watched from above the porch. I didn't hear what they were saying, but my mother came back after a long conversation. She was happy to tell me yes, on the condition that I would let her know if I wasn't happy and it didn't work out well.[13]

Lúcia began to feel more and more the desire to consecrate herself to the Lord. At first she was thinking about entering Carmel, but she decided instead on the Institute of Saint Dorothy, moved by the good example of her teachers in the school and also by a sense of gratitude.

Lúcia, a Dorothean Sister

The following details summarize Lúcia's early years in religious life. On October 24, 1925—which at that time was the feast of the Archangel Gabriel—Lúcia de Jesus arrived in the Dorothean convent of Túy, Spain, to start her postulancy. She was accompanied by the provincial superior and by Mother Meireles. The following day, she left for the convent at Travessa Isabel II in Pontevedra, Spain, where she spent the time of her postulancy (October 25, 1925 to July 20, 1926).

On October 2, 1926, she returned to Túy to begin the novitiate. When she arrived, she went to the Church of Saint Francis to receive Holy Communion, and from there to the Dorothean convent in Calle Martinez Padin. She was received there by the provincial superior, Mother Monfalim. Lúcia was entrusted to the care of the director of novices, Maria da Penha Lemos, and at once began the time of preparation to receive the habit. Lúcia made temporary vows on October 3, 1928, and she made her final vows six years later, on October 3, 1934. Then she was assigned again to the convent in Pontevedra and remained there until May 1937, when she returned to Túy.[14]

Lúcia's religious life progressed quite naturally; nothing occurred to draw people's attention. Just as she had always done, she continued to practice charity toward the most needy. She also used her special gift for dealing with children, which had been apparent from the days when the patio of her home was crowded with children while their mothers worked. "Lúcia is very good with children, and with everyone who approaches her. In the house she never attracts attention to herself, although she is witty and full of fun. If she stands out in any way, it is perhaps because of her spirit of prayer, her strict observance of the rule, and her love of Our Lady."[15]

During these years the promise made by Our Lady in the Cova da Iria on July 13, 1917, began to be fulfilled. She made two requests of Lúcia: the consecration of Russia, and the devotion of the first Saturdays. Lúcia received these requests in the Spanish towns of Tui and Pontevedra, where she was living as a Dorothean religious.

THE FIRST SATURDAYS
AND THE CONSECRATION OF RUSSIA

During the July apparition, after the frightening vision of hell, Our Lady made the three children a promise to take them all to heaven, but that Lúcia would stay longer on earth because she had a special mission. She was to spread devotion to the Immaculate Heart of Mary.

Lúcia received more instructions about this while she was in Pontevedra. One day while she was praying in her room, Our Lady appeared to her and made a particular promise. Lúcia describes what happened, using the third person to refer to herself in order to remain anonymous:

> On December 10, 1925, the most Holy Virgin appeared to her, and a child was by her side, suspended on a luminous cloud. The most holy Virgin rested her hand on her [Lúcia's] shoulder, and at the same time, she showed her a heart that she was holding in her hands, surrounded by thorns. At the same time, the child said: "Take pity on the heart of your most holy Mother, covered with thorns, with which ungrateful men pierce it at every moment. And there is no one to make an act of reparation to remove them."
>
> The Most Holy Virgin then said: "See, my daughter, my heart surrounded with thorns, with which ungrateful men pierce me at every moment by their blasphemies and ingratitude. You at least try to console me. Tell everyone who, on the first Saturday of five consecutive

months, shall go to confession, receive Holy Communion, recite five decades of the Rosary, and keep me company for fifteen minutes while meditating on the fifteen mysteries of the Rosary, with the intention of making reparation to me, that I promise to assist them, at the hour of their death, with all the graces necessary for the salvation of their souls."[16]

Lúcia later wrote a second account of this apparition when ordered to do so by her spiritual director.

Apparitions of the Child Jesus

Lúcia also received an apparition of the Child Jesus while she was at Pontevedra. The rainy season was beginning, and in that area of the country the rains are torrential. It was necessary to clean out all the drainpipes to prevent flooding.

Lúcia was still a postulant, and she was not spared certain seemingly humiliating trials. It was quite normal for the director in charge of her formation to try her in various ways, fearing that the devil could tempt Lúcia to pride since she had received so many graces. Perhaps that is why she was given the extremely difficult and unpleasant task of cleaning the drainpipes.

She took all the necessary tools and set off at once, without giving any excuses for not performing the task. She showed no sign of displeasure, nor did she complain. When she returned, the novice director was waiting at the top of the stairs to see how Lúcia had fared. With a certain admiration, the director saw that Lúcia came back radiantly happy. When she asked why she was so joyful, she told her quite simply what had just happened. She must have been referring to what she later wrote down regarding this meeting:

> On the fifteenth (of December 1925), I was occupied with my duties, and I wasn't remembering this at all.[17] I went outside to dispose of some garbage in the area beyond the vegetable garden. It was in the same location where I had met a child a few months earlier. I had asked him if he knew the Hail Mary, and when he said yes, I asked him to recite it for me. But he didn't even try to say it on his own, so I recited it with him three times. Then I asked him to recite it by himself. But he kept quiet. Because he couldn't say the Hail Mary alone, I asked him if he knew where the Church of Santa Maria[18] was, and he said yes, he did. I said that he should go there every day and pray: "O my

heavenly Mother, give me your Child Jesus!" I taught him this prayer and then left.

On February 15, 1926, I went there as I often did and I met a child, who seemed to be the same one. I asked him: "So then, did you ask our heavenly Mother for the Child Jesus?"

The child turned toward me and replied: "And have you spread throughout the world what our heavenly Mother asked of you?"

Thereupon he was transformed into a radiant child. Realizing then that it was Jesus, I said: "My Jesus, you know very well what my confessor told me in the letter that I read to you. He said that the vision had to be repeated, that more things must happen to prove its credibility, and that Mother Superior, by herself, could do nothing to spread this devotion." [19]

The letter Lúcia was referring to was one she received from Monsignor Pereira Lopes of Porto, who had been her confessor when she was at the school of the Dorothean Sisters, in Ruo do Vilar, Porto. After receiving his letter, Lúcia realized that she would not be able to carry out Our Lady's wishes just then. But she was at peace because she knew that obedience was most pleasing to God. For the time being she could only wait and carry on with her duties as best she could.

Difficulties in living the first Saturdays

It appeared that heaven was asking the impossible. It was not easy for a religious in the quiet of her room, isolated from the media of communication and wishing to remain anonymous, to fulfill the task that Our Lady had entrusted to her. Besides, Lúcia began to have doubts, but the Lord was to remove them. In describing her difficulties she continued to use the third person in order to hide her identity:

On February 15, 1926, the Child Jesus appeared to her again. He asked her if she had already spread the devotion to his most holy Mother. She put before him the confessor's difficulties, and said that Mother Superior was ready to spread it, but that the confessor had said she couldn't do anything by herself.

Jesus responded: "It is true that your superior can do nothing by herself, but she can do everything with the help of my grace."

She presented to Jesus the difficulty that some people had in going to confession on Saturday, and asked him if it would be valid to go to confession within eight days. Jesus replied: "Yes, and it could even be longer, as long as they are in the state of grace when they receive me, and have the intention to make reparation to the Immaculate Heart of Mary."

She further asked: "My Jesus, what if people forget to make this intention?"

Jesus said: "They can make the intention at their next confession, taking advantage of their earliest opportunity to go to confession."[20]

Lúcia continues to relate the sequence of events. The text which follows is a document written by Sister Lúcia at the end of 1927, by order of her spiritual director, Father Aparício, S.J. This document is, however, the second she wrote, identical to the first except that Lúcia added an introductory paragraph referring to the date, December 17, 1927, and explaining how she received permission from heaven to make known part of the secret.

This document is called "Text of the Great Promise of the Immaculate Heart of Mary." In effect, it is an expression of the merciful and gratuitous divine will, giving us an easy and sure means of salvation, since it is based on the soundest Catholic tradition, that of the saving efficacy of Mary's intercession.

In this text we can find the necessary conditions and the deepest intentions for answering the call of the five first Saturdays: reparation for injuries inflicted on the Immaculate Heart of Mary. In this text Lúcia again uses the third person:

> On December 17, 1927, she was before the tabernacle asking Jesus how she could carry out the task she had been given, that is, if the origin of devotion to the Immaculate Heart of Mary was part of the secret that the Most Holy Virgin had entrusted to her.
>
> Jesus, in a clear voice, let her hear these words: "My daughter, write down what they request, and also write everything that the Most Holy Virgin revealed to you in the apparition in which she spoke of this devotion. Continue to keep silence concerning the rest of the secret."[21]

Some days later, Sister Lúcia wrote her account as Jesus directed, which was sent to Monsignor Pereira Lopes, who later became vicar general of the Diocese of Porto. He had also been Lúcia's confessor while she was in the College of Vilar in the city of Porto.[22]

> Then he disappeared, and until today, I know nothing more about what heaven desires. And, as for me, I desire only that the flame of divine love should be enkindled in souls, and that, elevated by this love, they may greatly console the Sacred Heart of Mary.
>
> I, at least, want to greatly console my dear Heavenly Mother, suffering much for love of her; but right now I only have desires. When an

occasion arises for me to put up with a reprimand, a little word that wounds my self-love, or some small problem in my work, as soon as I can, I go to complain to Jesus in the Blessed Sacrament.

And sometimes I even complain to Mother Superior, telling her everything that happened. I hope that Jesus will tell me that he is pleased with me for keeping silent or for promptly carrying out the tasks I was given. And, if on some days I feel that Jesus is saddened with me, I simply feel like crying, and I don't know what to do to please him again. I must respectfully finish now, asking your Reverence to reply and let me know how I can best fulfill what heaven wants of me.[23]

Conditions for the devotion of the first Saturdays

Despite the difficulties, Lúcia committed herself to spreading the devotion of the first Saturdays. She had to follow a road similar to that of Saint Margaret Mary Alacoque, that is, Lúcia had to spread this devotion without identifying herself as the visionary of Fátima or speaking of the revelations that she had received about it.

Some people made known to Lúcia that they had found certain difficulties when they tried to live the devotion of the first Saturdays. So Lúcia asked Our Lady for explanations. When the Child Jesus appeared in the garden of Pontevedra and asked her if she had forgotten to spread the devotion of the First Saturdays, Lúcia answered:

> "But my confessor wrote to me that this devotion is not lacking in the world, because there are many souls who receive you on the first Saturdays, in honor of Our Lady and of the fifteen mysteries of the Rosary."
>
> [Jesus replied:] "It is true, my daughter, that many souls begin them [the first Saturdays], but few finish them, and those who do finish them do it because they want to receive the graces that are promised thereby. It would please me more if they completed five with a fervent spirit, having the intention to make reparation to the Heart of your heavenly Mother, than if they did fifteen in a lukewarm way...."[24]

The first measures taken to spread this devotion

Lúcia sought various ways to spread this devotion that Our Lady had requested. Lúcia approached people privately, carefully maintaining her anonymity. In a letter to her mother, besides comforting her in the

202 THE SHEPHERDS OF FÁTIMA

suffering caused by her own absence, Lúcia spoke enthusiastically about the devotion of the first Saturdays.

> I wish you would give me the consolation of embracing a devotion [the first Saturdays] that I know is pleasing to God and that was asked for by our dear Heavenly Mother. As soon as I came to know about it, I wanted to practice it and I wanted everyone else to practice it as well. I hope, dear Mother, that you will write and tell me that you have done so and have tried to get everyone around you to embrace it too. You could give me no greater consolation than this. It only entails doing what is written on this little holy picture. Confession can be on another day, but the fifteen minutes [of meditation] may cause the most confusion.
>
> But it's very easy. Is there anyone who cannot think about the mysteries of the Rosary? About the Annunciation of the angel and the humility of our dear Mother who, upon being so exalted, calls herself a servant? About the passion of Jesus, who suffered so much for our love? And our blessed Mother beside Jesus on Calvary? Thinking about these holy things, who could not spend fifteen minutes with our Mother, the most tender of mothers?
>
> Good-bye, dearest Mother. Console our heavenly Mother in this way, and try to get many other people to console her also; thus you will give me, too, unspeakable happiness.[25]

Lúcia also wrote to Dona Filomena Morais Miranda Santo Tirso, her confirmation sponsor. In a letter dated November 1, 1927, the visionary said:

> I don't know if you have heard about the devotion of the five Saturdays in reparation to the Immaculate Heart of Mary.... This is what it consists of: for five months, on the first Saturday, to receive Jesus in Holy Communion, to recite the Rosary, to spend fifteen minutes in the company of Our Lady while meditating on the mysteries of the Rosary, and to go to confession. Confession may be made some days before, and if we forgot to place that intention in the previous confession, we can place that intention in the next confession. On the first Saturday, however, we must be in the state of grace and have the intention to offer reparation for offenses committed against the Most Holy Virgin, which grieve her Immaculate Heart....[26]

The request that Russia be consecrated

When Lúcia was in the convent at Túy, another important development took place concerning the request for the conversion of Russia. This happened while Lúcia was praying in the convent chapel:[27]

Father José Bernardo Gonçalves came several times to hear confessions in our chapel. I made my confession to him. Because I felt he understood me well, he was my confessor for the three years that he was here as the socius.[28]

During this time Our Lady let me know that the time had arrived when she would share with the Holy Church her desire to have Russia consecrated [to her Immaculate Heart] and her promise to convert it.... This was her message:

June 13, 1929. I had received the permission I had asked for from my superiors and my confessor to make a holy hour every Thursday night, from eleven o'clock until midnight.

Alone one night, I knelt down between the altar rails in the middle of the chapel, to recite the angel's prayers prostrate on the floor. Because I was tired, I stood up and kept on reciting these prayers while I stretched out my arms like a cross. The only light came from the sanctuary lamp.

In a flash the entire chapel was lit by a supernatural light. A cross of light appeared above the altar, reaching to the ceiling. A brighter light on the upper part of the cross showed the face of a man and his body down to the waist, a dove of light on his breast, the body of another man nailed to the cross.

Just below the waist, a chalice and a very large Host could be seen suspended in the air. Drops of blood were falling on them from the face of the Crucified One and from the wound on his side.

These drops ran down onto the Host and then fell into the chalice. Our Lady was under the right arm of the cross ("she was Our Lady of Fátima with her Immaculate Heart ... in her left hand ... without a sword or roses but with a crown of thorns and flames ...") with her Immaculate Heart in her hand.... Under the left arm of the cross, large letters, like crystal clear water flowing down upon the altar, formed these words: "Grace and Mercy."

I understood that the mystery of the Blessed Trinity had been shown to me, and I received lights about this mystery that I am not allowed to reveal.

Then Our Lady said to me: "It is now the time when God is asking the Holy Father, in union with all the bishops of the world, to consecrate Russia to my Immaculate Heart, promising to save it by this means. So many souls are condemned by God's justice for sins committed against me that I have come to seek reparation: sacrifice yourself for this intention and pray."

I told this to my confessor and he told me to write down Our Lady's wishes.[29]

Lúcia wrote to her confessor, Father José Bernardo Gonçalves, S.J.:

What do I think happened between God and my soul regarding the devotion of reparation to the Immaculate Heart of Mary and the persecution of Russia?

It seems to me that our good God, in the depths of my heart, is insisting that I should ask the Holy Father to approve this devotion of reparation. God himself and the most holy Virgin deigned to ask for it in 1925, so that, in view of this small devotion, the grace of forgiveness will be granted to those souls who had the misfortune of offending the Immaculate Heart of Mary. The most holy Virgin promises those souls who seek to make reparation in the following manner that she will assist them at the hour of death with all the graces necessary for salvation.

The devotion consists of the following [practices] on the first Saturday of five consecutive months: to receive Holy Communion, to pray the Rosary, and to spend fifteen minutes in company with our Lady, meditating on the mysteries of the Rosary, and to go to confession for the same intentions. This [confession] may take place on another day. If I am not mistaken, the good God promises to end the persecution in Russia if the Holy Father deigns to make, together with the bishops of the Catholic world, a solemn and public act of reparation and consecration of Russia to the most holy Hearts of Jesus and Mary. As a response to the end of this persecution, His Holiness must approve and recommend the already indicated practice of the devotion of reparation.

I declare that I very much fear being mistaken. And the reason for this fear is that I did not personally see Our Lord, but only felt his divine presence.[30]

Sister Lúcia had already given the reasons why she found it so difficult to speak of this to her superior, admitting, among other possibilities, the action of the spirit of darkness.

Lúcia again wrote to her spiritual director, Father Gonçalves on October 28, 1934, and on January 21, 1935. She insisted on the necessity of the Holy Father consecrating Russia to the Immaculate Heart of Mary. "Three years ago, Our Lord was very displeased because his request had not been fulfilled."[31]

This consecration was finally made on March 25, 1984, by Pope John Paul II in Saint Peter's Square. The Pope made this consecration in front of the statue from the Chapel of the Apparitions in Fátima. The Bishop of Leiria, Alberto Cosme do Amaral, had brought the statue with him at the Holy Father's request. Pope John Paul II had spent the previous night in his private chapel, in a vigil of prayer in front of the statue. Before a crowd of 200,000 people, the Pope knelt before the statue and solemnly consecrated the world to the Immaculate Heart of Mary in union with the bishops of the whole world. Thus, according to Sister Lúcia, Our Lady's request was completely fulfilled.[32]

In a letter from Coimbra, dated November 8, 1989, to Walter N. Noelker, with reference to the consecration, Sister Lúcia said:

> The same supreme pontiff, John Paul II, wrote to all the bishops of the world, asking each one to make this consecration in his own diocese, with the People of God entrusted to him, in union with the Pope. He asked that the statue of Our Lady of Fátima be brought to Rome, and in front of it, in union with the bishops of the whole world [who were] in communion with the Pope, and in union with all the People of God, he made this consecration in Rome, publicly, in front of the statue of Our Lady of Fátima, on March 25, 1984. I have been asked since whether the consecration has been made as Our Lady requested. I responded that it was.

Sister Lúcia gave the same answer on November 21, 1989, to Father Paul Kramer.[33] Russian Communism began to break up, the Berlin Wall fell, and changes took place in the countries of Eastern Europe that had been under Communist rule.

Wars

Lúcia—already a Dorothean Sister—lived through the civil war that sowed death and destruction throughout Spain from 1936 to 1939. The confusion and antireligious persecution of these years originated from almost the first days of the Republic, in the early 1930s.[34] Fortunately, the Galicia region was not devastated by this whirlwind that bathed the people of Spain in tears and blood.

Communism here made a first attempt to impose, by force, its atheistic political system. Soviet soldiers and members of the Communist party from all over the world went to Spain to join in the fight.

A few months after the roaring cannons had ceased, World War II broke out. On September 1, 1939, the conflagration began in Europe when Hitler's troops invaded Poland. The war would last until 1945. In the apparition of July 13, 1917, Our Lady told the children that another war would break out if people did not stop sinning.

In 1925, Our Lady had promised that, by a special grace from her Immaculate Heart, Portugal would be preserved from this war. Sister Lúcia recorded this promise in a letter, which she carefully sealed.

At nightfall on January 25, 1938, Europe saw with amazement what
the scientists called an unusual aurora borealis, Lúcia recalled that this
was the sign Our Lady had foretold in July 1917. As September 1, 1939
approached, various attempts at reconciliation spurred hopes that the
danger had passed. Lúcia, however, insisted that the war was certainly
coming and that it would be terrible.

In a letter that she gave the Bishop of Leiria, who passed it on to
Cardinal Gonçalves Cerejeira, Lúcia said that Our Lady had promised
that Portugal would not be involved in the war, by a special privilege of
her Immaculate Heart. In one of the moments of greatest perplexity,
the cardinal showed this letter to the president of the council who
answered more or less as follows: "Only by a great miracle!"

Meanwhile the Portuguese bishops had made a vow to erect in
Lisbon, as had already been done in Rio de Janeiro, a statue of the
Sacred Heart of Jesus facing the city. Standing beside the Tagus, in
Almada, the statue is a perpetual memorial to this singular grace.

Lúcia enters Carmel

Sister Lúcia remained in Spain until May 1946, when she was
allowed to return to Portugal. She spent some days at home and again
visited the places connected with the apparitions: the Loca do Cabeço,
the well at Arneiro, Valinhos, and the Cova da Iria. She was assigned to
the convent in Sardão, in Villa Nova da Gaia near Porto. Feeling an ever
stronger attraction to the silence and enclosed life of Carmel, she
obtained from Pope Pius XII permission to transfer from the Dorothean
Sisters to the Carmel of Saint Teresa in Coimbra. She was received
there on March 25, 1948, the solemnity of the Annunciation of the
Lord. In Carmel she was known as Sister Maria Lúcia de Jesus e do
Coração Imaculado.

She went several times to the Sanctuary of the Immaculate
Conception at Monte Sameiro in Braga,[35] directing the work of reno-
vating a house that had been offered in the Bom Jesus sanctuary as a
Carmelite convent. She recalled the time she had spent vacations there
with the Pestana family of Porto, who had later offered her a house in
which to establish another Carmel. This dream was realized only when
Don Francisco Maria da Silva became Archbishop of Braga.

For the rest of her life, Lúcia visited Fátima only a few more times. She went to the Cova da Iria on May 13, 1967, for the visit of Pope Paul VI to the Sanctuary of Fátima. She went again on May 13, 1982, when Pope John Paul II came to Fátima to thank Our Lady for having saved his life during the assassination attempt. On this occasion she had a private meeting with the Holy Father in the basilica. Finally, she returned to Fátima on May 13, 1991, when John Paul II visited the shrine on the tenth anniversary of the attempt on his life, and again on May 13, 2000, when John Paul II beatified Francisco and Jacinta Marto.

Lúcia, the writer

Our Lady had told the three children to go to school and learn to read. Lúcia obeyed this command, and went on to write so much that the Fátima apparitions are the best documented in the history of the Church. Always obedient, Lúcia spent her life writing. Besides thousands of letters, she wrote six *Memoirs*. The first four are collected in one volume; the last two in a second volume.

In 2001, Sister Lúcia gave us another book: *Calls from the Message of Fátima*.

Coincidences

While she was still in Túy an interesting event occurred. Sister Lúcia met Josemaría Escrivá, founder of Opus Dei.

The Bishop of Túy-Vigo, José López Ortiz arranged this meeting. He had been a friend of Escrivá since their university days in Madrid. The bishop asked Sister Lúcia's superior to allow her to go to the bishop's residence. The bishop had arranged a code with the superior to indicate when Sister Lúcia could go to the residence. This code conveyed no information to indiscreet people who might be listening on the telephone, something that often happened during the post-war years. The message was: "Send me flowers!"

Sister Lúcia and Josemaría Escrivá had never met. All the same, Lúcia said emphatically to him: "Go as soon as possible to Portugal and found Opus Dei there!" He answered that he did not have a passport for Portugal, so she herself offered to negotiate with the civil authorities in

the district of Viana do Castelo to facilitate his entry into Portugal. That
was in 1945.

Sister Lúcia's death

Lúcia lived a long life as a Carmelite, offering her prayers and
sacrifices as Our Lady had requested. After many years of suffering and
prayer, she died on February 13, 2005, at the age of ninety-seven. People
all over the world mourned for her with a great outpouring of affection
and prayers. Lúcia was buried at the Carmelite cemetery in Coimbra
while a tomb for her was being prepared at the Basilica of Fátima. Her
body was later transferred there, where she lies next to her cousins,
Blesseds Jacinta and Francisco. On the third anniversary of her death,
February 13, 2008, Pope Benedict XVI waived the five-year waiting
period so that her cause for beatification could proceed.

CHAPTER 12

The Beatification of Francisco and Jacinta

THE FIRST STEPS were taken to open the cause of beatification for Jacinta and Francisco in 1946. This preliminary process began officially with a decree from the Bishop of Leiria, José Alves Correia da Silva, dated December 21, 1949. It wasn't until April 20, 1952, however, that the diocesan informative process was initiated (in the episcopal curia of Leiria). The process closed in 1979, under Bishop Alberto Cosme do Amaral.

Francisco's cause comprised seventy-nine sessions, of which sixty-three were held in Fátima and sixteen in Coimbra, in order to hear testimony from Sister Lúcia. Twenty-five witnesses were deposed, including his parents, four siblings, seven cousins, Father Manuel Nunes Formigão, and Father Manuel Ferreira Gonçalves, vicar of the district of Batalha. The process was concluded on August 3, 1979.

Jacinta's cause comprised ninety-eight sessions, of which seventy-eight were held in Fátima and twenty in Coimbra. Twenty-seven witnesses gave testimony, most of them the same people who had testified for Francisco. But they also included some persons who had been with the little girl in Lisbon during the last month of her life. The process was concluded on July 2, 1979, and the official documents were sent to the Congregation for the Causes of Saints in Rome.

On December 14, 1979, Father Paul Molinari, postulator general of the Society of Jesus, was appointed postulator for the cause of the visionaries of Fátima in Rome. Father Luis Kondor, of the Society of the Divine Word, was named vice-postulator of the same cause in Portugal.

Such a long delay was due first of all to the slowness of the process demanded by current canon law—the process could be introduced only after fifty years; information had to be collected in the home diocese; and the process itself had to be completed in Rome. Besides this, in the case of the little shepherds, another obstacle had to be overcome: the idea that children of that age could not practice virtue to a heroic degree. In fact, some theologians maintained that these children, young as they were, were not capable of living a virtuous life to a heroic degree. This hesitation held up the process considerably. But it is impossible to read Lúcia's words about her cousins, along with the depositions of the witnesses at the diocesan process, without being deeply impressed by the lives of these children.

Toward the end of December 1988, Cardinal Pietro Palazzini, who until recently had been prefect of the Congregation for the Causes of Saints, held a news conference and touched on this question. He spoke of the possibility of children practicing virtue to a heroic degree and therefore able to be beatified and canonized. He did not refer to the little shepherds of Fátima, however, and neither did he declare that they would soon be beatified, an idea that the media spread. Despite the lack of reference, it was concluded that the cardinal wanted to refer to Francisco and Jacinta, so much so that he had seated next to him the relator of the cause, Father Peter Gumpel, S.J.[1]

An enormous amount of documentation on the cause, meticulously copied and checked, arrived in Rome and was entrusted to Father Gumpel. After reading and studying all the documents, he drew up, with the collaboration of a competent Portuguese canonist, the so-called *Positio*, or report, about the lives of Francisco and Jacinta. This report was given to the theologians of the Congregation for the Causes of Saints, who unanimously agreed that the little shepherds had practiced the virtues to a heroic degree.

The process was concluded in May 1989, and the joyful news arrived in Fátima and the whole world that the heroicity of the virtues of the two little shepherds had been recognized.[2] On May 13, 1989, at a solemn celebration, the Bishop of Leiria-Fátima announced that the Holy Father, Pope John Paul II, had declared the heroicity of the virtues of the Servants of God Jacinta and Francisco Marto, granting them the title Venerable. Now all that was needed to beatify the two children was a duly approved miracle.

A miracle was in fact performed, and on June 28, 1999, it received official recognition. The miracle had taken place in Leiria and was received by Maria Emília Santos, a resident of the Saint Francis home who had been paralyzed for twenty-two years. On the night of March 25, 1987, through the intercession of Jacinta, Maria succeeded in sitting up in bed. The following is the decree from the Congregation for the Causes of Saints:

> With the beatification in view, the postulation submitted to the Congregation for the Causes of Saints for examination a presumed miraculous cure, attributed to their intercession. The case in question is that of Maria Emília Santos, Portuguese, who, in 1946, when she was sixteen, began to suffer from rheumatic fever, with a slight difficulty in walking. Two years later she had more severe pains in her legs, with loss of movement. She was thought to suffer from inflammation of the spinal marrow, probably of tubercular origin. She was subject to a surgery of the vertebral column, but it was not successful and she could no longer walk, due to severe pains in her lower limbs.
>
> In the University of Coimbra, she was operated on a second time. Her situation deteriorated still further, with paraplegia of her lower limbs. Maria Emília lay in a hard bed, and could move only her head and her hands. She was hospitalized in 1978 in the hospital of Leiria because of inexplicable feverish symptoms; she remained there for six years without obtaining any precise diagnosis.
>
> Given the failure of science, the patient, after twenty-two years of immobility, turned in confidence to divine help through the intercession of the Servants of God Jacinta and Francisco Marto. On March 25, 1987, the patient felt unexpected warmth in her feet and managed to sit up, something which she had found impossible for a long time. On February 20, 1989, she was able to get up and spontaneously took her first steps without any pain, after which she walked without difficulty, with the help of a cane.
>
> In 1997 the cúria of Leiria set up a diocesan inquiry into the cure, which was considered miraculous; the juridical validity of the final decision was recognized by the Congregation for the Causes of Saints by a decree of November 21 of that same year.
>
> The medical college of the dicastery, in the session of January 28, 1999, declared unanimously that the cure had been rapid, complete, lasting, and scientifically inexplicable.
>
> On March 7, 1999, the special meeting of the theological consultors was held, and on the following June 22, an ordinary session of the

cardinals and bishops, including the promoter of the cause, Cardinal Andrzej Maria Deskur. In both meetings, that of the consultors and that of the cardinals and bishops, a doubt was expressed as to whether the cure was a divine miracle, but the answer was affirmative.

Finally, the Holy Father John Paul II was given a careful account of all these facts by the prefect. Accepting the votes of the Congregation for the Causes of Saints, His Holiness ordered that the decree announcing the miraculous nature of the cure in question be promulgated. When all the above proceedings were concluded, a meeting was held with the Holy Father; present were the above-mentioned prefect, the cardinal promoter of the cause, and myself, the bishop secretary of the congregation, as well as all those who are normally present at such meetings. In the presence of all, the Holy Father declared:

"It appears that a miracle has been granted by God through the intercession of the Servants of God Francisco Marto, a boy, and Jacinta Marto, a girl. This miracle concerns the rapid, complete, and lasting cure of Maria Emília Santos of a paraplegia caused by a probable transverse myelitis that had lasted for twenty-two years; there was no question of any psychopathology."

His Holiness wished also that this decree should be made public and that it should be written into the acts of the Congregation for the Causes of Saints.[3]

Testimony of Maria Emília Santos

Maria Emília Santos described the great event in her life to a journalist from the newspaper *Correio da Manhã*.

Only one day was left in the novena that I was making to Jacinta Marto. On March 25, about 11:30, I had just finished praying the Rosary with one of the assistants. When she left I turned to Jacinta Marto and said out loud to her: "Oh, Jacinta, Our Lady appeared to you and asked you to pray for peace in the world, for the conversion of sinners, and for the sick, but for me, nothing!" And I closed my eyes.

When I closed my eyes, I felt a sensation that I cannot explain throughout my whole body. There was a buzzing noise in my head and I heard a voice saying to me: "Sit up, because you can!"

Then, I folded back the bedclothes, turned on my side and sat on the bed, clasping my Rosary in my right hand, as I do so often when going to sleep. When I sat up, the room was completely dark, and I started to think: "If I lie down again, tomorrow they won't believe that I actually sat up."

I put out my right hand, rang the bell, and began to call for someone. The assistant appeared, opened the door but didn't turn on the light. I said to her: "Maria, aren't you going to turn on the light?" She did so. She was astonished to see me sitting up and began to shout: "Oh, Our Lady! Oh, Our Lady!"

From then on, Maria Emília began to move about in a wheelchair. She prayed every day to Jacinta, hoping that she would be able to walk again someday, even after twenty-two years. On the night of February 20, 1989, thirty-two months after the day when she sat up in bed, she was again making a novena when she suddenly recovered the ability to walk!

After she became able to move around, she returned to a normal life, acting as receptionist and answering the telephone in the Saint Francis home, where she had been bedridden for years. The doctors who had attended Maria Emília over the years have never found a convincing scientific explanation for her cure.[4]

The beatification

At the beginning of the Great Jubilee of 2000, rumors began to circulate that Francisco and Jacinta would soon be beatified and that John Paul II might go to Fátima for the occasion. In the Cova da Iria, it seemed that everything was being prepared for some great event: the crown on top of the basilica was gilded, the entire building was washed, and some repairs were made. In February, the beatification was made definitive, though news of it was restricted to a few people. Before Easter the news was made official that the Pope would travel to the Cova da Iria, and great joy spread throughout Portugal.

On March 25, 2000, the Portuguese bishops issued a pastoral letter about the coming beatification of Francisco and Jacinta and called on the people to prepare spiritually for this event. They asked people to accept the message that Mary had given at Fátima and to live more intensely this baptismal commitment.

The great day

John Paul II landed at the military airport (Figo Maduro) in Lisbon on the afternoon of March 12, 2000. He was received and welcomed by Dr. Jorge Fernando Branco de Sampaio, the president of the Republic, and by António Guterres, the prime minister. After the military honors, the president greeted the Pope in his welcome address, and then John Paul II gave a speech.[5]

After these ceremonies, the Holy Father left at once for Fátima by helicopter, landing in the sports center. From there he went with the pontifical escort straight to the Chapel of the Apparitions. Although the distance was only about three kilometers, it took quite a while to travel because the love and enthusiasm of the crowds were indescribable, making it very difficult for the cars to get through. When John Paul II arrived at the chapel, the many thousands of Portuguese people who were awaiting him greeted him affectionately.

The Pope wanted also to renew his gratitude to the Virgin Mary for her protection during his pontificate. He entered the Chapel, knelt down, and remained there in prayer in front of the statue of Our Lady for some moments, during which the crowd kept a respectful silence. Next followed prayers in honor of the Mother of God, interspersed with the singing of "Totus Tuus."

After the final blessing, the Pope made an unexpected and significant gesture. He gave Our Lady of the Capelinha the ring Cardinal Stefan Wyszynski, Archbishop of Warsaw, had given him after his election as Pope, saying: "You will lead the Church into the third millennium."

At about 9:30 P.M. a prayer vigil was held in the great esplanade of the Sanctuary, preceded by the traditional candlelight procession with the statue of Our Lady and the singing of the Fátima Ave. The statue was decorated with many beautiful flowers.

The glory of the altar

Saturday, May 13, was a beautiful sunny day. The great square filled quickly with pilgrims, estimated at about a million.[6] Before the concelebrated Mass that morning, the Holy Father met Sister Lúcia for a few moments in the house of Our Lady of Mount Carmel in Coimbra. It must have been a thrilling moment for Lúcia.

Two flags were hung on the sides of the Basilica—that of the Holy See and that of Portugal. The flags covered two large portraits of the little shepherds, Jacinta and Francisco, until the time of their beatification. At 9:00 A.M., the Holy Father came into the sanctuary. Awaiting him were the Cardinal Secretary of State Ângelo Sodano; José Saraiva Martins, prefect of the Congregation for the Causes of Saints; the apostolic nuncios of Portugal and Spain; and many Portuguese bishops, along with bishops from Spain and other countries. There were nine cardinals and about a thousand priests.

Five hundred children occupied the steps of the altar in the square and the chairs in front, near the concelebrants. White doves made their appearance, too, perched on the steps, as if to take part in the great event.

At the beginning of the Mass, the Bishop of Leiria, Serafim de Sousa Ferreira e Silva, addressed the Holy Father, asking him to beatify the two little shepherds. Then he read a short account of their lives. John Paul II, visibly moved, declared the two children Blessed, while, at the same time, the two flags came down so the crowd could see the two large portraits. In the tower, the bells rang out to let the whole world know of the joy of the entire Church at the glorification of Jacinta and Francisco. The applause of the crowd mingled with the voices of the Sanctuary choir which, for the first time, sang the hymn of the little shepherds.

Let us all sing with joy, in one voice: *Francisco and Jacinta, pray for us!*[7]

Reflection on the lives of the children

For his homily, the Holy Father chose the prayer of Jesus: "I thank you, Father, Lord of heaven and earth, because you have hidden these things from the wise and the intelligent and have revealed them to infants" (Mt 11:25). He reflected on the lives of Francisco and Jacinta, emphasizing the different ways by which the Holy Spirit led each of them. Francisco was especially moved to think of how sad Jesus was over the sins committed against him. The little boy wanted to console Our Lord and make him happy. For Jacinta, the vision of hell had so deeply moved her that she offered herself and her sufferings for the conversion of sinners. She joyfully endured tremendous pain and suffering during her final illness for that intention that she took so much to heart. The Pope then spoke of the message of Fátima as a call to conversion. Finally, he addressed a beautiful message to the children, many of them dressed like Francisco and Jacinta. He urged them to go to the "school" of Our Lady in order to imitate the virtues of the little shepherds.

Along with their cousin, these two children, Francisco and Jacinta, were chosen by God for a special mission in the Church and in the world. While the message that Our Lady gave them had a particular significance for the twentieth century, it is a timeless message rooted in the essence of the Gospel: prayer, penance, and conversion of life. In their simplicity, these children showed us how to live the two great commandments, love of God and love of one's neighbor. The same road to holiness is open to us all.

Blesseds Jacinta and Francisco are commemorated in the liturgy on February 20, the anniversary of Jacinta's death.

Our hope in Fátima

In the early years of the twentieth century, Our Lady came to the Cova da Iria. The series of apparitions to three little shepherds occurred while the Bolshevik revolution was beginning in Russia. Mary came to bring from heaven a message of love, a message that would have the power to counteract the forces of hatred and evil in the world.

From 1917 to the present, the history of the Church has been full of remarkable events. We have only to remember the Second Vatican Council, a gift of the Holy Spirit for which we can never be sufficiently grateful; the breath of new life animating the Church in every continent, despite difficulties; the marvelous saga of John Paul II, the good shepherd, who traveled all over the world and won hearts everywhere. Never, in the history of the Church, did such huge crowds gather to hear the words of the Vicar of Christ on earth.

We are beginning to recognize once again the primacy of love, as in the first years of Christianity, though it is always a challenge to live the life of love. Mary came to ask for conversion of hearts. She promised that in the end, her Immaculate Heart would triumph. On March 25, 1984, Pope John Paul II, in union with all the bishops, consecrated the world to the Immaculate Heart of Mary. Not long after, the Berlin Wall—"the wall of shame," symbol of the slavery imposed on the world by Communism—began to crumble. The political system that had seemed so threatening and invincible collapsed like a house of cards.

The message of Fátima remains a call to each of us. Mary asks us to give God the first place in our lives. More than anyone, the little shepherds of Fátima took this message to heart and lived it out. In their simple lives, with the innocence of children, they prayed and did penance as the Lady had asked. Can we do anything less?

Notes

Preface

1. Cf. A. M. Martins, S.J., *Novos Documentos de Fátima* (Porto: Livraria A. I., Braga: Editorial Franciscana, 1984), p. 132. (Hereafter cited as *Novos Documentos.*)

2. *Novos Documentos*, concerning the order of Benedict XV to which the text alludes, cf. AAS 9 (1917), 266. This invocation is translated "Queen of Peace, pray for us!"

3. *Memoirs of Sister Lúcia*, III, no. 4, pp. 44–45. (Hereafter cited as MIL).

4. Sebastião Martins dos Reis. *The Visionary of Fátima: Dialogues and Answers About the Apparitions.* The author's edition (Braga: Franciscan Publications, 1980). Interrogation of P. H. Iongen, p. 78. Lúcia is referring, naturally, to the Foundress of the Dorothean Sisters. (Hereafter referred to as S.M.R.)

5. "Not a few people have expressed considerable surprise at the memory that God has deigned to give me. In this matter indeed I have, through his infinite goodness, been quite favored in every respect. Where supernatural things are concerned, this is not to be wondered at, for these are imprinted on the mind in such a way that it is almost impossible to forget them. At least, the meaning of what is made known is never forgotten unless it be that God wills that this, too, be forgotten." MIL IV, II, Epilogue, p. 174. Cf. MIL II, Epilogue, no. 3, p. 99.

CHAPTER 1
The Little Shepherds' Families

1. Irmã Lúcia de Jesus e do Coração Imaculado, *Apelos da Mensagem de Fátima*, p. 23. (Hereafter cited as *Apelos da Mensagem.*)

2. "In the past, widowhood was seen as a problem for the stability of the family. As well as loneliness, there were the material difficulties of keeping a family, so

most widows and widowers married a second time and had children in the second marriage" In *Aljustrel, Uma Aldeia de Fátima: o Passado e o Presente* (Fátima, 1993), p. 248.

3. José Fernandes da Rocha was born October 13, 1850. While he was emigrating to Brazil, his ship was wrecked. "He was saved, swimming on a plank, imploring all the time the protection of Our Lady of the Rosary, and was rescued by an English packet which brought him to Mozambique, where he worked for a few years and then returned to Aljustrel" (MIL V, no. 2, p. 48).

4. MIL V, no. 2, p. 11.

5. MIL I, no. 6, p. 28.

6. MIL I, no. 2, p. 23.

7. João de Marchi. I.M.C., *Era uma Senhora mais Brilhante Que o Sol* (Fátima: Edições Consolata, 13th edition, 1991), p. 162. (Hereafter cited as *Era uma Senhora.*)

8. Answer to positions and articles for Jacinta's process in *Novos Documentos*, p. 354.

9. MIL, V, no. 2, p. 19.

10. S.M.R., p. 28, note no. 10 of footnote.

11. Cf. *Era uma Senhora*, p. 18.

12. MIL, I, 1, no. 11, p. 34.

13. *Novos Documentos*, p. 374.

14. Cf. *Era uma Senhora*, p. 49.

15. *Novos Documentos*, p. 374.

16. *Era uma Senhora*, p. 58.

17. Ibid., p. 20.

18. S.M.R., p. 28, no. 10.

19. MIL V, no. 3, p. 53.

20. Ibid., Prologue, no. 3, pp. 53–54.

21. We should be deeply grateful to the rector of the Sanctuary of Fátima, Monsignor Canon Dr. Lúciano Guerra, for sending to Sister Lúcia a questionnaire that was handed to her by the Carmelite provincial, Father Jeremias Carlos Vechina, on October 11, 1986, "with the direction to answer as soon as possible." On April 14, 1988, he personally repeated this request; on October 20, he reminded her of the urgency of this work by means of the new provincial, Father Pedro Ferreira, and in a letter of November 23, 1988, he returned to the subject. Without this fortunate diligence in requesting the visionary to write down everything she remembered about her parents, not only would the image of her father have remained distorted for history, but the shining virtues of this home would have been lost forever. Cf. MIL V, no. 3, p. 8.

22. MIL V, no. 3, p. 8.

23. Ibid., pp. 15–16.

24. MIL VI, pp. 78–79.

25. MIL V, no. 3, p. 24.

26. Ibid., p. 16.

27. Ibid., p. 17.

28. *Apelos da Mensagem*, p. 23.

29. MIL V, no. 3, pp. 19–21.

30. Cf. Ibid., no. 2, p. 11.

31. Ibid., no. 3, p. 25.

32. Ibid., no. 4, pp. 31–33.

33. Ibid., no. 2, pp. 14–15.

34. Ibid., pp. 14–15.

35. Ibid., no. 3, p. 20.

36. Ibid., no. 2, p. 13.

37. Ibid., no. 3, p. 20.

38. Ibid.

39. Ibid., p. 23.

40. Ibid., no. 2, p. 16.

41. Ibid., no. 3, pp. 23–24.

42. Ibid., p. 27.

43. Ibid., pp. 27–29.

44. Maria de Belém, *Uma Família de Fátima* (Paulinas Editora, 1996), p. 22. (Hereafter cited as *Uma Família*.)

45. MIL V, no. 3, pp. 27–29.

46. MIL VI, no. 41, p. 132.

47. Ibid., no. 42, p. 134.

48. Ibid.

49. MIL V, no. 4, p. 33.

50. MIL VI, no. 28, p. 108.

51. It seems the disagreement concerned renovations being carried out in the church.

52. MIL II, p. 91.

53. MIL V, no. 4, p. 33.

54. Cf. *Uma Família*, p. 11; cf. no. 33, MIL II; S.M.R., p. 28.

55. Cf. Proverbs 31:10–13, 19–20, 29–31.

56. MIL VI, no. 3, p. 50.

57. Cf. Ibid., p. 54.

58. Ibid., no. 45, p. 138.

59. Ibid., no. 20, p. 92.

60. *Apelos da Mensagem*, pp. 25–26.

61. MIL I, II, no. 10, pp. 32–33.

62. MIL VI, no. 39, p. 126.

63. Ibid., no. 47, p. 140.

64. Ibid., no. 49, pp. 141–142.

65. Ibid., p. 141.

66. Ibid., no. 73, p. 174.

67. Ibid., no. 74, p. 175.

68. MIL II, no. 17, p. 83.

69. MIL VI, no. 74, pp. 174–175.

70. Ibid., no. 77, pp. 177–178.

71. Ibid., p. 182.

72. Ibid., no. 78, p. 182.

CHAPTER 2

The Shepherds: Lúcia, Francisco, and Jacinta

1. S.M.R., pp, 29–31.

2. MIL V, no. 2, p. 13.

3. Ibid., p. 12.

4. Ibid.

5. MIL V, no. 2, pp. 13–14.

6. Novais Granada, *Fátima, Pastorinhos no Altar, fascículo VIII,* Sunday magazine of *Correio da Manhã e do Comércio do Porto,* September 26, 1999, p. v.

7. MIL VI, no. 21, p. 96.

8. Cf. *Era uma Senhora,* p. 13.

9. Ibid., p. 12.

10. Ibid.

11. MIL II, Epilogue, no. 2, p. 98.

12. MIL II, I, no. 2, p. 52.

13. Ibid.

14. Ibid.

15. *Novos Documentos,* p. 27.

16. MIL VI, no. 20, pp. 92–93.

17. Ibid., no. 15, pp. 75–76.

18. Ibid., no. 22, pp. 98–99.

19. Ibid., no. 26, pp. 103–104.

20. Ibid., no. 27, p. 107.

21. The first four *Memoirs* were written in the novitiate of the Dorothean Sisters in Túy, Galicia, Spain, under rather unfavorable conditions, "in a remote corner of the attic … lit by a single skylight.… My lap serves me as a table, and an old trunk as a chair." MIL IV, Preface, no. 2, p. 118. The first was finished on Christmas Day, 1935; the second on November 21, 1937; the third on August 31, 1941; the fourth on December 8, 1941; the fifth, in the Carmel of Coimbra, on February 23, 1989; and the sixth there on March 25, 1993.

22. Cf. MIL II, I, no. 3, p. 54.

23. In a footnote, Lúcia identifies him as the Venerable Father Francisco Cruz (d. 1948).

24. MIL II, no. 3, pp. 54–55.

25. Ibid. This beautiful statue still stands in the parish church of Fátima. After reconstruction, which gave the church two side aisles besides the already existing central nave, the statue was placed on the right side when one is facing the altar, in front, near the door to the sacristy. Still, today, the tradition is kept about the place where the statue smiled at Lúcia when she went to pray in front of it, as we were told in January 1999 by the woman who looks after the church.

26. MIL II, no. 4, pp. 55–56.

27. Ibid., no. 5, p. 56.

28. Ibid., nos. 5–6, pp. 56–57.

29. At that time, the Church prescribed a complete fast from midnight until after Holy Communion the following day; even water was not allowed.

30. MIL II, I, nos. 5–6, p. 57.

31. Ibid., no. 6, p. 57.

32. That year, the feast of the Sacred Heart fell on May 30. *Ed.*

33. Cf. MIL VI, no. 28, p. 109.

34. MIL IV, I, no. 2, p. 122.

35. MIL II, no. 3, p. 64.

36. Ibid., no. 10, pp. 78–79.

37. MIL II, III, no. 6, p. 91.

38. MIL IV, I, no. 13, p. 140.

39. Ibid., no. 1, p. 120.

40. *Era uma Senhora*, p. 23.

41. Ibid., p. 17.

42. Ibid., p. 22.

43. *Novos Documentos*, p. 27.

44. MIL IV, I, no. 1, p. 120.

45. Ibid., no. 15, pp. 141–142.

46. Ibid., I, no. 1, p. 121.

47. *Era uma Senhora*, p. 19.

48. Ibid., p. 20.

49. Ibid.

50. Ibid.

51. Ibid., p. 22.

52. MIL IV, I, no. 1, p. 120.

53. Ibid.

54. Ibid., no. 4, p. 125.

55. Ibid., no. 14, p. 141.

56. Ibid., no. 11, p. 137.

57. Ibid., no. 9, p. 130.

58. Ibid., no. 12, pp. 137–138.

59. Ibid., no. 1, p. 121.

60. Ibid., no. 2, pp. 121–122.

61. Ibid., no. 14, p. 143.

62. Ibid., no. 15, p. 143.

63. Ibid.

64. Ibid., no. 12, p. 138.

65. Ibid., no. 1, p. 121.

66. Ibid.

67. *Era uma Senhora*, p. 21.

68. Ibid., p. 19.
69. Ibid., p. 17.
70. S.M.R., interview with Dr. Goulven, pp. 28–29.
71. *Novos Documentos*, p. 27.
72. MIL I, I, no. 1, p. 22.
73. Ibid., no. 2, p. 23.
74. Ibid., no. 6, p. 27.
75. Ibid., no. 6, pp. 27–28.
76. Ibid., no. 6, p. 28.
77. Ibid., no. 14, p. 37.
78. Ibid.
79. MIL IV, p. 120.
80. MIL I, I, no. 1, p. 21.
81. Ibid., no. 1, p. 22.
82. Ibid., no. 1, pp. 21–22.
83. Ibid., no. 2, p. 23.
84. Ibid., no. 7, p. 29.
85. MIL I, II, no. 5, pp. 40–41.
86. MIL I, I, no. 5, p. 24.
87. Ibid., no. 8, p. 30.
88. Cf. MIL, I, II, no. 2, p. 38.
89. MIL I, I, no. 5, pp. 24–25.
90. Ibid., no. 5, pp. 25–26.

Chapter 3

At the School of the Angel of Peace

1. Cf. MIL II, II, 2, p. 62.

2. Oliveros de Jesus Reis, *Mesangem de Fátima Dada ao Mundo*, pp. 17–18. "Besides the liturgical feast, many confraternities were started during these centuries in honor of the angel of Portugal. The churches of Bucelas and Saint Francis in Évora also have signs of homage to the guardian angel of the nation, the latter in the form of a famous panel, a sixteenth century work of the Ferreirim Masters" (p. 18).

3. Ibid., p. 17.

4. Ibid.

5. The Estrumeira da Conceição, belonging to José Francisco Marto, from Casa Velha, in a place called Esbarradoiro or Escorregadoiro, on the sloping boulders of which the children used to play, letting themselves slip down by holding onto the hanging branches of the pines and holm oaks. Here, around 1915, took place the first apparition of the angel, which left them perplexed and impressed, S.M.R., pp. 32–33.

6. MIL II, II, no. 1, p. 60.

7. Ibid., p. 61.

8. Ibid.

9. "I cannot fix the dates exactly, because at that time I didn't know how to count the years, nor months, nor even the days of the week. It seems to me, however, that it must have been in the spring of 1916 that the angel came the first time at the Loca do Cabeço." MIL IV, II, no. 1, p. 152.

10. MIL II, II, no. 2, pp. 62–63; cf. MIL IV, II, no. 1, pp. 155–156.

11. MIL IV, II, no. 1, p. 152; cf. MIL II, II, no. 2, p. 63.

12. MIL, II, II, no. 2, p. 63; cf. MIL IV, II, no. 1, p. 152.

13. MIL IV, II, no. 3, p. 152.

14. MIL IV, I, no. 3, p. 126.

15. MIL II, II, no. 2, p. 62. Cf. S.M.R. In an interview with Sister Lúcia, Dr. Goulven asked her specifically whether the angel had said "your country." She answered in the affirmative.

16. MIL IV, II, no. 1, pp. 152–153.

17. MIL IV, I, no. 3, p. 126.

18. MIL II, II, no. 2, pp. 62–63; cf. MIL IV, I, no. 1, p. 153.

19. Cf. MIL IV, I, no. 3, p. 125.

20. Ibid.

21. S.M.R., pp. 34–35.

22. Ibid., p. 36.

23. Ibid., p. 57.

24. Ibid., p. 55.

25. Ibid., p. 56.

26. MIL IV, II, no. 1, p. 153.

27. Costa Brochado, *Fátima in the Light of History* (Lisbon: Portugália Editora, 1948), pp. 142–144. (Hereafter cited as *Fátima*.)

28. See *Fátima*, pp. 144–145.

29. MIL IV, no. 3, p. 9.

30. See MIL IV, I, no. 28, p. 143.

31. MIL II, III, no. 7, p. 96.

32. Ibid., no. 8, p. 97.

33. S.M.R., p. 77.

34. Ibid. pp. 77–78.

CHAPTER 4

May 13: An Unforgettable Day

1. On this subject, see, among others, *Fátima*, pp. 108–125.

2. *Fátima*, pp. 115–116.

3. Ibid., p. 135.

4. *Era uma Senhora*, p. 29.

5. Ibid.

6. Cf. *Era uma Senhora*, p. 42.

7. Cf. MIL IV, no. 1, p. 177.

8. Cf. Ibid., p. 144.

9. MIL IV, I, Preface, p. 180.

10. *Era uma Senhora*, p. 61.

11. MIL IV, no. 8, p. 177.

12. Cf. S.M.R., interview with Bishop José Pedro da Silva, no. 10, p. 58.

13. MIL IV, IV, Preface, p. 180.

14. This "seventh time," refers to June 16, 1921, on the eve of Lúcia's departure to the College of Vilar in Porto. The apparition in question had a personal message for Lúcia, which she did not consider necessary to relate here. Cf. note 12, MIL IV, no. 3, p. 161.

15. MIL IV, no. 3, pp. 162–164.

16. Ibid.

17. *Era uma Senhora*, p. 45.

18. S.M.R., p. 58.

19. Cf. *Era uma Senhora*, pp. 47–48.

20. MIL IV, I, no. 4, p. 125.

21. *Era uma Senhora*, p. 50.

22. Letter of Dr. Carlos de Azevedo Mendes to his fiancée, of September 8, 1917, in *Novos Documentos*, p. 27.

23. *Era uma Senhora*, p. 56.

24. MIL IV, I, no. 4, pp. 125–127.

CHAPTER 5

The Apparition of June 13

1. Cf. *Era uma Senhora*, p. 57.

2. MIL II, II, no. 4, p. 66.

3. *Era uma Senhora*, p. 58.

4. Cf. Ibid.

5. Answer to the positions and articles for Jacinta's process, in *Novos Documentos*, p. 359.

6. *Novos Documentos*, p. 359.

7. MIL II, II, no. 5, p. 66.

8. *Novos Documentos*, p. 362.

9. Cf. *Era uma Senhora*, p. 60.

10. Cf. Ibid., p. 60.

11. Cf. Ibid., p. 61.

12. MIL IV, II, no. 5, pp. 161–162.

13. *Era uma Senhora*, p. 62.

14. Documentação Crítica de Fátima, II, p. 102.

15. *Era uma Senhora*, p. 63.

16. Documentação Crítica de Fátima, II, p. 103.

17. Cf. Ibid., II, p. 104.

18. *Era uma Senhora*, pp. 64–65.

19. Ibid., p. 67.

20. MIL II, II, no. 5, p. 67.

21. Ibid., pp. 67–68.

22. MIL I, II, no. 10, p. 33.

CHAPTER 6
Events in July

1. MIL, II, II, no. 6, p. 68.

2. Ibid.

3. Ibid.

4. Ibid.

5. Ibid.

6. Ibid., p. 69.

7. Cf. Ibid., no. 5, pp. 67–68; *Era uma Senhora*, p. 75.

8. MIL, IV, I, no. 6, p. 128.

9. MIL, II, II, no. 6, p. 69.

10. Ibid.

11. Ibid., pp. 69–70.

12. Ibid., p. 70.

13. *Era uma Senhora*, p. 76.

14. Ibid., p. 77.

15. *Fátima*, p. 213.

16. *Era uma Senhora*, p. 77.

17. Ibid., p. 78.

18. MIL IV, II, no. 5, p. 162.

19. It should be noted that it is a question of one secret that has three parts. Here, Lúcia describes the first two. The third was written down early in 1944 and was made known to the world in Fátima on May 13, 2000, after the beatification of Francisco and Jacinta.

20. We have chosen the text in MIL IV, although Sister Lúcia had already written, with slight differences, the two parts of the secret in MIL III, Preface, nos. 1–2, pp. 104–105.

21. The third part of the secret would follow here. It was revealed with the Holy Father's permission on May 13 in the Year of the Great Jubilee 2000.

22. MIL, IV, II, no. 5, pp. 166–171. The silence about the three parts of the secret was Our Lady's suggestion. As she received permission, Sister Lúcia made public each one of the parts of the secret.

23. On the occasion of his third visit to Fátima, May 13, 2000, John Paul II beatified Francisco and Jacinta; on the same day, the Cardinal Secretary of State, Angelo Sodano, announced that the text of the third secret would shortly be made public. This was carried out by the Congregation for the Doctrine of the Faith on June 26, 2000.

24. See Cardinal Tarcisio Bertone, *The Last Secret of Fatima* (New York: Double-day, 2008), p. 36.

25. Congregation for the Doctrine of Faith. *The Message of Fátima (The Secret)* Ed. (Lisbon: Paulus Editora, 2000), p. 7. The diary of Blessed John XXIII records that on August 17, 1950, he had an "Audience with Commissar of the Sacred Office, who brought me the letter that contains the third part of the Secret of Fátima. I am keeping it to read with my confessor."

26. Cf. *Era uma Senhora*, p. 67; MIL II.

27. MIL III, Preface, no. 3, p. 107.

28. MIL I, I, no. 8, pp. 30–31.

29. A little village to the north of the Cova da Iria.

30. MIL I, I, no. 9, pp. 31–32.

31. MIL IV, I, no. 7, p. 131.

32. *Apelos de Mensagem*, pp. 14–15.

33. Ibid., p. 56.

34. Ibid., p. 57.

35. Ibid., pp. 57–63. Subtitles added.

CHAPTER 7

August: Month of Trials

1. Artur de Oliveira Santos was born in Vila Nova de Ourém on January 1, 1884. On November 3, 1907, he founded the Democratic Republican Center. He emigrated to Spain in 1931 and was there until 1940; he died in Lisbon June 27, 1955. Cf. *Grande Enciclopédia Portuguesa e Brasileira*, Vol. 27, pp. 344–345.

2. Cf. *Fátima*, p. 176; and *Era uma Senhora*, p. 95.

3. Cf. Ibid., p. 177.

4. MIL II, II, no. 8, p. 72.

5. MIL VI, no. 40, p. 127.

6. Ibid.

7. Ibid., no. 8, p. 72.

8. Ibid.

9. MIL II, II, no. 8, p. 72.

10. MIL VI, no. 40, p. 127.

11. Documentação Crítica de Fátima, II, Doc. 4, p. 66.

12. *Fátima*, p. 180.

13. MIL VI, no. 40, p. 128.

14. MIL II, II, no. 11, p. 74.

15. *Fátima*, p. 181.

16. Ibid., p. 182.

17. Documentação Crítica de Fátima, pp. 377–378.

18. *Fátima*, pp. 182–183.

19. Ibid.

20. MIL I, I, no. 12, p. 35.

21. Ibid.

22. Ibid., no. 13, p. 35.

23. Ibid., p. 36.

24. Ibid.

25. Ibid., no. 12, pp. 36–37.

26. Documentação Crítica de Fátima, I, Doc. 54, pp. 379–380.

27. Ibid., pp. 381–382.

28. Ibid.

29. MIL IV, I, no. 8, p. 133.

30. *Fátima*, p. 187.

31. Ibid.

32. MIL VI, no. 40, p. 129.

33. *Novos Documentos*, p. 170. The manuscript of the deposition is dated 1923.

34. MIL II, II, no. 12, p. 77.

35. S.M.R., interrogation by Dr. Goulven, no. 31, p. 44.

36. MIL II, II, no. 11, p. 74.

37. *Novos Documentos*, p. 20. This is an incomplete letter—the beginning and the end are missing—from the seminarian Joel Magno to Cânon Félix, rector of the seminary of Santarém, definitely written in August 1917.

38. *Novos Documentos*, p. 21.

39. Cf. *Fátima*, p. 135.

40. Documentação Crítica de Fátima, II, Doc. 4, p. 67.

41. Cf. *Novos Documentos*, pp. 22–23.

42. The attitude of João was fully justified. He was hoping to see Our Lady. Then he thought better of it and he went off because he thought the Mother of God was waiting for his sister to arrive before appearing. Although he was present during the apparition, he saw nothing.

43. MIL IV, II, no. 6, p. 167.

44. *Novos Documentos*, pp. 270–271.

45. MIL IV, II, no. 6, p. 167.

46. MIL II, II, no. 11, p. 74.

47. *Novos Documentos*, p. 171.

48. Cf. Documentação Crítica de Fátima, II, Doc. 4, p. 67.

49. *Era uma Senhora*, pp. 122–123; cf. *Novos Documentos*, p. 171.

50. Ibid., p. 123.

CHAPTER 8

The Apparition of September 13

1. Documentação Crítica de Fátima, I, Doc. 56, p. 395, no. 2.

2. Ibid., p. 396.

3. MIL II, II, no. 12. p. 76.

4. MIL IV, no. 7, p. 168.

5. Documentação Crítica de Fátima, I, Doc. 56, p. 396.

6. Ibid., II, Doc. 4, p. 82.

7. Ibid. Inquérito Paroquial de Fátima, fl. 15.

8. Cf. *Fátima*, p. 214.

9. Documentação Crítica de Fátima, Vol. I, p. 27.

10. MIL IV, II, no. 7, p. 170; cf. MIL II, II, no. 12, p. 77.

11. MIL II, II, no. 12, p. 75.

12. Ibid., no. 13, p. 77.

13. MIL IV, II, no. 7, p. 170.

14. Documentação Crítica de Fátima, Vol. I, p. 22.

15. Ibid., Doc. 56, p. 396. In his deposition sent to the Bishop of Leiria on September 13, 1927, Dr. Carlos de Azevedo Mendes says: "I carried Lúcia in my arms" (no. 10).

16. During the apparitions of the angel and of Our Lady, Francisco saw but did not hear. At the end of each apparition his cousin and his sister had to tell him what had been said.

17. MIL II, II, no. 13, p. 78.

18. Documentação Crítica de Fátima, Vol. II, p. 82.

CHAPTER 9

A Great Miracle

1. MIL II, II, no. 16, p. 80.

2. Ibid.

3. MIL IV, no. 8, p. 170; cf. MIL II, II, no. 16, pp. 79–80.

4. MIL IV, IV, no. 3, p. 182.

5. Cf. *Fátima*, p. 297.

6. MIL IV, II, no. 8, p. 172.

7. Cf. Documentação Crítica de Fátima, I, fl. 13, p. 23.

8. MIL IV, II, no. 8, p. 172.

9. *Fátima*, pp. 213–215.

10. Cf. *Era uma Senhora*, p. 123.

11. MIL IV, II, no. 8, p. 172.

12. Former seminarian of the Santarém seminary. He was a Freemason, a free-thinker, and an ardent anticlerical who in the weekly *Lanterna* wrote pages of unbelievable criticism of priests and religion, descending to terrible blasphemy. Cf. *Fátima*, p. 251; S.M.R. in *Na Órbita de Fátima, Rectificações e Achegas* (Évora, Portugal: Cláudia Ribeiro, 1958), pp. 17–65. It is impossible to give the whole article; the quotes are the most significant part of the text.

13. This fact is even more significant because this professional writer had left with the editor of his paper an article to be published on the thirteenth, mocking the apparitions.

14. *Novos Documentos*, pp. 52–56. Transcribed from *O Século* of October 15, 1917.

15. Ibid., pp. 60–61; cf. *Fátima*, pp. 297–303. The text was taken from Visconde de Montelo, *Os Episódios Maravilhosos de Fátima*, Guarda, Portugal, 1921, pp. 20–24.

16. *Novos Documentos*, pp. 58–59.

17. This event was reported by the Cardinal Legate Frederico Tedeschini on October 13, 1951, at the closing of the Holy Year, in Fátima. Pius XII had seen in about 1950, in the Vatican Gardens, the Miracle of the Sun. It was the Holy Father himself who described this extraordinary fact. "It was October 30, 1950, two days before that day so longed for throughout the Catholic world when the solemn definition of the dogma of the Assumption of Our Lady into Heaven was to be proclaimed. At about 4:00 P.M., I was taking my usual walk in the Vatican Gardens, reading and studying as always various official documents.... At a certain moment, lifting my eyes from the documents in my hand, I was surprised by a phenomenon I had never witnessed before. The sun, which was still fairly high in the sky, appeared like an opaque globe of a yellowish color, circulating around a luminous halo which, however, did not prevent one in any way from gazing directly at the sun, nor did it cause the slightest discomfort. In front there was a small, very light cloud. The opaque globe moved on the outside, turning slowly and moving from left to right and vice versa. But on the inside, one could see quite clearly and uninterruptedly very pronounced movements. The same phenomenon was repeated on October 31 and on November 1, the day of the definition; later, on November 8, octave of the same solemnity. Since then, nothing more." Américo S. Inverno in *Stella*, no. 523. This author adds a curious note: "It remains to be added that the Pilgrim Statue of Our Lady of Fátima was in Rome when these phenomena were observed by Pius XII: the statue was in a convent of nuns near the Vatican and remained in Rome from October 28, 1950 until November 2, 1950.

18. MIL II, II no. 16, p. 80.

19. MIL IV, IV, no. 3, p. 182.

20. MIL IV, I, no. 9, p. 131.

CHAPTER 10

Witnesses of the Message

1. MIL II, II, no. 12, p. 76.

2. MIL IV, I, no. 4, p. 125.

3. MIL II, II, no. 14, p. 78.

4. MIL IV, no. 2, pp. 183–184.

5. MIL I, no. 4, pp. 39–40.

6. MIL IV, no. 9, p. 131.

7. MIL I, I, no. 2, pp. 38–39.

8. MIL IV, I, no. 15, pp. 143–144.

9. Ibid., p. 144.

10. Documentação Crítica de Fátima, *Interrogatórios aos Videntes*, 1917.

11. MIL I, II, no. 3, p. 40.

12. Documentação Crítica de Fátima, I, Doc. 55, pp. 391–392.

13. MIL I, I, no. 2, p. 38.

14. In their fervor, the children performed penances in a way that was almost extreme and could have damaged their health. Later Lúcia followed the advice of prudent spiritual guides on this matter. *Ed.*

15. MIL I, I, no. 9, pp. 31–32.

16. Ibid.

17. MIL IV, I, no. 9, p. 131.

18. MIL II, II, no. 12, p. 75.

19. MIL IV, II, no. 7, p. 170.

20. MIL II, III, no. 7, p. 92.

21. Ibid., p. 93.

22. MIL IV, I, no. 27, p. 128.

23. Ibid., no. 13, p. 139. While Lúcia places this vision in the "Great Barrancos" in the hamlet of Pedreira, Sebastião Martins dos Reis situates it in Várzea, on land belonging to the parents of Francisco and Jacinta. Cf. S.M.R., p. 33.

24. MIL IV, I, no. 15, p. 142.

25. Ibid., pp. 142–143.

26. MIL III, no. 7, p. 112.

27. MIL IV, I, no. 7, p. 129.

28. MIL IV, II, no. 4, p. 162.

29. Documentação Crítica de Fátima, Vol. II, p. 183.

30. Ibid.

31. Teresa de Jesus was married to Anastácio Vieira, from Aljustrel. She was the aunt and godmother of Lúcia's father. She died February 10, 1929.

32. MIL II, III, no. 7, p. 91.

33. MIL IV, I, no. 16, p. 144.

34. MIL II, III, no. 7, p. 92.

35. MIL IV, V, no. 4, p. 187.

36. Ibid.

37. MIL IV, V, no. 4, p. 187.

38. Ibid., no. 4, p. 188.

39. MIL IV, I, no. 12, p. 141.

40. Ibid., no. 17, p. 146.

41. *Era uma Senhora*, p. 235.

42. MIL IV, I, no. 16, p. 145.

43. Ibid.

44. Ibid., no. 17, p. 148.

45. Cf. S.M.R., no. 41, p. 46.

46. MIL I, III, no. 1, p. 41.

47. MIL III, no. 9, pp. 112–113.

48. MIL I, I, no. 11, p. 39.

49. MIL III, no. 9, p. 112.

50. MIL I, I, no. 11, pp. 34–39.

51. MIL I, III, no. 11, p. 34.

52. MIL III, no. 6, p. 111.

53. Ibid., 6, p. 112.

54. MIL I, III, no. 1, p. 41.

55. MIL II, III, no. 7, p. 91; cf. MIL I, III, no. 1, p. 42.

56. Ibid.

57. MIL II, III, no. 7, p. 92.

58. MIL I, III, no. 1, p. 42.

59. Ibid.

60. Ibid.

61. MIL II, III, no. 7, p. 92.

62. MIL I, III, no. 1, p. 42.

63. MIL II, III, no. 7, p. 93.

64. Ibid.

65. Ibid., p. 92.

66. MIL I, III, no. 2, p. 43.

67. Ibid.

68. Cf. S.M.R., no. 48, p. 47.

69. MIL I, III, no. 5, pp. 45–46.

70. Ibid., no. 2, p. 43.

71. Ibid.

72. MIL I, III, no. 4, p. 40.

73. MIL IV, III, no. 2, pp. 175–176.

74. Ibid., no. 1, pp. 174–175.

75. MIL I, III, no. 3, p. 44.

76. Ibid., no. 4, p. 44.

77. Ibid.

78. Maria da Purificação Godinho was born on July 24, 1877, and belonged to the Order of Poor Clares of Reparation. In 1913 she founded the orphanage of Our Lady of Miracles in Lisbon.

79. *Era uma Senhora*, p. 253.

80. MIL I, III, no. 6, p. 46.

81. This could be the apparition that took place at the Cova da Iria where Lúcia went to bid farewell the morning she was to leave for Porto.

82. Documentação Crítica de Fátima, Vol. II, p. 186.

83. Monsignor José Manuel Pereira dos Reis was parish priest of Anjos from 1918. In 1931 he was appointed rector of the seminary in Olivais. He was greatly devoted to the liturgy. He died on May 13, 1960.

84. Cf. *Fátima*, p. 83.

CHAPTER 11

Lúcia's Journey

1. MIL II, no. 15, p. 78. In a note at the end of *Memoir* II, the real reason for the priest's departure is explained. He left, in fact, because of a difficulty that arose with the parishioners over the building of the new church.

2. MIL II, III, no. 8, p. 93.

3. MIL VI, no. 56, p. 151.

4. Cf. MIL VI, no. 66, pp. 162–163.

5. Ibid., no. 68, p. 165.

6. Ibid., no. 71, p. 172.

7. Cf. Ibid., no. 72, pp. 172–173.

8. Ibid., no. 73, pp. 173–174.

9. Ibid., no. 74, p. 174.

10. Ibid., no. 70, p. 170.

11. MIL I, Introduction, p. 9.

12. It was called, as stated, Quinta da Formigueira, in the parish of Frossos, on the outskirts of Braga. The estate was later sold, but the house where Lúcia and her mother spent some time has been preserved.

13. MIL VI, no. 74, pp. 174–175.

14. Cf. S.M.R., no. 62, p. 50.

15. S.M.R., p. 67.

16. The Text of the Great Promise of the Immaculate Heart of Mary, in the *Memoirs*, Appendix I, p. 230. It will be referred to as the Great Promise.

17. Lúcia is certainly referring to the apparition she had in her room.

18. The Church of Santa Maria is next to the Dorothean convent in Ponte-vedra. There may be seen the statue in front of which Lúcia sent the Child Jesus to pray.

19. *Novos Documentos*, pp. 115–116.

20. The Great Promise, pp. 198–199.

21. Ibid., p. 200.

22. This unedited document was published by Sebastião Martins dos Reis in the book *A Life Spent in the Service of Fátima*, pp. 336–337.

23. Letter from Sister Lúcia to Monsignor Pereira Lopes, her spiritual director, while she was in Porto. *Novos Documentos*, p. 116.

24. The Great Promise, p 200.

25. Letter of July 24, 1927.

26. The text of this letter and the one previously quoted is published in *Novos Documentos*, pp. 118–119.

27. Today this chapel has been dismantled for renovations, and the altar is now in the convent of Pontevedra. The text of this appendix is not a manuscript written by Sister Lúcia, but it has all the guarantees of authenticity, because it was her spiritual director at that time, Father José Bernardo Gonçalves, S.J., who transcribed it directly and literally from her notes. She had the vision mentioned in the text on June 13, 1929, in the convent chapel at Túy, Spain. She begins by narrating the vision of the Most Holy Trinity, which accompanied the vision of Our Lady showing her heart, as in the June and July apparitions in 1917. The promise made then now became a reality. And Sister Lúcia heard the Virgin Mary asking for the consecration of Russia to her Immaculate Heart in very carefully defined circumstances.

28. A socius is an assistant to the provincial in the Jesuit order. *Ed.*

29. *Novos Documentos*, pp. 121–122.

30. Ibid.

31. *Novos Documentos*, p. 139.

32. Lúcia also confided this to Cardinal Tarcisio Bertone. See *The Last Secret of Fátima* (New York: Doubleday, 2008).

33. See Father Fernando Leite in *Revista Cruzada*, January 2001.

34. During the Spanish Civil War, 13 bishops, 4,184 priests (13 percent of priests in Spain), 2,635 men religious (23 percent of the male religious in Spain), and 283 women religious were killed. Besides these, countless lay men and women were martyred. Cf. Gonsalo Redondo *La Iglesia en el Mundo Contemporâneo 1878-1939*, II (Pamplona, Spain: Ediciones Universidad de Navarra, 1979), p. 275.

35. A story connected with Fátima is told about the statue venerated in this Marian sanctuary. Dr. Eurico Lisboa, a native of Viana do Castelo and Jacinta's doctor during the time she was a patient in the Estefânia Hospital in Lisbon, brought a collection of pictures of Our Lady one day to show her. He asked her which of them was most like the Lady she had seen in the Cova da Iria. Jacinta looked carefully at them all and then pointed to Our Lady of Sameiro. Monsignor Abílio, the first rector of the sanctuary, told the writer that he had received this testimony from Lisboa himself.

CHAPTER 12

The Beatification of Francisco and Jacinta

1. A relator is affiliated with the Congregation for the Causes of Saints, and works with the postulator in reviewing the documentation of a cause. *Ed.*

2. Cf. Father Fernando Leite, in *Celebração Litúrgica*, no. 4 (Year C/1988/1989), pp. 1340–1341.

3. The decree has the following date and signatures: "Given in Rome, on June 28 in the year of the Lord, 1999. José Saraiva Martins, C.M.F., Titular Archbishop of Thubumica, Prefect; Edward Nowak, Titular Archbishop of Luni, Secretary."

4. Novais Granada, in Fátima. "Little Shepherds Raised to the Altar," sheet IX, supplement to the *Correio de Manhã e Comércio do Porto*, October 3, 1999.

5. Accompanying the Holy Father on this trip were Cardinals Ângelo Sodano, Roger Etchegaray, and Camilo Ruini, and various prelates including: Giovanni Re, substitute at the Secretariat of State; José Saraiva Martins, prefect of the Congregation for the Causes of Saints; José da Cruz Policarpo, president of the Portuguese Episcopal Conference; and Serafim de Sousa Ferreira e Silva, Bishop of Leiria-Fátima.

6. This number was also calculated by the Portuguese edition of *L'Ósservatore Romano*, May 20, 2000, no. 21.

7. The text was written by Heitor de Morais, S.J., and the music is by Manuel Cartageno.

Bibliography

Brochado, Costa. *Fátima à Luz da História*. Lisbon: Portugália Editora, 1948.

Congregação Para a Doutrina da Fé, *A Mensagem de Fátima*. Lisbon: Paulus Editora, 2000.

Cosme Do Amaral, Don Alberto, *Francisco e Jacinta, Virtudes Heroiças*. Braga: Edições CAS, 1991.

de Belém, Maria, *Uma Família de Fátima, Carolina, Irmã da Vidente Lúcia*. Lisbon, Paulinas, 1996

De Marchi, João, *Era Uma Senhora mais Brilhante Que o Sol*. 13th ed. Fátima: Edições Consolata, 1991.

de Jesus Reis, Oliveiros, *Mensagem de Fátima Dada ao Mundo*. Lisbon: Rei dos Livros, 1977.

Documentação Crítica de Fátima, I, *Interrogatórios aos Videntes–1917*, Edição Santuário de Fátima, 1992.

Documentação Crítica de Fátima, II, *Processo Canónico Diocesano (1922–1930)* Edição Santuário de Fátima, 1999.

Irmã Lúcia de Jesus e do Coração Imaculado, *Memórias da Irmã Lúcia*, I (I to IV). 6th ed. Fátima: Vice-Postulação, 1980.

Irmã Lúcia de Jesus e do Coração Imaculado, *Memórias da Irmã Lúcia*, II (V and VI). Fátima: Vice-Postulação, 1996.

Irmã Lúcia de Jesus e do Coração Imaculado, *Apelos da Mensagem*. Fátima: Secretariado dos Pastorinhos, 2000.

Leite, Fernando, S.J., *Jacinta*. Braga: A. O., 2000.

Martins, A. M., S.J., *Novos Documentos de Fátima*. Braga: Livraria A. I., 1984.

Martins Dos Reis, Sebastião, *A Vidente de Fátima Dialoga e Responde pelas Aparições.*
    Author's ed. Braga: Editorial Franciscana, 1980.

Pasquale, Humberto *Eu Vi Nascer Fátima.* Vila do Conde: Edições Salesianas, 1968.

Vários, *Aljustrel, Uma Aldeia de Fátima: o Passado e o Presente.* Fátima: Torres Novas Gráf.
    Almondina, 1993, p. 248.

BOOKS & MEDIA

A mission of the Daughters of St. Paul

As apostles of Jesus Christ, evangelizing today's
world:

We are CALLED to holiness
by God's living Word and Eucharist.

We COMMUNICATE the Gospel message
through our lives and through all
available forms of media.

We SERVE the Church
by responding to the hopes and needs
of all people with the Word of God,
in the spirit of St. Paul.

For more information visit our Web site:
www.pauline.org.

auline
BOOKS & MEDIA

The Daughters of St. Paul operate book and media centers at the following addresses. Visit, call or write the one nearest you today, or find us on the World Wide Web, www.pauline.org.

CALIFORNIA

3908 Sepulveda Blvd, Culver City, CA 90230	310-397-8676
2640 Broadway Street, Redwood City, CA 94063	650-369-4230
5945 Balboa Avenue, San Diego, CA 92111	858-565-9181

FLORIDA

145 S.W. 107th Avenue, Miami, FL 33174	305-559-6715

HAWAII

1143 Bishop Street, Honolulu, HI 96813	808-521-2731
Neighbor Islands call:	866-521-2731

ILLINOIS

172 North Michigan Avenue, Chicago, IL 60601	312-346-4228

LOUISIANA

4403 Veterans Memorial Blvd, Metairie, LA 70006	504-887-7631

MASSACHUSETTS

885 Providence Hwy, Dedham, MA 02026	781-326-5385

MISSOURI

9804 Watson Road, St. Louis, MO 63126	314-965-3512

NEW JERSEY

561 U.S. Route 1, Wick Plaza, Edison, NJ 08817	732-572-1200

NEW YORK

150 East 52nd Street, New York, NY 10022	212-754-1110

PENNSYLVANIA

9171-A Roosevelt Blvd, Philadelphia, PA 19114	215-676-9494

SOUTH CAROLINA

243 King Street, Charleston, SC 29401	843-577-0175

TENNESSEE

4811 Poplar Avenue, Memphis, TN 38117	901-761-2987

TEXAS

114 Main Plaza, San Antonio, TX 78205	210-224-8101

VIRGINIA

1025 King Street, Alexandria, VA 22314	703-549-3806

CANADA

3022 Dufferin Street, Toronto, ON M6B 3T5	416-781-9131

¡También somos su fuente para libros, videos y música en español!